Fashion Patternmaking Techniques

HAUTE COUTURE
[VOL.1]

Haute Couture Models,
Draping Techniques,
Decorations

Antonio Donnanno

promopress

Fashion Patternmaking Techniques Haute Couture [Vol. 1]
Haute Couture Models, Draping Techniques, Decorations

Original title:
La tecnica dei modelli
Alta Moda vol. 1

Translation: Katherine Kirby

ISBN: 978-84-16504-66-4

Promopress is a brand of:
Promotora de prensa internacional S.A.
C/ Ausiàs March 124
08013 Barcelona, Spain
Tel.: 0034 93 245 14 64
Fax: 0034 93 265 48 83
Email: info@promopress.es
Facebook: Promopress Editions
Twitter: Promopress Editions @PromopressEd

First published in English: 2017

Sketches: Nadia Bonzi
Patternmaker's assistants: Marisa Cassera, Cinzia Traversi
Painting on fabric: Mary Laurora
Draping: Herman Waugh
Graphics: Emanuela Donnanno
Runway photographs: Indigitalitalia srl Milano

Cover design: spread: David Lorente with the collaboration of Noelia Felip
Photo cover design: Blugirl S/S 2011

Printed in Spain

PREFACE

In the fashion world, the patternmaker is a very important professional figure. He or she plays a strategic role for haute couture designers, prêt-à-porter clothing manufacturers and accessories producers. The patternmaker transforms the designer's drawing or sketch into a paper pattern, making the stylist's ideas material. He or she gives a more concrete shape to the garment in the correct measurements and proportions. This ensures the correct fit and line as the patternmaker studies the best way to cut the fabric while keeping any financial restraints imposed by the company in mind. He or she oversees the creation of the prototype or even makes it him/herself to ensure the designer's original vision is adhered to while uniting creative sensibility with the garment's technical demands. Sometimes the patternmaker implements modifications or discreetly suggests suitable solutions to the designer without offense and without altering the basis of the creation.

In the clothing industry, the designer's sketch may be turned into a pattern directly at the graphics workstation then transferred to a digital or paper format to be used in the subsequent cutting phase. At this point, the expert patternmaker uses Cad Modelli, a special computer program which allows the user to quickly optimise his or her time, even when fine-tuning the changes he or she would like to make. This technical ability comes from proper schooling and should be enriched with useful knowledge, such as an understanding of industrialisation and cost analysis, and familiarity with sewing machines, various fabrics, leathers, threads, and a number of garment finishing techniques. Experience and professionalism are gained by working in studios that use cutting-edge technology, where it is necessary

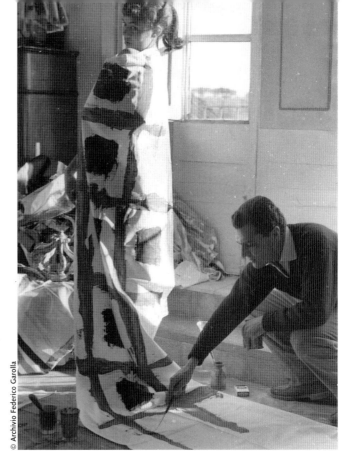

© Archivio Federico Garolla

to try new things, deepen one's knowledge and even make mistakes in order to improve. Even when a good patternmaker has a behind-the-scenes role, his or her work is valued by stylists and fashion houses because it is a fundamental cornerstone for the success of a garment or collection.

Above: Naples, 1957. The designer Livio De Simone painting on a piece of fabric for a dress already draped on the shoulders of the actress Giorgia Moll. Below: Rome, 1953. The Fontana Sisters in their atelier.

TABLE OF CONTENTS

Rotary cutter

Tailor's scissors

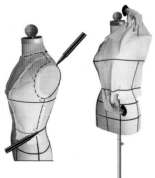

HIGH FASHION

High fashion is synonymous with enchantment, fairy tales, the shaping of desires, and sartorial and stylistic perfection. It is creative freedom: a chance for inventive expression without restrictions of any kind. Luxury products have no price limit and, as a result, they allow the designer to create with few restrictions. Makers of high fashion are regarded as creative geniuses who don't follow the market's rules when they attempt to satisfy the tastes of a demanding clientele.

Some fashion houses - including a few very well established ones - are known specifically because of their great designers. These individuals are responsible for world-famous brands. With the intention of anticipating fashion trends, they present their innovative creations on fashion runways before the press and buyers. The great Italian designers give life to collections that bestow prestige on those who wear them and enthral even those who cannot afford a garment of such workmanship or at such a price.

High fashion is the driving force behind the entire garment industry. It's the search for and study of fashion solutions in the form of textiles or styles and patterns. But what is fashion?

© Archivio Federico Garolla

© Archivio Federico Garolla

In its broadest definition, fashion is an expression of culture, imagination, innovation, taste, provocativeness and one's personality. It's an intertwining of economic and social anthropological phenomena, but it's also a reflection of the trends in a given era. Fashion is distinct from the parallel phenomenon of traditional costumes because of its transitory and fickle nature. In contrast to the persistence of habits and customs in the traditional dress of past centuries, fashion stands out owing to its fleetingness, variety and novelty.

It's a capricious phenomenon defined by the rhythm of short periods of time. The roots of the Italian and French words for "fashion" (moda and mode, respectively) reveal this sense of transience and a strict connection to the present. While the English word "costume" derives from the Italian costume, which in turn derives from the Latin consuetudo ("custom," "habit"), the etymology of moda and mode can be traced back to the Latin word modus, which means "measurement," "time" or "rhythm." It is thus an idea inherently tied to the times and closely linked to the present.

Naturally, traditional costumes are not entirely rigid and variations - even if only slight - do exist. But unlike fashion, costumes came about at the end of an evolutionary process which, when finished, did not allow for further changes. A quintessential example of a custom is the unchanging costumes associated with a particular nationality, locality, profession or association.

The persistence of a fixed costume was and still is mainly influenced by a people's history and traditions. Variations certainly do occur, but they usually involve the garment's details rather than its essential lines

Above: *Rome, 1956. Irene Galitzine, spring/summer collection.*
Left: *Florence, 1956. Germana Marucelli, autumn/winter collection.*

6

1. STYLE, FABRIC, FASHION

STYLE

Style is the synthesis of our attitudes and our way of being and living. The sensibilities we use to perceive, appreciate, and refute what surrounds us inevitably shape our lives and thus also our style. The phenomenon of style is different from fashion because it is more permanent over time.

The word "style", stile in Italian, derives from the Latin stilo, meaning "dagger", which in turn comes from the root word stei, to prick or jab (as a stimulus), incite, and distinguish. While the costume has the purpose of keeping a determined social, economic, or moral situation stable, style seems to have the ability to spur, to stimulate, and solicit a specific mode of expression or form. The former is a passive way to adhere to a customary way of dressing; the latter plays a particularly active role in determining tendencies, which it tries to maintain in order to establish itself. For this reason, we cannot underestimate the way in which stylistic creativity determined artistic tendencies, such as those seen in the Renaissance, Baroque, Rococo, Neoclassicism, Impressionism and Surrealism. Over time, these movements invaded every form of social expression beyond clothing, to include painting, architecture, literature and art in general.

Style is unlike fashion, the bearer of constant changes

and innovation, in that it establishes itself thanks to its intrinsic significance. It is more permanent, with a duration that often lasts long, historic periods of time. Fashion tends to be more dynamic: it changes and shakes up tradition. Of course this doesn't mean that the two phenomena aren't often intertwined or that a specific style can't arise from a series of homogeneous fashions or trends.

Because style can take on a wider sense or meaning, within a single style we may find numerous various on the same theme. For example, fashion designers all have their own style (just think of Valentino, Armani, Versace, etc.) which remains over the years. However, this does not exclude the need for "propulsive thrusts" of innovation as appropriate to social, economic, artistic or moral development.

FASHION AS TRANSGRESSION

Fashion remains a phenomenon of deviation with respect to costumes and style. As Renè König proposed, change in fashion is unique because it is based on the prerogative of elevating the deviation from costume up until that moment understood and held as binding as the norm, just as happened before with behaviour which respected the rules.

Compared to costumes or style, fashion is a "continuous attempt" to deviate from a pre-established reality. In a few aspects, it comes up against opposition from conformist society precisely because it is transgression. To better understand the phenomenon of fashion in the various stages of its formation, it is interesting to refer to the work of the French philosopher and sociologist Marc-Alain Descamps. In *Psychologie de la Mode*, he provides a table which divides fashion into five different degrees:

- The first degree is the sudden spread of an object or a use. For example, the use of forks in the 1600s became a part of culture as the centuries went on. In this case, the adoption of a useful object goes beyond fashion to be absorbed into the customs of a civilisation.
- The second degree involves diffusion with a smaller reach, influenced by personal or social taste, such as the collection of detective novels, opera, etc.
- In the third degree we find fleeting enthusiasm for fashion; where a trend is spread suddenly but short-lived and with little justification. Descamps remarks, "Infatuation tells us that something, in some way, involves us in a sort of exaggerated enthusiasm that doesn't last." It's interesting to note that the English language is meticulous and clear about this term: the word "fashion" corresponds to something which is semi-institutional, while short-lived infatuations are referred to with words like "fads" for things that are frivolous, "crazes" for the subversive, "rags" for what's popular, "booms" for that which is spectacular and dramatic.
- In the fourth degree, we find the word "mode" (fashion) defined as a slow, uninterrupted circulation, similar to tide of successive waves, with one dominating characteristic: cyclical reappearance. One example is the gauzy, bell-shaped skirt worn by women in Crete in the fifteenth century B.C. and in Spain by Don Margarita of Austria in the 1660s.
- In the fifth degree, on the other hand, we find a rapid, sudden succession and diffusion. In other words, current fashion with changes and a seasonal rhythm.

Within the larger phenomenon of fashion, we can also highlight different trends which distinguish different social strata. For example, the haute-couture of great designers who create luxurious dresses for special occasions are quite distinct from the more common ready-to-wear fashions - those which are made in a series and intended for daily use.

Juan B. Martinez del Mazo, Infanta Margarita Teresa in a Pink Dress, *1660.*

FASHION AND CLOTHING

Fashion may thus be an attitude, an appearance or a way of acting or speaking which can be used to create one's identity or to stand out. To adhere to a certain fashion one needn't be original or have a capacity for reflection. The only requirement is the desire to follow the fashion itself.

It goes without saying, however, that fashion's favourite playground is clothing - that thin layer of material which covers the human body. We'll try to understand what exactly fashion is and how to recognise it.

Fashion in clothing is a system of transformations which take place over time and which relate to three axes around which the garment takes shape:

1. Enhancement of the parts of the body, which can be accentuated or highlighted, such as padded shoulders, tight-fitting hips, etc.

2. Accentuation and consideration of verticality and height. For example, the wearer can appear taller by wearing high heels or a long skirt or with a certain hair style.

3. Highlight the body's movements by adding, for example, undulating attachments that oscillate when the body moves. This includes feathers, wide sleeves, wide skirts or trains, and the use of soft, flowy fabrics. The overlap and composition of these elements combine to create taste - the aesthetics of dressing which every fashion interprets.

Armani privé S/S 2009

Armani privé S/S 2011

Dior S/S 2011

Accentuation of the shoulders and waist.

Y.S. Laurent, S/S 2009

Dior A/W 2010

Chanel S/S 2010

Accentuation of height, with high heels and hairstyles.

There are thus a few traits which characterise the garments they modify. For example, in a given historical period, the neckline of a blouse must be open and not buttoned to be considered up-to-date. However, the variation of a few traits does not guarantee that a certain fashion will take hold. The change must be seen as a type of excess or provocation.

As we have seen, fashion over the centuries has asserted itself in its extravagance, its audacity and even its "craziness". Women's magazines underline and emphasise the aspect of newness and the provocation that new fashions bring with them. Understood in this way, a fashionable look must be considered the bearer of not just a variation, but also understood as a case of an extravagant variation that drums up enthusiasm. The enthusiasm for a specific fashion is then translated into success and spread when that fashion's followers place it in relation to a specific, extremely variable meaning, which may consist only of being fashionable.

There are different categories of production in the fashion industry, divided according to their target consumers, aesthetic canons, and the price point of the final product: high fashion, ready-to-wear designs, bridge, mass market, better collections, junior, and budget.

As we have seen, the high fashion industry may:
- Enhance a part of the body (with padded shoulders, décolleté, and wrapped hips).
- Accentuate verticality (with high heels and hairstyles, and long skirts).
- Highlight movement (with feathers, wide sleeves, and flowing skirts).

Enhancing the body, décolleté.

Accentuation of verticality and movement.

Emphasising movement.

THE FABRIC-CLOTHING SUPPLY CHAIN

There are numerous steps carried out in numerous distant locations that transform the first fibres into to the finished garment. When taken all together, this set of phases is called the "textile supply chain".

1. Fibre production. Fibres are the basis of creating fabrics and textiles. These raw materials can be natural in origin, including those from plants, such as cotton, linen, hemp or coconut fibre, or they may come from animals, such as sheep's wool, or goat, rabbit and llama hair, etc. Fibres may also be artificial, using cellulose for example, or synthetic, deriving from petroleum, natural gas or carbon.

2. Yarn production. After being stretched, washed and combed, the fibres have to be pressed and spun to create a continuous thread called yarn.

3. Fabric creation. There are three main types of fabric: weaves, knits and non-woven fabric.

Woven fabric is made from vertical and horizontal rows of yarn arranged at right angles to each other. Called weaving, this process involves two main elements: the warp, which runs longitudinally and which is held to the loom, and the weft, which runs across it (alternating over and under). Knit fabrics are made from a single piece of yarn which is looped into stitches arranged in a line or a tube. The loops are interlocked along a series of consecutive rows, which can be arranged horizontally or vertically using a variety of stitches.

Non-woven fabric is a generic term used to indicate an industrial product similar to fabric but made from procedures other than knitting or weaving. In non-woven fabric, the fibres have a more random, unstructured arrangement and are impossible to distinguish individually.

4. Textile finishing. In general, finishing treatments are done at the end of the production process to change one or more of the following characteristics, as requested by the client: appearance, colour, print, feel, dimensional stability, physiological comfort, and technical characteristics (such as light fastness and resistance to washing and sweat, etc.).

5. Production. Here the roads travelled by various textiles diverge. Some of them are used in the clothing industry to make dresses, jackets, trousers, shirts, jumpers and many other garments. Others are used by the textile industry to produce items such as woollen blankets, car seats, bandages, safety belts, parachutes, curtains, etc.

6. Distribution. The finished fabric or clothing finally arrives to the shops! They travel by sea, air or land, shipped across the globe. This allows us to purchase, say, a jacket made in the United States of America or any other country, in Italy or Germany.

7. Use. No matter what we do for a living or where we reside, we are surrounded by textiles such as sheets, towels, carpets, rucksacks and clothes, of course. It's difficult to imagine a world without them!

8. Care. In order for fabrics to last a long time, we must be sure to care for them correctly. For this reason, it's important to check the washing and care instructions on the label.

9. Duration and disposal. Every year in Italy, each person buys an average of 35 kg (77 lbs) of fabric. That's a lot!

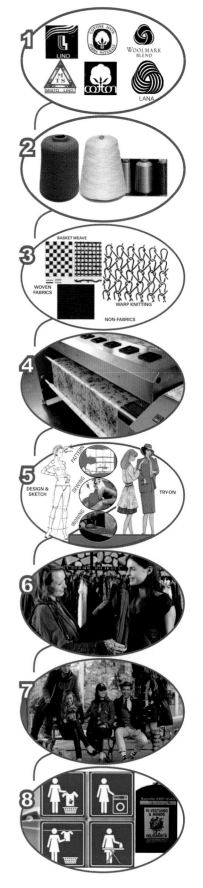

FIBRE
NATURAL
SYNTHETIC

YARN
WITH DISCONTINUOUS FIBRES
WITH CONTINUOUS FIBRES

FABRIC (OR TEXTILES)
WOVEN
KNIT
NON-WOVEN FABRIC

FINISHING
DYING
PRINTING
IMPREGNATING

PRODUCTION
HAND-MADE
INDUSTRIAL

SALES
WHOLESALE
RETAIL

USE
PRACTICAL USE
MAINTENANCE

DISPOSAL
RE-USE
INCINERATION
LANDFILL

Much of that is never used, however. It would be ideal if unused and disposed of garments were collected and used in some way. For example, they could be sold at flea markets and second-hand stores, or taken to used clothing collection bins and organisations.

FABRIC AND EMOTIONAL PERCEPTION

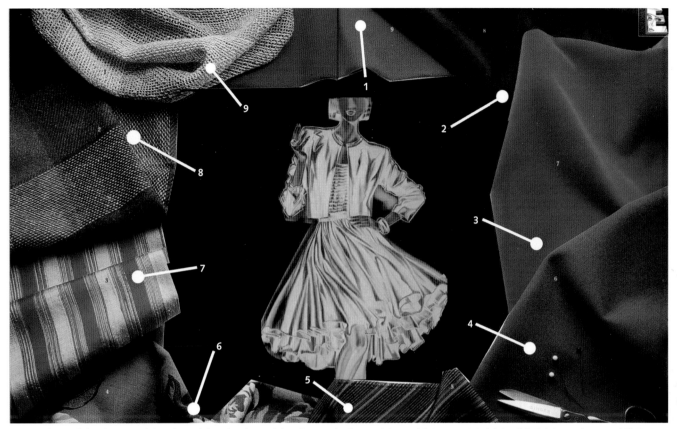

(1) Corduroy. (2) Velveteen. (3) Velvet. (4) Gabardines. (5) Fabric with diagonal lines. (6) Large-print fabric. (7) Fabric with rows. (8) Tartan. (9) Loose weave fabric.

Psychologists have always said that erogenous pleasure stimulated by temperature is one of the important components of sexuality. Humans need warmth not just to protect the body, but also for the sensual role it plays. The pleasurable sensation of heat, and the unpleasant sensation of cold, are as old as hunger and the need to eat. Often the choice of one fabric over another coincides in a real way with one's personality and character. We can thus confirm that the cloth chosen by each individual reveals his or her personality. In particular, there are those who prefer wool, or silk, or cotton, or linen, etc. according to their traits: extroverted, introverted, shy or uninhibited.

WOOL
Due to its symbolic ambivalence, wool is known for two different effects on different subjects.
On one hand, it's a symbol of purity and feminine chastity (pure "virgin" wool). Thus wearing and preferring wool is a symbolic way to satisfy the unconscious desire to maintain a warm, soft link to one's mother, tied in to the childhood memory of when she made knit garments.
On the other, opposite, hand, there are wool allergies. For some subjects, wool is associated with itchy, stinging or irritated skin, causing immediate heat. Wool is thus loaded with dual sensations, warmth-goodness and itch-irritation, which give rise to feelings of nervousness or increase sexual urges. Symbolically, if wool is perceived to be itchy and irritating, the wearer has the sensation of rejection, loss of maternal love, and punishment.

SILK
The word silk derives from the Old English word seoloc or sioloc, based on the Latin sericum, which in turn has its origins in the Greek word Serikos, the name given to the people from Asia from whom the Greeks got their silk. Like wool, silk is also ambivalent from a psychological point of view.
On one hand, studies carried out by Dichter (an Austrian psychologist and marketing expert who worked in the United States, considered the father of research on motivation) in the 1960s show that silk is an aphrodisiac which awakens sensuality in men, even more than in women. He described it as personal, secret and intimate, evoking the nude body, while also being refined, supple, elegant, and luxurious. It's functional in that it's cool in the summer and warm in the winter, while maintaining a sense of something royal, exotic, the height of refinement and evocative of oriental luxury.
Silk is worn and used by those with extroverted, unpredictable personalities often as an object of seduction.
However, there are also people who base their inner sense of security on the fact that they are able to defend against both sexual and aggressive impulses through an inaccessible plate of armour. To them, silk may also carry unpleasant and disturbing skin sensations, pushing them to overall insecurity precisely due to its smooth, draping qualities. These people reject silk as a formidable weapon for its illusory stability.

Armani, S/S 2013

Dolce&Gabbana, A/W 2012

COTTON

Originally considered a substitute for wool (consider the German word baum-wolle, where baum = tree and wolle = wool), albeit a wool coming from a plant, cotton is a symbol of innocence, childhood and the simplicity of emotions. Those who wear garments made of cotton, a fresh, soft and reassuring fabric, feel protected and defended. Cotton doesn't evoke dark sensations; rather it instils the wearer with the happy tranquillity of childhood.

For young people in particular, fondness for cotton garments such as t-shirts, jumpers or jeans indicates a desire to remain connected to the recreation-sports world, to a sense of being carefree and a lack of responsibilities, or a rejection of the obligations and duties imposed by society and adults.

LINEN

From a psychological point of view, linen causes sensations of rigidity and freshness in some, which represents moral integrity and self-respect. It's preferred, precisely for its coolness, by people who do not accept transgressions and who impose strict, rigid behaviour on themselves. For others, as it can also be seen as light, clean, and happy, even associated to childhood and femininity, linen sheds its sense of austerity.

SYNTHETIC FABRICS

Synthetic fabrics generally have a negative connotation related to their tendency to trap body odours. Intolerance of the artificial and chemical, often manifested in itchy reactions, redness or other outbreaks on the skin, emphasise some people's need for contact with nature.

Psychologically, as shown in a study by Dichter in 1964 among young housewives, these fibres are often criticised. As he states, they are known for their coldness and lack of warmth and genuineness, even if they are simultaneously appreciated for a few positive qualities, such as their ease of washing and drying, durability and low prices. These characteristics thus make synthetic textiles a common choice when buying.

COMMERCIAL CATEGORIES OF FASHION

Fashion production and its market, like in other industries, are divided into categories, each with its own buyers, based on production costs, sales prices, style and quantity of product. It's helpful to know these sectors and the differences between them, even if only to make informed business decisions. The main, best-known categories are: high fashion, ready-to-wear (prêt-a-porter), bridge, mass market, better collections, budget and junior.

High fashion includes the most expensive items, with prices that are generally quite prohibitive and within reach of very few. Such haute couture garments require the work of highly specialised professionals trained in the utmost attention to details, applications, and construction. They're checked after each step by the same designer, the one who created them, from the start. The creation of a high fashion garment requires hours of work, prized fabrics, precious and unique accessories, exclusive prints, particular patterns, innovative production processes and hand-finishing.

Ready to wear (prêt-a-porter) indicates the clothing sector made up of garments which are not custom made for the client, but sold as finished products in standard sizes. These garments are ready to be worn and presented to buyers and the fashion press each season. Clothing in this category is made with high-quality materials and fine, careful construction. They often take on added prestige in that they often benefit from advertising campaigns and proper marketing. Recently, most fashion houses have dedicated their efforts to the production of ready to wear garments, especially in order to push their cheaper collections through franchising.

The bridge category, in use in America starting from the 1970s in particular, is made up of classic sports clothing and women's suits. This sector's prices were originally almost as high as those seen in high fashion, but today bridge collections are undergoing numerous changes. Their price point is more attainable and their styles are more innovative, in part because suits are worn less and less by the enthusiasts of this category.

Better garments, destined for large retail stores and shopping centres, vary from casual to office wear. Most clothing in this area is inspired by the collections of great stylists, or is a reworking of the successful garments of the previous season. Better clothing generally is divided into two sub-categories: new garments and basic garments. The former follow fashion trends and usually bring greater customer satisfaction. The latter are found in more classic colours and models, perhaps with some detail that sets them apart, and they also have a bedrock market of buyers.

The budget sector includes garments destined for a lower target market. As a consequence, the budget to create them is much tighter. To respect this cost limit, these items are made with lower quality fabrics which are at times damaging to buyers and to the environment when they are disposed of. Those who make budget clothing are also impacted by this low budget: they are often paid very little and under the table.

Juniors clothing is made for those between 9 and 17 years of age. It's a quite developed sector, aimed at both parents, who wish to help their children develop a sense of identity, and by the children themselves who, for the same reasons, wish to distinguish themselves from their parents and older generations.

CLOTHING REQUIREMENTS

The main requirements for clothing are: functionality, appearance, longevity, ease of maintenance and physiological suitability.
- Functionality: it should have a protective, aesthetic and social identification function.
- Appearance: it should be well-suited to the person wearing it and confer him/her with the appearance s/he desires.
- Longevity: it should be resistant and durable over time.
- Ease of maintenance: it should be washable, withstand dry-cleaning treatments and not prone to deformities.
- Physiological suitability: it should ensure the well-being of the person wearing it in various situations.

CLOTHING AS A PRIMARY NEED

Clothing, as with food and housing, is one of mankind's primary needs and has various functions: it protects the body, which otherwise is nude and vulnerable, from harm in the environment, be it weather (cold, rain, sun, etc.) or insects, toxic substances and other risks to personal safety.

Each garment also has cultural and social meaning.

Human beings are the only mammals which wear clothes, aside from domesticated animals who are dressed by their owners.

Generally, by clothing we exclusively mean that series of objects which human beings wear, not practices which change the appearance of an individual. So, the decoration of the human body itself (make-up, cosmetics, etc.) or modifications made to its physical characteristics (cutting and colouring hair/beard/moustache, tattoos and piercings) are not necessarily clothing. The same is true for complementary items, often called accessories (bags, umbrellas, canes).

Clothing may be studied from an anthropologic-ethnographic point of view (from the moment the evolution of costume is documented), or from a socio-economic one, as a product of the textile industry (linked to technological development), of fashion and of consumerism. Man has displayed extreme creativity in finding new solutions for suiting practical needs, and the distinction between garments and other protective items isn't always cut and dry. For example, there are clothes with air conditioning, armour and bulletproof vests, bathing costumes, bee-keeper suits, motorcycle jumpsuits and reflective safety gear.

John Galliano, S/S 2008

Valentino, S/S 2008

Missoni S/S 2008.

Dior, ss2010.

Valentino S/S 2009.

B.Johnson S/S 2009.

THE PHYSIOLOGY OF CLOTHING

The science which concerns the interaction between the body and clothing in various weather conditions is called the physiology of clothing.

Generally, humans are exposed to various climatic conditions and the body may react in numerous different ways, depending on the situation. When moving, the body produces heat in proportion to the intensity of said movement. Excess heat is then removed through the skin and breath.

Skin tends to favour dispersion through clothes, approximately 90% of body heat, while only the 10% remaining is expelled through respiration. If there is more heat produced than dispersed, there is an excess of warmth which the body reacts to by sweating.

When sweat evaporates from the skin it produces an intense sensation of cooling for the body. If more heat is dispersed than is produced, we start to feel cold. To create a sense of wellbeing, clothing must favour the ratio of interactions between the body and the weather through insulation, aeration, and the absorption and transportation of humidity. By properly choosing clothing, we can compensate for even the most extreme weather conditions, reaching thermic equilibrium.

CLOTHING'S FUNDAMENTAL FUNCTIONS

Clothing has three fundamental functions: protection, aesthetics, and identification.

PROTECTION

Clothing is necessary to:

1. protect from weather conditions such as heat, wind, rain, snow, etc.

2. protect from possible injuries, such as in the workplace, in traffic, when playing sports, etc.

3. assist in the body's natural temperature regulation. In warmer parts of the globe perhaps people could go without clothing, if it wasn't for the no-less important function of covering the nude body.

AESTHETICS

In addition to its protective function, clothing has always played various roles in terms of aesthetics, conferring the wearer with a specific, personal character.

IDENTIFICATION

Often in civil society, one's belonging to a certain category or group of people is recognised from how someone dresses. Examples of this are the traditional costumes which determine ethnic groups; uniforms for soldiers, police officers, firemen, etc.; outfits worn by young cultural or trendy groups, such as punks, hippies, football fans, etc.

Moncler Gamme Rouge A/W 2015

INSULATION

Insulation is necessary to make sure the body doesn't get excessively cold. Usually our blood and skin act like an A/C and heating unit, just like the water in the radiator of a car: warm blood leaving the internal organs is cooled as it moves towards the skin. When we feel cold, however, many capillaries in our skin contract, reducing the blood flow to approximately one fifth of the average amount. As a result, the skin acts as a radiator which dissipates the heat into a cover which conserves it. The efficacy of this epidermal cover depends in part on the thickness of the layer of fat just below it. In general, people with a good amount of well-distributed fat tolerate the cold better than thin people.

The conservation of body heat depends in part on that which the body or clothing is in contact with.

Insulation comes from: 50% from the air captured by the garment, 30% by the layers of air which adhere to the garment, and 20% of the thermal conductivity of the fibres which it is made of.

Almost everyone thinks that wool is the ideal fabric to keep warm. However, the insulating effect is not due to the fabric itself, rather to the air which remains trapped between its fibres. It's the thickness of the layer of air encapsulated that really counts. The superiority of wool over cotton in this regard depends thus on its elasticity more than anything else. Wet or dry, wool tends to quickly return to its initial thickness after being compressed, and thus englobes more air.

It should be added that while still air is a wonderful insulating 'material', moving air quickly sweeps warmth away. Just a breeze is enough to dissipate a quantity of internal heat eight times than that lost to still air. For this reason, winter clothing made of good quality wool loses approximately half of its insulating power when the wearer walks quickly, due to the air currents which the movement provokes within the clothing. The large garments of seal furs and walrus skins worn by Eskimos are almost perfect for cold weather. During the hunt, when the Eskimo is tracking his prey, the frozen air stops the body from overheating. Then, when the hunter rests, the garment sticks more closely to the body and creates a hard-to-beat level of thermal insulation.

The movement of air is necessary to maintain the proper balance between heat and humidity in the microcli-

J. Linderberg A/W 2015

Diagram showing clothing's thermal insulation.
(from UNI, 2004)

1. Layer of surface air
2. Clothing
3. Layer of internal air
4. Body
T = Total insulation, clo
Id = Intrinsic insulation, clo
Ia = Superficial insulation, clo

mate which is created between the skin and the garment. The movement of air essentially depends on three factors.

1. Fabric structure, that is, the type of fibre, yarn, weave, and fabric finishing.

2. Cut of the garment. In fact, with garments which are too close-fitting there is no air movement and those who wear these garments generally feel hot and sticky from sweat. Loose-fitting garments with large openings, on the other hand, favour ventilation.

3. Ventilation, that is, the movement of air deriving from wind, be it natural, from a fan, produced by riding a bicycle or a motorbike, etc.

BODY HUMIDITY

The human organism emits heat in order to regulate itself and react to the weather. Depending on the intensity of heat which the body is subjected to, it contains a greater or lesser amount of humidity which must be absorbed and evaporated through the garment in contact with the skin. Thus it's necessary to use hygroscopic fibres: fibres which attract water vapour and wick it away. In this way, the fabric doesn't become wet and stick to the skin, impeding the transportation of the humidity formed by the water vapour. It should be emphasised that stagnant humidity gives the impression of being cold. Thus, when the body is sweating a lot, it's important for the sweat to be quickly distanced from the skin and towards the external layer of the clothing. This is why sports clothing is often made with two layers: one made of synthetic fibres which come into contact with the skin and which are able to transport humidity away with their capillary action towards the exterior, and a second layer of hydrophilic fibres, such as cotton, which accumulate humidity and release it slowly.

THE PATTERN AND THE DESIGN

In a global market, the challenge for creative professionals, managers and entrepreneurs is the union of creativity and entrepreneurship. Globalisation changes fashion and technology becomes strategic. Fashion companies are facing an important moment of transformation: young, international creative teams are taking the place of individual designers, and companies and designers work and collaborate at great geographical distances.

Fashion is losing any local connotations and technology is becoming a way to optimise and quicken the entire value chain, allowing responsiveness and dynamism.

The challenge of maintaining the design's integrity during the entire production cycle is overcome thanks to the aid of new technological instruments which are increasingly powerful and sophisticated.

Today's true necessity thus isn't having a broad vision and using technology as a simple application or single solution. Rather, it is that of planning and implementing a strategy to manage complexity and growth.

A young professional who wishes to establish him/herself today must be a concrete dreamer: a dreamer because s/he must pursue the ideas about fashion s/he would like to present, but also concrete because s/he must face a series of undeniable realities. Thus the combination of creativity and imagination and the ability to support industrial processes is a winning one, as Italy has managed to do what no other country has: industrialise luxury and offer it at accessible prices. Technology becomes fundamental to lowering costs, obtaining a good time-to-market, communicating and sharing information even between geographically distant places,

Venice, 1968. Roberta di Camerino in her laboratory.

Armani S/S 2012

and bringing about those changes which make the creation more efficient and appreciated by the client in real time. In fact, we are standing before a market in which the client is an increasingly important player in the creation of the product, clearly voicing preferences and tastes. Virtuality is the response to this demand, a virtuality which today is made possible by technology and software.

THE IMPORTANCE OF THE PATTERN MAKER

Even if the fashion sketch is the main star in the creation of clothing, the pattern maker and his/her ability to create a pattern faithful to the drawing is just as important, along with the creation of the prototype and the industrialisation of the paper pattern used for production.

The designer tends to draw upon freedom of expression, which allows him or her to spontaneously "play" with ideas, colours and forms. What's important, however, is that the project can actually be created. At first this may seem obvious, but it is often necessary to create innovative pattern solutions which conform to the lines, the volume and the style of the drawing. The patterns which we present in this and in other "High Fashion" books are all made with some sort of non-standard detail. However, they all are connected to the basics and the creative patterns already explained in the first three volumes of *Fashion Patternmaking Techniques.*

The creation of a high fashion dress pattern can be compared to the creation of an architectural blueprint. There are so many parallels between the two fields that they almost seem to be one and the same at times. They are similar in terms of lifestyle and the implementation of style and when, responding to the functions assigned to them, they are able to conveniently fit in to the space, time and environment which is to host them. Observing a well-made work of architecture and a high-fashion dress, we note the same harmony of the elements, the same guaranteed functionality, equal balance, a competition between multiple technical elements and a hard-to-find creative flair. In addition to the designers, the driving force behind these fine results is the technicians responsible for their implementation: architectural engineers for buildings and patternmakers for haute couture creations.

© Archivio Federico Garolla

MEASUREMENTS FOR HAND-MADE GARMENTS

The creation of made-to-measure patterns, such those for high fashion, like those in the other volumes of *Fashion Patternmaking Techniques*, requires utmost attention when taking the client's measurements. To be precise and objective, use a non-elastic tape measure which isn't worn out.

All measurements should be taken snugly, but not too tightly, ensuring that the client is standing normally and relaxed. The subject should not be wearing bulky garments which may alter the contours of the figure. Measurements should be written down immediately on a special notebook or on a personal client card. The ease of the garment to be made, based on the type of fabric to be used and found in the attached chart, should be added to the measurements. In addition, it's a good idea to note (discretely of course), any defects in the subject's anatomy and posture which will be essential when making the pattern.

The measurements to take depend on the type of garment to be made. However, keep in mind that any measurements relevant to compensating for irregular conformations and body types (explained in previous volumes) will be necessary, in addition to the standard measurements. It's important to remember the necessity of applying corrections in order of importance and of possibly combining them to simplify and streamline the process.

Obviously, the possibility of streamlining, being dependent on the capacity for combination with the corrections, is implicitly relative to the exercise, to the study and to the experiences which one may have. Tailoring knowledge tells us that a defect on the final product is the manifestation of an error in construction or of making the pattern and that the correction it requires is the result of initial carelessness

Measurements of Circumference and Width
Neck Cir. - Chest Cir. - Bust Cir. - Waist Cir. - Lower Ab. Cir. - Hip Cir. - Arm Cir. - Elbow Cir. - Wrist Cir. - Thigh Cir. - Knee Cir. - Ankle Cir. - Back Shoulder Width - Front Chest Width - Bust Divergence - Shoulder Measurement.

Length Measurements
Back Waist Length - Front Waist Length - Shoulder Drop - Bust Height - Side Height - Crotch Height - Total Crotch Measurement - Knee Height - Total Leg Length from Waist - Total Rear Measurement Without Heels - Head Height - Total Stature - Sleeve Length at Elbow - Total Sleeve Length.

Measurements to Check
Upper Spinal Curvature Depth - Buttock Protrusion - Belly Protrusion - Armscye Drop.

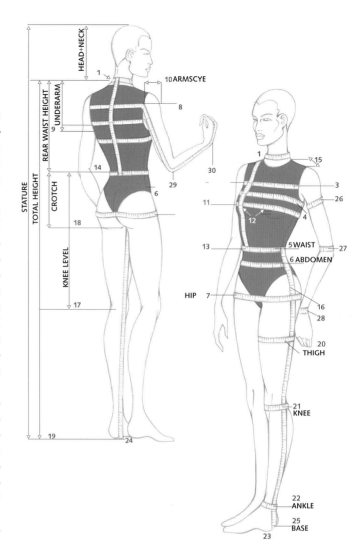

SIZE CHART WITHOUT EASE
WOMEN

Circumference measurements	CM/IN	CM/IN	CM/IN	CM/IN	CM/IN	CM/IN
SIZE	40	42	44	46	48	50
Torso circumference	84/33.07"	86/33.86"	89/35.04"	92/36.22"	96/37.80"	100/39.37"
Bust circumference	89/35.04"	92/36.22"	96/37.80"	100/39.37"	105/41.34"	110/43.31"
Waist circumference	66/25.98"	68/26.77"	72/28.35"	76/29.92"	81/31.89"	86/33.86"
Hip circumference	89/35.04"	92/36.22"	96/37.80"	100/39.37"	105/41.34"	110/43.31"
Length of front torso *(including darts)	36.1/14.21"	37.1/14.61"	38.9/15.31"	40.5/15.94"	42.5/16.73"	44.5/17.52"
Length of back shoulders	35.3/13.90"	36.5/14.37"	37.9/14.92"	39.5/15.55"	41.5/16.34"	43.5/17.13"
Neck circumference	36/14.17"	37/14.57"	38/14.96"	39/15.55"	40.5/15.75"	41/16.14"
Back neckline	7.5/2.95"	8/3.15"	8.5/3.35"	9/3.54"	10/3.94"	11/4.33"
Length and width measurements						
HEIGHT	164/64.57"	166/65.35"	168/66.14"	170/66.93"	172/67.72"	174/68.50"
Bust divergence	17/6.69"	18/7.09"	19/7.48"	20/7.87"	21/8.27"	21/8.27"
Shoulder width	12/4.72"	13.5/5.31"	13.5/5.31"	14/5.51"	14.5/5.71"	15/5.91"
Back waist width	39.1/15.39"	40/15.75"	40.9/16.10"	41.8/16.46"	42.7/16.81"	43.6/17.17"
Front waist width	40.4/15.91"	41.5/16.34"	42.6/16.77"	43.7/17.20"	44.8/17.64"	45.9/18.07"
Bust depth	21.8/8.58"	22.5/8.86"	23.2/9.13"	23.9/9.41"	24.6/9.69"	25.1/9.88"
Side depth	19.6/7.72"	20/7.87"	20.4/8.03"	20.8/8.19"	21.2/8.35"	21.6/8.50"
Crotch depth	23.5/9.25"	24/9.45"	24.6/9.69"	25.2/9.89"	25.8/10.16"	26.5/10.43"
Knee depth	575/22.64"	58.5/23.03"	59.5/23.43"	60.5/23.82"	61.5/24.21"	62.5/24.61"
Outer leg length	102/40.16"	104/40.94"	105/41.34"	106/41.73"	107/42.13"	108/42.52"
Upper arm circumference	28/11.02"	29/11.42"	30/11.81"	31.5/12.40"	33/12.99"	35/13.78"
Wrist circumference	18/7.09"	19/7.48"	20/7.87"	20/7.87"	21/8.27"	21/8.27"
Sleeve length	57/22.44"	58/22.83"	59/23.23"	60/23.62"	61/24.02"	61/24.02"

*Control measurements

EASES BASED ON GARMENT TYPE

TYPE OF GARMENT	Costumes and bodysuits	Tops and bodices	Shirts, dresses and waistcoats	Boleros, shaped jackets	Loose-fitting jackets, shaped coats	Outerwear	Dusters, Macs, Capes	Padded heavy jackets
Torso circumference	-4 /-2 (-1.57/-0.79")	0 / 2 (0 / 0.79")	4 / 8 (1.57 / 3.15")	10 / 12 (3.94 / 4.72")	14 / 16 (5.51 / 6.30")	18 /20 (7.09 / 7.87")	22 /24 (8.66 / 9.45")	28 / 32 (11.02 / 12.60")
Bust circumference	-4 /-2 (-1.57/-0.79")	0 / 2 (0 /0.79")	4 / 8 (1.57 / 3.15")	10 / 12 (3.94 / 4.72")	14 / 16 (5.51 / 6.30")	18 /20 (7.09 / 787")	22 /24 (8.66 / 9.45")	28 / 32 (11.02 / 12.60")
Waist circumference	-2.5 / 1 (0.98/0.39")	0 / -1.5 (0/ -0.59")	2.5 / 4 (0.98 / 1.57)	5 / 6 (1.97 / 2.36")	8 / 10 (3.15 / 3.94")			
Hip circumference	-4 /-2 (-1.57/-0.79")	0 / 2 (0/0.79")	4 / 8 (1.57/ 3.15)	10 / 12 (3.94 / 4.72")	14 / 16 (5.51 / 6.30")	18 /20 (7.09 / 7.87")	22 /24 (8.66 / 9.45")	28 / 32 (11.02 / 12.60")
Upper arm circumference	-1.5 / -0.5 (-0.59 / 0.20")	0 / 1 (0 / 0.39")	1 / 1.5 (0.39 / 0.59")	1.5 / 2 (0.59-0.79")	2.5 / 5 (0.98 / 1.97")	3.5 / 7 (1.38 / 2.76")	4.5 / 8.5 (1.77 / 3.35")	6 / 10 (2.36 / 3.94")
Back shoulders width	-1.5 / -0.5 (-0.59 / 0.20")	0 / -0.5 (0 / -0.20")	1 - 2 (0.39-0.79")	2.5 - 3.5 (0.98 - 1.38")	3.5 - 4 (1.38 - 1.57)	4.5 - 5 (1.77 - 1.99")	5 - 5.5 (1.99 - 2.17")	7 - 8 (2.76 - 3.15")
Front torso width	-1.5 / -0.5 (-0.59 / 0.20")	0 / -0.5 (0 / -0.20")	1 - 2 (0.39-0.79")	2.5 - 3.5 (0.98 - 1.38")	3.5 - 4 (1.38 - 1.57)	4.5 - 5 (1.77 - 1.99")	5 - 5.5 (1.99 - 2.17")	7 - 8 (2.76 - 3.15")
Waist width (front and back)	-	-	-	1 (0.39")	2 (0.79")	2 (0.79")	2 (0.79")	3 / 4 (1.18 / 1.57")

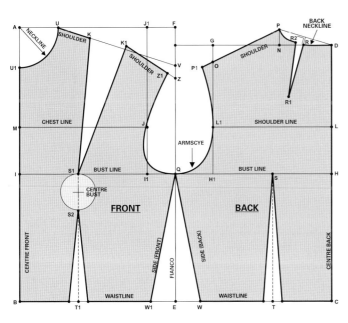

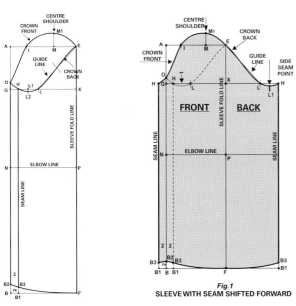

Fig.1
SLEEVE WITH SEAM SHIFTED FORWARD

THE BASE BLOCKS

To construct the patterns found in this book, as for the variations and the creative versions in the previous volumes of "Fashion Patternmaking Techniques", you should always begin with the base block of the garment to be made. Thus the explanations of the models presented here begin from the base blocks already illustrated precisely and clearly in depth in those three volumes. For that reason, it will be useful for those who own said volumes to review the various base blocks. We recommend that those who do not currently own the books get them to better construct the patterns presented here, as well as in future volumes of *High Fashion Patternmaking Techniques.*

1st Volume:

- Pencil Skirt and Variations - 1/4 Circle Skirt - 1/2 Circle Skirt - Circle Skirt and Variations - Hemmed "Square" Skirt - Culottes and Variations - Women's Trousers and Variations - Bodice with Darts and Set-in Sleeve - Bodice without Darts and Set-in Sleeve - Form-fitting Shirt - Loose-fitting Shirt - Defect Correction - Necklines and Collars - Linings - Men's Shirt and Related Sleeves and Collars - Men's Trousers and Defect Correction - Size Grading for Skirts, Culottes and Trousers.

2nd Volume:

- Base Bodice Variations - Short Kimono with Gusset - Long-sleeve Kimono - Long-sleeve Kimono with Gusset - One-piece Kimono - Seamless Kimono - Kimono-based Raglan Sleeves - Set-in Raglan Sleeves - Shirt Variations - Jumpsuits and Overalls - Dress with Darts and Sleeves, plus Variations - Dress without Darts, with Sleeves and Creative Variations - Creative Dresses - Set-in, Raglan and Kimono Sleeve Variations - T-shirts and Derivatives - Vests - Sweatshirts made of Knits - Unitards and Sleeves - Bodysuits and Swimwear and Variations - Underwear and Variations - Bras and Variations - Men's Jacket, Sleeves, Collars, and Variations - Men's Waistcoat and Variations - Correcting Defects for Men's Garments - Size Grading for Dresses, Jumpsuits and Jackets.

3rd Volume:

Women's Waistcoats and Variations - Fitted Women's Jacket and Relative Sleeves, Collars and Variations - Loose-fitting Jacket and Set-in Sleeve - Raglan Sleeve Jacket - Kimono Sleeve Jacket - Creative Jackets - Women's Blouses and Coats - Women's Winter Jackets - Fitted Women's Overcoats and Relative Set-in Sleeve - Loose-fitting Coats and Relative Set-in Sleeve - Creative Variations on Outerwear, Raglan Sleeves and Kimonos - Macs (Trench) and Related Sleeves and Collars - Cape - Variations and Creative Capes - Hoods and Variations - Men's Overcoats and Relative Set-in Sleeve and Collar - Loose-fitting Men's Outerwear and Relative Sleeve and Collar - Men's Macs (Trench) and Relative Sleeve and Collar - Raglan Overcoat - Montgomery - Men's Winter Jacket and Relative Sleeve.

2. PLEATS, DRAPES AND FRILLS

DRESS WITH A PLEAT ON THE CHEST AND SIDE PANELS

CHEST   CHEST

BUST   BUST   BUST

FRONT   **FRONT**   **BACK**

CENTRE FRONT   CENTRE FRONT

3 CUT WAIST   CUT   WAIST 9.5   3 WAIST CUT   CUT 1

DISCARD 3 8.5   DISCARD CLOSE 1.5 1.5 CLOSE   3

CUT AND OPEN
CUT AND OPEN

SIDE   SIDE   SIDE   SIDE

HIP   HIP   HIP

CENTRE FRONT

CENTRE BACK

SHOULDERS

2

A 14.5
CUT AND OPEN
"
"
"
" 10 " DISCARD 3 WAIST

BUST   BUST

FRONT   B **FRONT**

FOLD 3.5 CLOSE 3 C WAIST 9.5

8
10
20
3.5

LEFT SIDE

BUST

FRONT

ENTIRE CENTRE FRONT   SEW   SIDE   WAIST 9.5

BACK

WAIST   WAIST

CENTRE BACK

Construct this pattern by using the base of the
dress with darts and set-in sleeve, transforming it
as illustrated here.

DRESS WITH A PLEAT ON THE CHEST AND SIDE PANELS

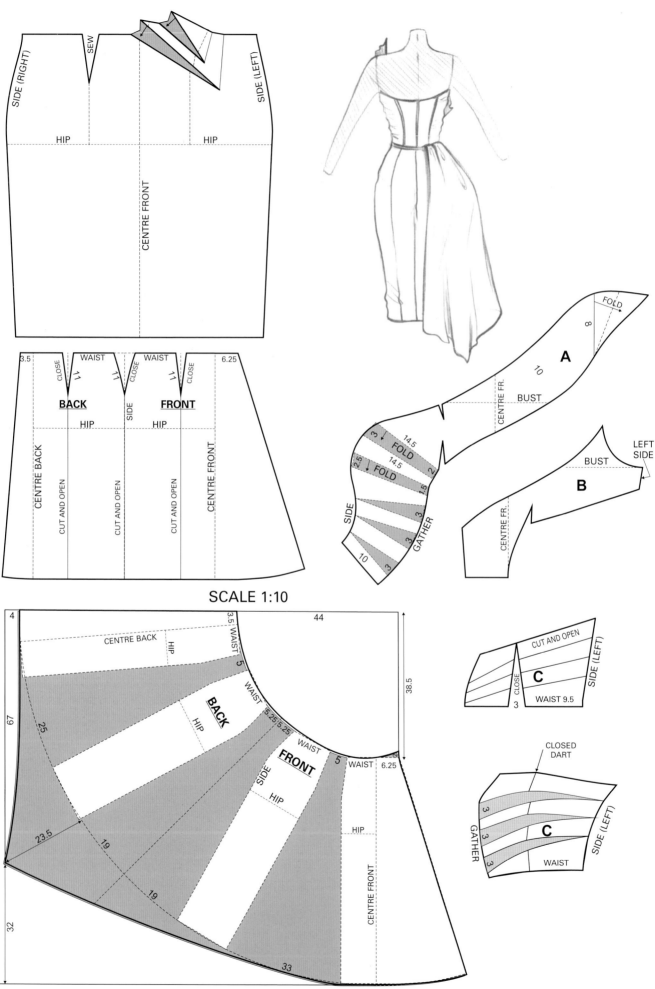

SCALE 1:10

DRESS WITH FOLDED DRAPING AND BELL-SHAPED SKIRT

LONGER IN THE BACK

DRESS WITH FOLDED DRAPING AND BELL-SHAPED SKIRT

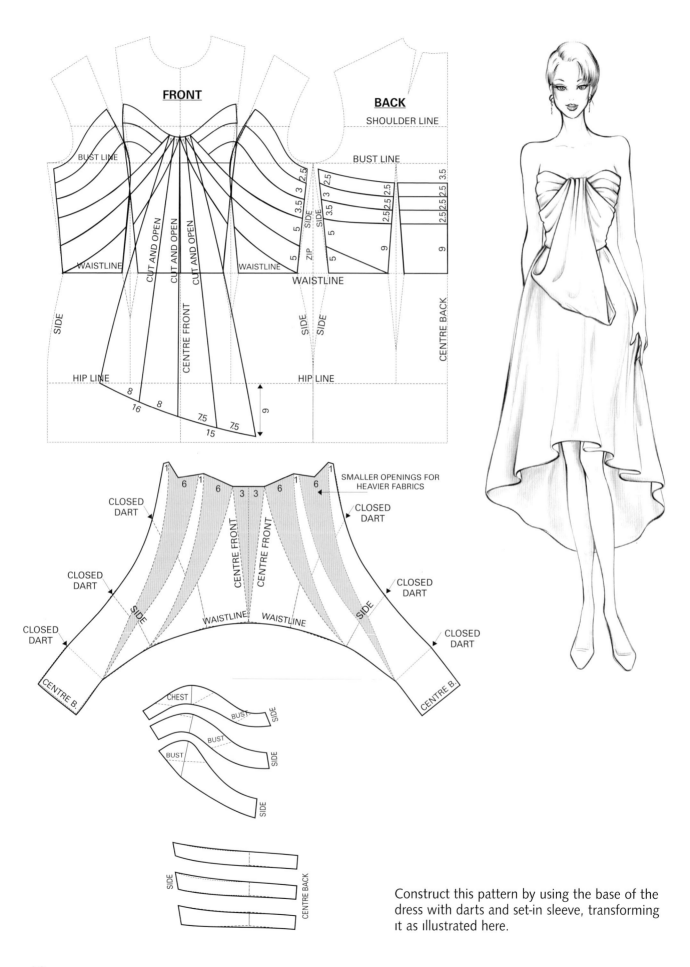

Construct this pattern by using the base of the dress with darts and set-in sleeve, transforming it as illustrated here.

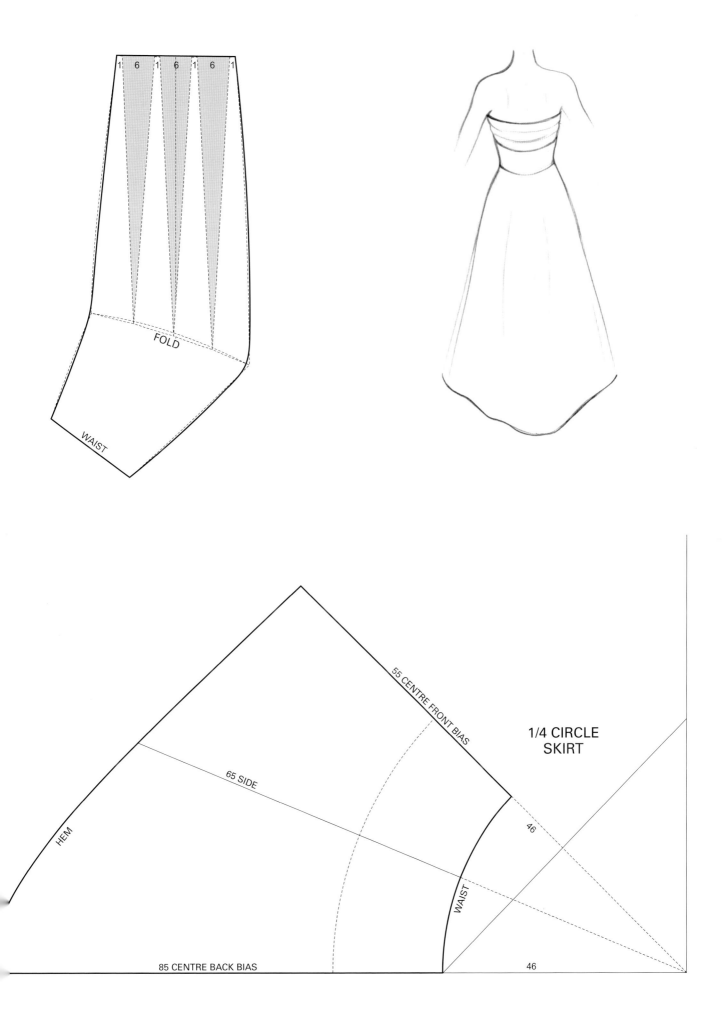

1 6 1 6 1 6 1

FOLD

WAIST

1/4 CIRCLE
SKIRT

55 CENTRE FRONT BIAS

65 SIDE

HEM

46

WAIST

85 CENTRE BACK BIAS

46

DRESS WITH CRISSCROSSED DRAPING
FRONT FLOUNCES AND WINGS ON THE DÉCOLLETÉ

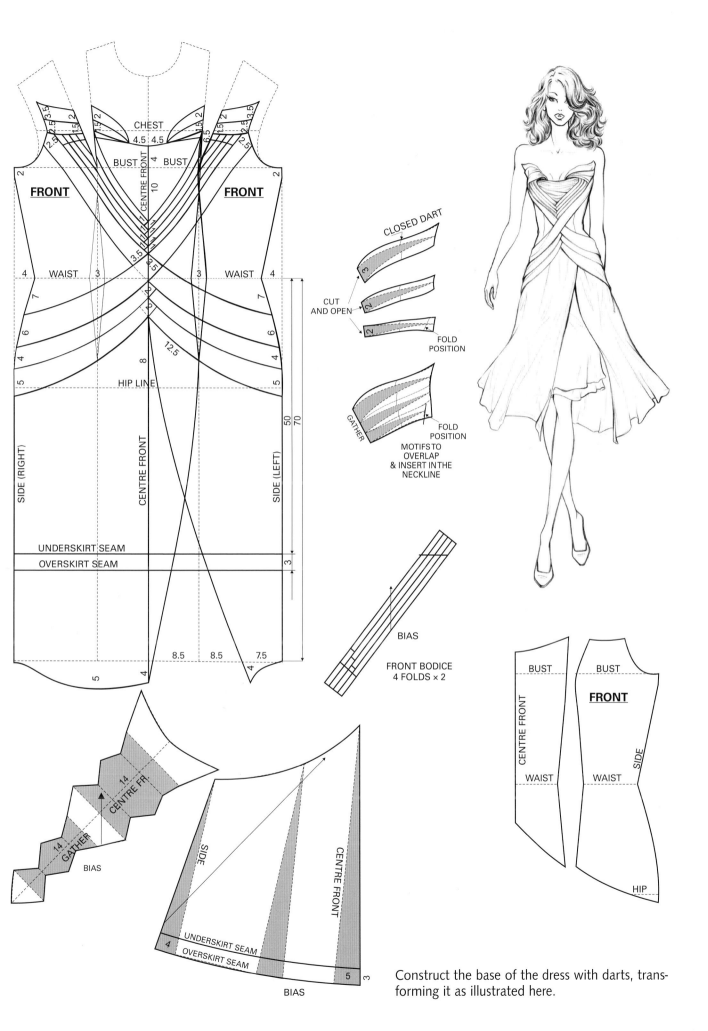

Construct the base of the dress with darts, transforming it as illustrated here.

DRESS WITH CRISSCROSSED DRAPING

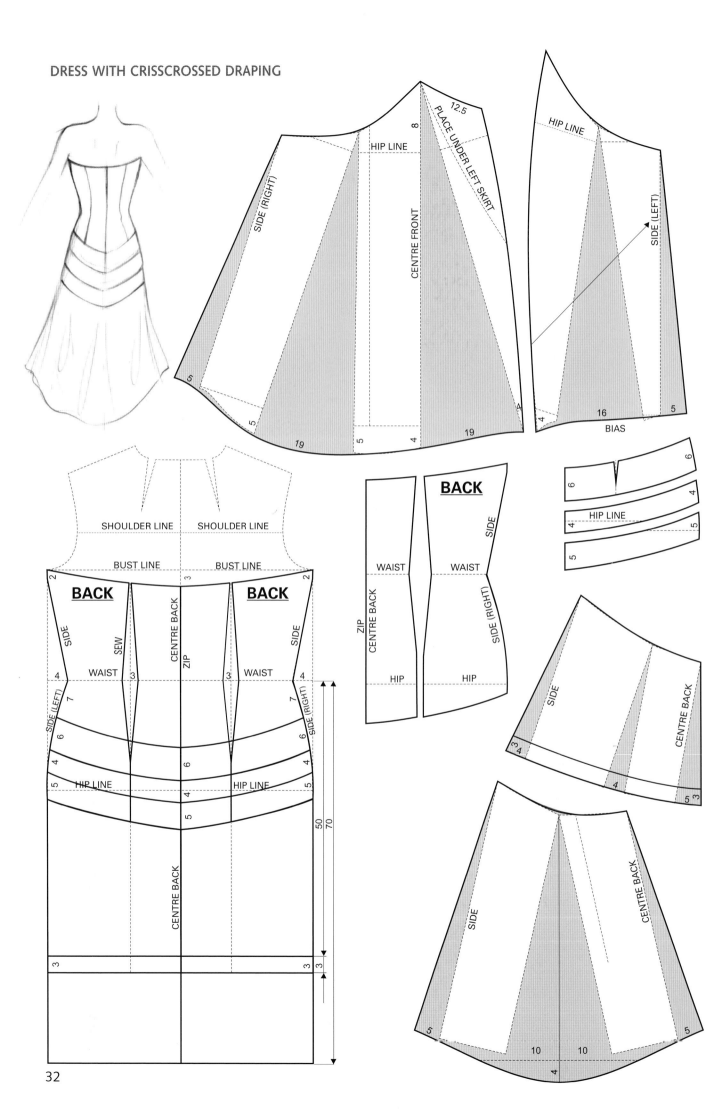

SIDE (RIGHT)

HIP LINE

12.5

8

PLACE UNDER LEFT SKIRT

CENTRE FRONT

5

19

5

5

5

19

4

HIP LINE

SIDE (LEFT)

BIAS

4

16

5

SHOULDER LINE   SHOULDER LINE

BUST LINE   BUST LINE

BACK   **BACK**

2   3   2

SIDE   SEW   CENTRE BACK   SIDE

SIDE (LEFT)   WAIST   ZIP   WAIST   SIDE (RIGHT)

4   3   3   4

7   7

6   6

4   6   4

5   HIP LINE   HIP LINE   5

4

5

50   70

CENTRE BACK

3   3   3

BACK

ZIP   CENTRE BACK   WAIST   WAIST   SIDE   SIDE (RIGHT)

HIP   HIP

6   6

HIP LINE   4   5

5

SIDE   CENTRE BACK

3   4

4

5   3

SIDE   CENTRE BACK

5   5

10   10

4

32

DRESS WITH ASYMMETRICAL NECKLINE AND A-LINE SKIRT

DRESS WITH ASYMMETRICAL NECKLINE AND A-LINE SKIRT

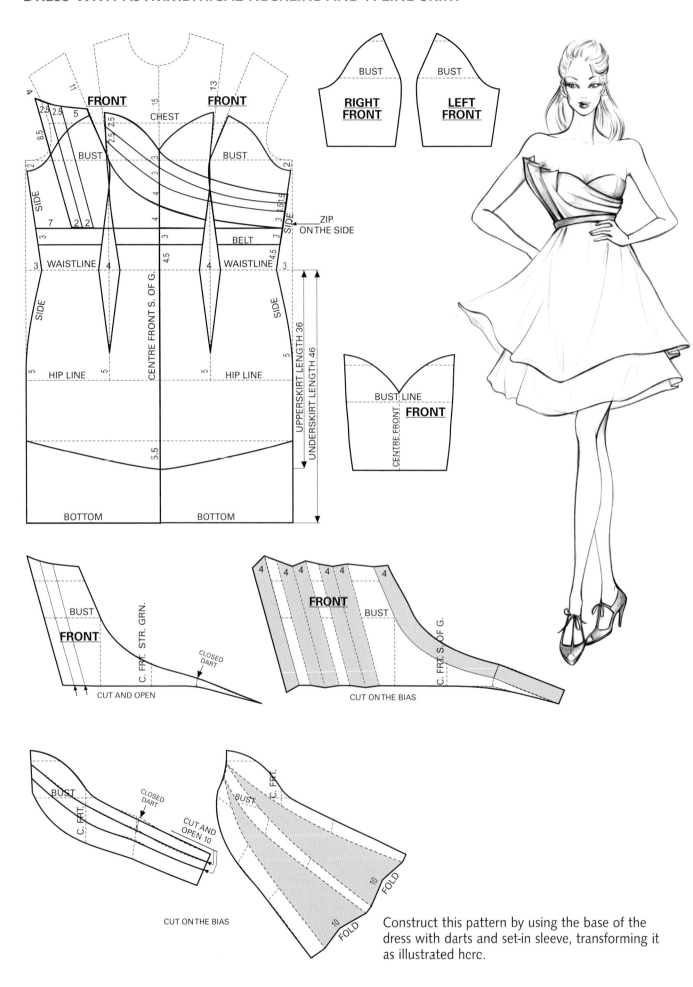

Construct this pattern by using the base of the dress with darts and set-in sleeve, transforming it as illustrated here.

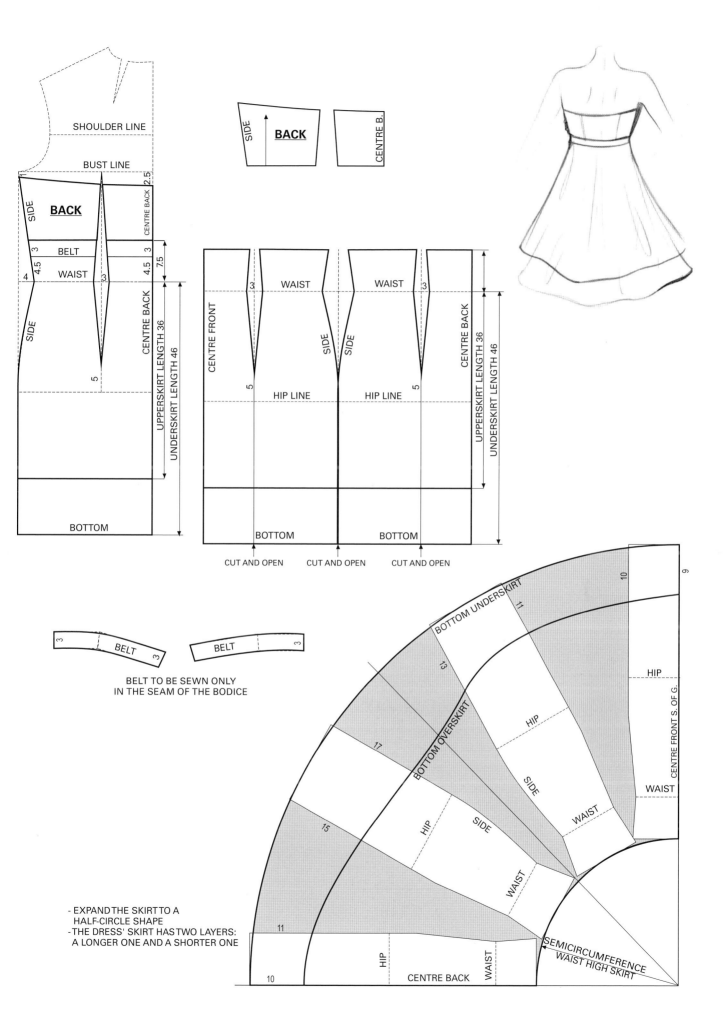

SHOULDER LINE

BUST LINE

SIDE **BACK** CENTRE BACK 2.5

BELT 3

4.5 WAIST 4.5 7.5

4 3

SIDE CENTRE BACK

5 UPPERSKIRT LENGTH 36

UNDERSKIRT LENGTH 46

BOTTOM

SIDE **BACK** CENTRE B.

CENTRE FRONT WAIST 3

3 WAIST

5 HIP LINE SIDE SIDE HIP LINE 5

CENTRE BACK UPPERSKIRT LENGTH 36

UNDERSKIRT LENGTH 46

BOTTOM BOTTOM

CUT AND OPEN   CUT AND OPEN   CUT AND OPEN

3 BELT 3

BELT 3

BELT TO BE SEWN ONLY
IN THE SEAM OF THE BODICE

- EXPAND THE SKIRT TO A
  HALF-CIRCLE SHAPE
- THE DRESS' SKIRT HAS TWO LAYERS:
  A LONGER ONE AND A SHORTER ONE

BOTTOM UNDERSKIRT

10 9

11

13 HIP

BOTTOM OVERSKIRT SIDE HIP

17 WAIST

HIP SIDE

15 WAIST CENTRE FRONT S. OF G.

WAIST

11 SEMICIRCUMFERENCE
WAIST HIGH SKIRT

10 HIP WAIST
CENTRE BACK

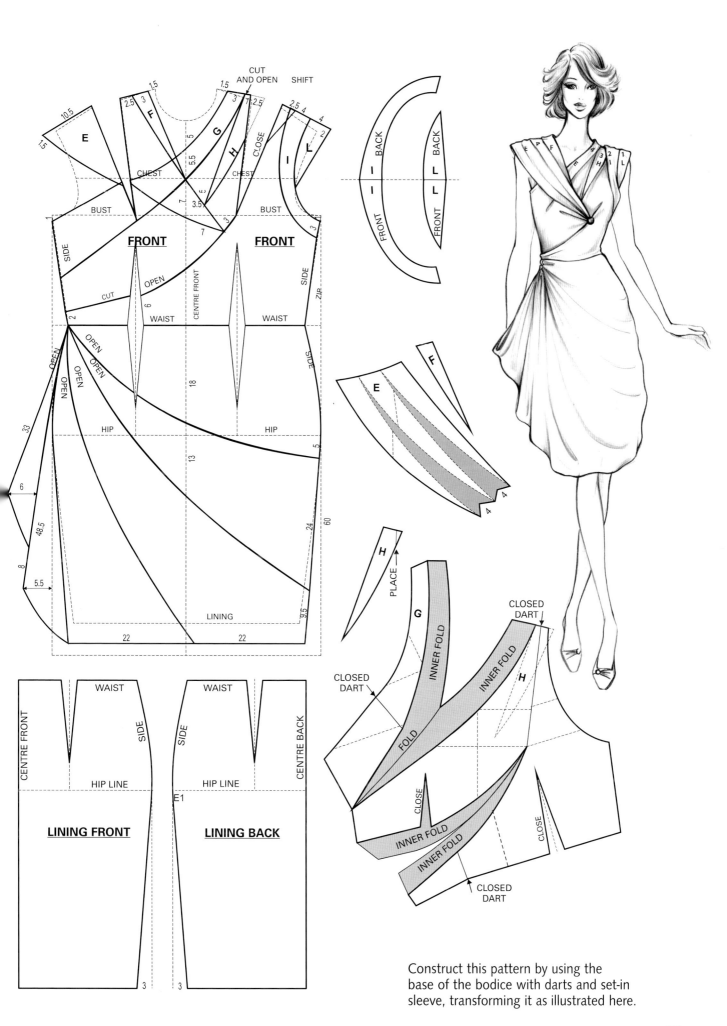

Construct this pattern by using the base of the bodice with darts and set-in sleeve, transforming it as illustrated here.

DRESS WITH PLEATS ON THE SHOULDERS AND GATHERING AT THE SIDE

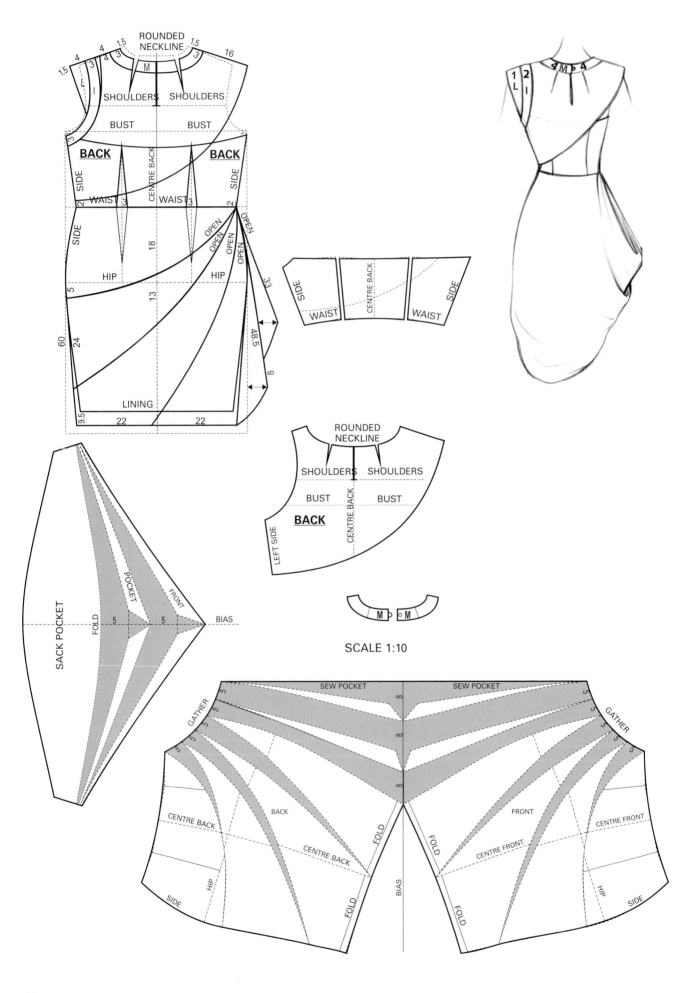

ROUNDED NECKLINE

SHOULDERS   SHOULDERS

BUST   BUST

BACK   **BACK**

SIDE   CENTRE BACK   SIDE

WAIST   WAIST

SIDE   OPEN   OPEN   OPEN   OPEN

HIP   HIP

LINING

SIDE   CENTRE BACK   SIDE

WAIST   WAIST

ROUNDED NECKLINE

SHOULDERS   SHOULDERS

BUST   CENTRE BACK   BUST

BACK

LEFT SIDE

M   M

SCALE 1:10

SACK POCKET   POCKET   FRONT

FOLD   5   5   BIAS

SEW POCKET   SEW POCKET

GATHER   GATHER

CENTRE BACK   BACK   FRONT   CENTRE FRONT

CENTRE BACK   FOLD   BIAS   FOLD   CENTRE FRONT

HIP   SIDE   FOLD   FOLD   HIP   SIDE

DRESS WITH BUBBLE SKIRT
WITH FOLDED "ORIGAMI" BODICE

DRESS WITH BUBBLE SKIRT

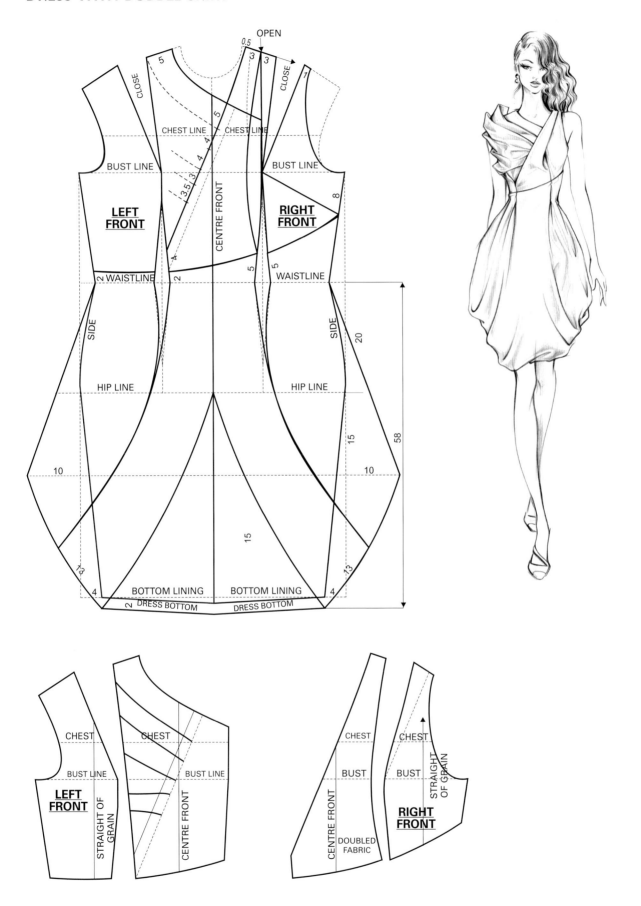

Construct this model from the base of the dress with darts and set-in sleeves, transforming it as illustrated here.

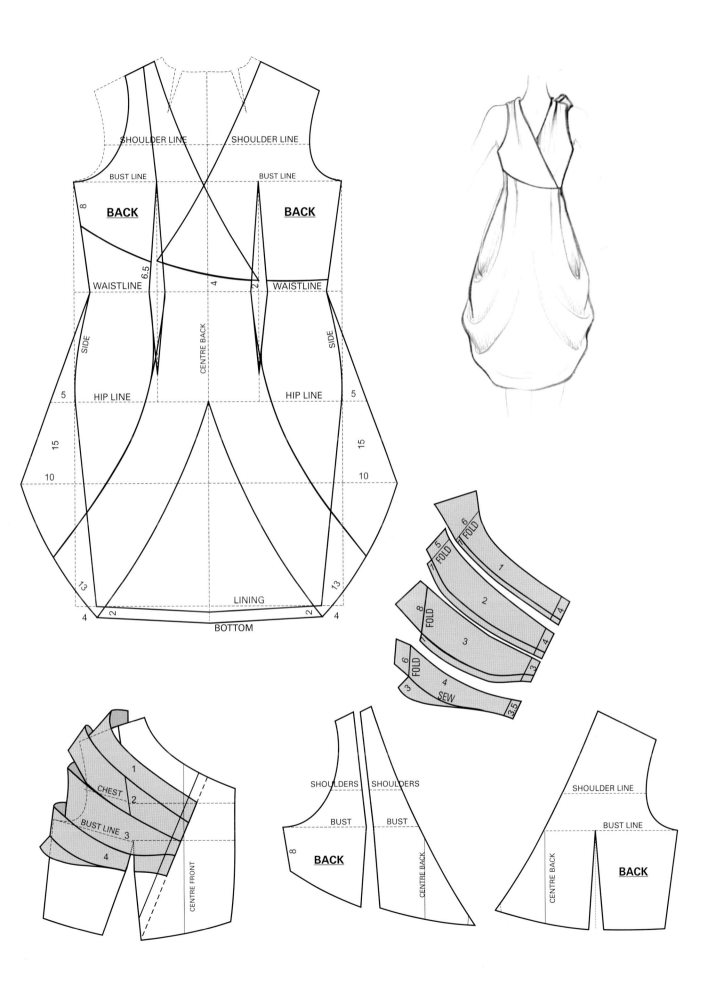

BACK

SHOULDER LINE   SHOULDER LINE

BUST LINE   BUST LINE

8   BACK   BACK

6.5   4   2

WAISTLINE   WAISTLINE

SIDE   CENTRE BACK   SIDE

5   HIP LINE   HIP LINE   5

15   15

10   10

13   13

LINING

4   2   2   4

BOTTOM

5   6
FOLD   FOLD
1
4
8
FOLD   2
3   4
6
FOLD   3
3   4
SEW   3.5

1
CHEST   2
BUST LINE   3
4
CENTRE FRONT

SHOULDERS   SHOULDERS

BUST   BUST

8   BACK   CENTRE BACK

SHOULDER LINE

BUST LINE

CENTRE BACK   BACK

DRESS WITH BUBBLE SKIRT

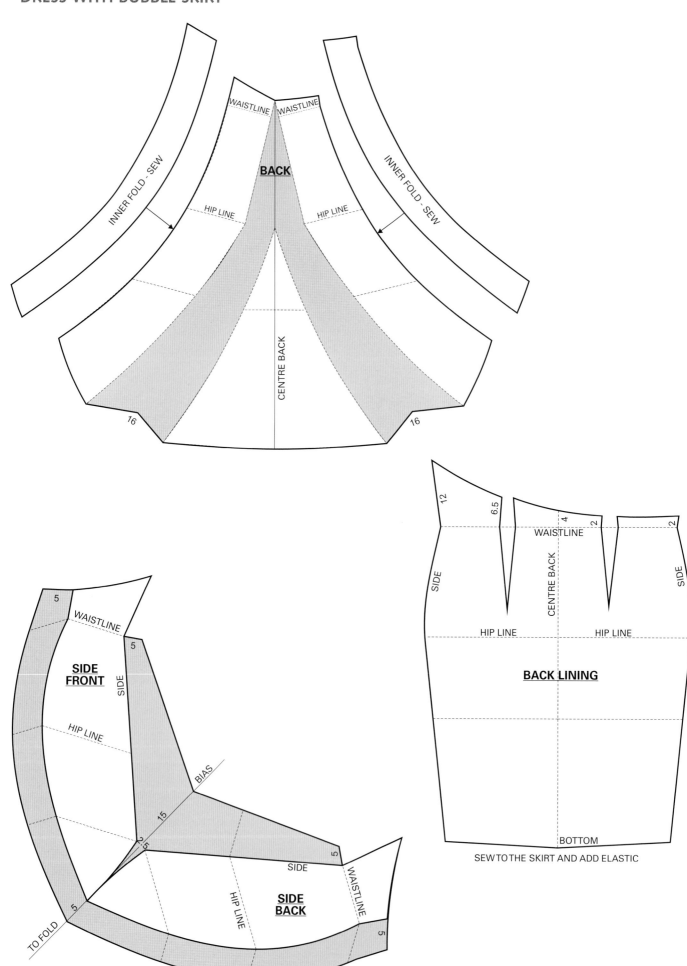

BACK

WAISTLINE WAISTLINE

INNER FOLD - SEW

INNER FOLD - SEW

HIP LINE

HIP LINE

CENTRE BACK

16

16

SIDE FRONT

5

5

WAISTLINE

SIDE

HIP LINE

BIAS

15

2.5

SIDE

5

SIDE BACK

HIP LINE

WAISTLINE

5

TO FOLD

5

5

BACK LINING

12

6.5

4

2

WAISTLINE

CENTRE BACK

SIDE

SIDE

2

HIP LINE

HIP LINE

BOTTOM

SEW TO THE SKIRT AND ADD ELASTIC

DRESS WITH HALTER NECK

WITH FRONT EMBELLISHMENT AND OVERLAPPING PANELS

DRESS WITH HALTER NECK

BODICE
- Draw the base of the bodice with darts with the appropriate ease.
- Draw the neckline and the band as shown in the figure.
- Draw the shaped embellishment panels.
- Take up the neckline after having closed the dart.

- Take up the band on the front and back, close the darts and smoothly join the two.
- Take up the single pieces of the front embellishment.
- Take up the front and back bodice and close the dart.

SKIRT

Add the measurement of the internal fold multiplied by the number of pleats to the waist semi-circumference. This pattern shows 4+4 cm (1.57+1.57") because there are two pleats, multiplied by the desired quantity (6 double pleats).

(E.g.: waist semi-cir. 36 + 48 (6x8) = 84)
- OA 26.76 cm (84 : 3.14 = 26.76 cm) / 10.54".
- Draw the arch AB ½ waist cir. + pleats.
- Draw the arch DC centred on O with AD equal to the desired skirt length (58 cm/ 22.83").
- Divide the arch CD into two equal parts. Point G.
- Draw the straight line OG. Hip division line.

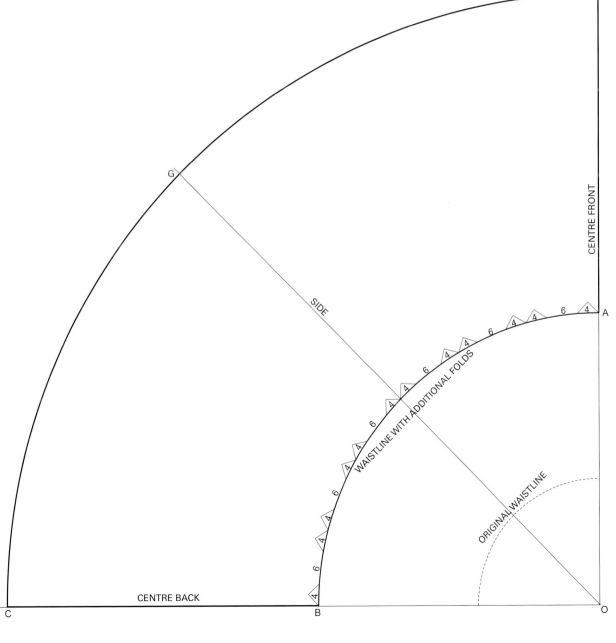

45

SINGLE-SHOULDER DRESS
WITH BOW DETAIL AND DRAPING

Construct this pattern by using the base of the dress with darts and set-in sleeve, transforming it as illustrated here.

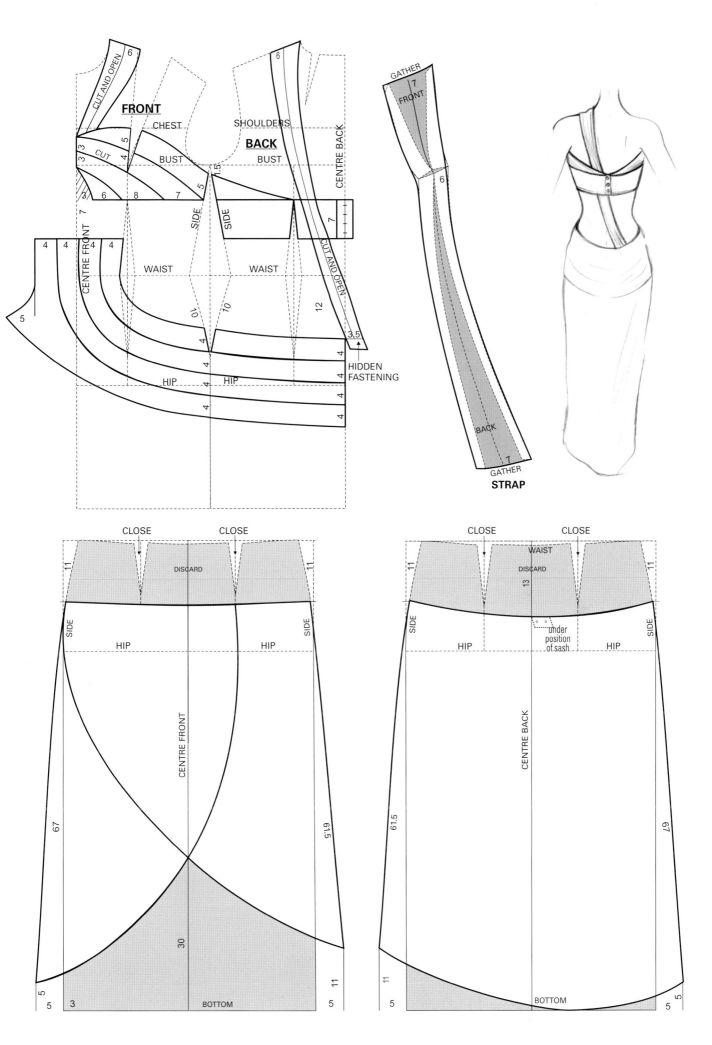

FRONT

BACK

CHEST

SHOULDERS

CUT AND OPEN

CUT

BUST

BUST

CENTRE BACK

CENTRE FRONT

SIDE

SIDE

WAIST

WAIST

CUT AND OPEN

HIDDEN FASTENING

HIP

HIP

GATHER

FRONT

BACK

GATHER

STRAP

CLOSE

CLOSE

DISCARD

SIDE

SIDE

HIP

HIP

CENTRE FRONT

BOTTOM

CLOSE

CLOSE

WAIST

DISCARD

under position of sash

SIDE

SIDE

HIP

HIP

CENTRE BACK

BOTTOM

47

SINGLE-SHOULDER DRESS

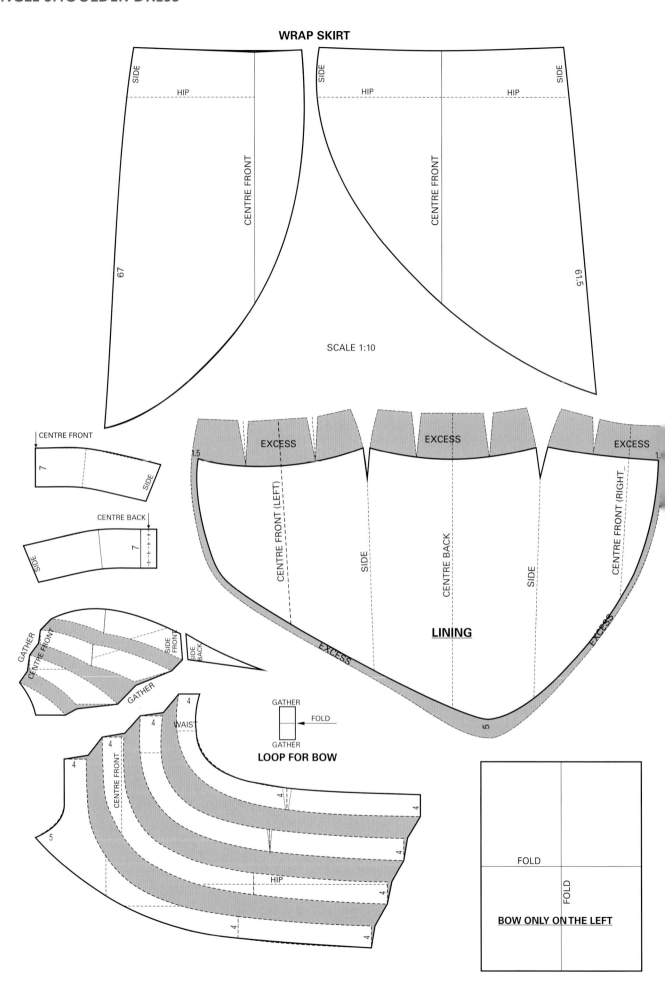

WRAP SKIRT

SIDE

HIP

CENTRE FRONT

67

SIDE

HIP

CENTRE FRONT

HIP

SIDE

61.5

SCALE 1:10

CENTRE FRONT

7

SIDE

CENTRE BACK

SIDE

7

1.5

EXCESS

EXCESS

EXCESS

CENTRE FRONT (LEFT)

SIDE

CENTRE BACK

SIDE

CENTRE FRONT (RIGHT)

LINING

EXCESS

EXCESS

5

GATHER

CENTRE FRONT

GATHER

CENTRE FRONT

SIDE FRONT

SIDE BACK

GATHER

GATHER

FOLD

LOOP FOR BOW

4

4

WAIST

4

4

CENTRE FRONT

4

5

4

4

4

HIP

4

4

4

FOLD

FOLD

BOW ONLY ON THE LEFT

48

BLOUSE WITH SHORT KIMONO SLEEVES
STAND-UP COLLAR, OVERLAPPING PANELS ON THE FRONT

BLOUSE WITH SHORT KIMONO SLEEVES

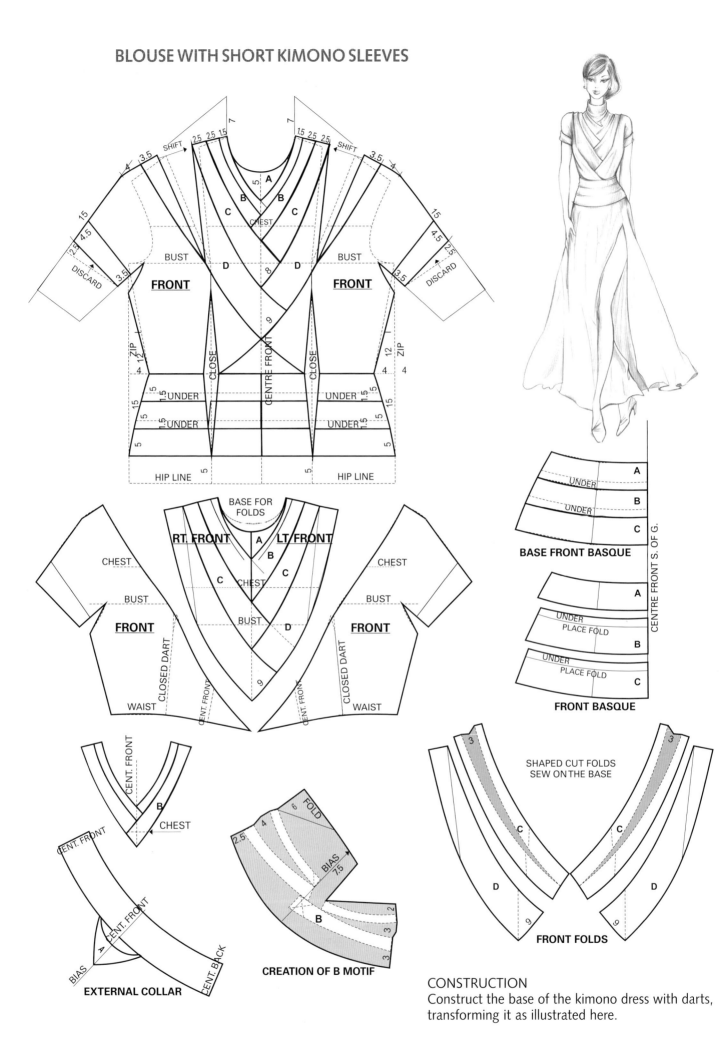

CONSTRUCTION
Construct the base of the kimono dress with darts, transforming it as illustrated here.

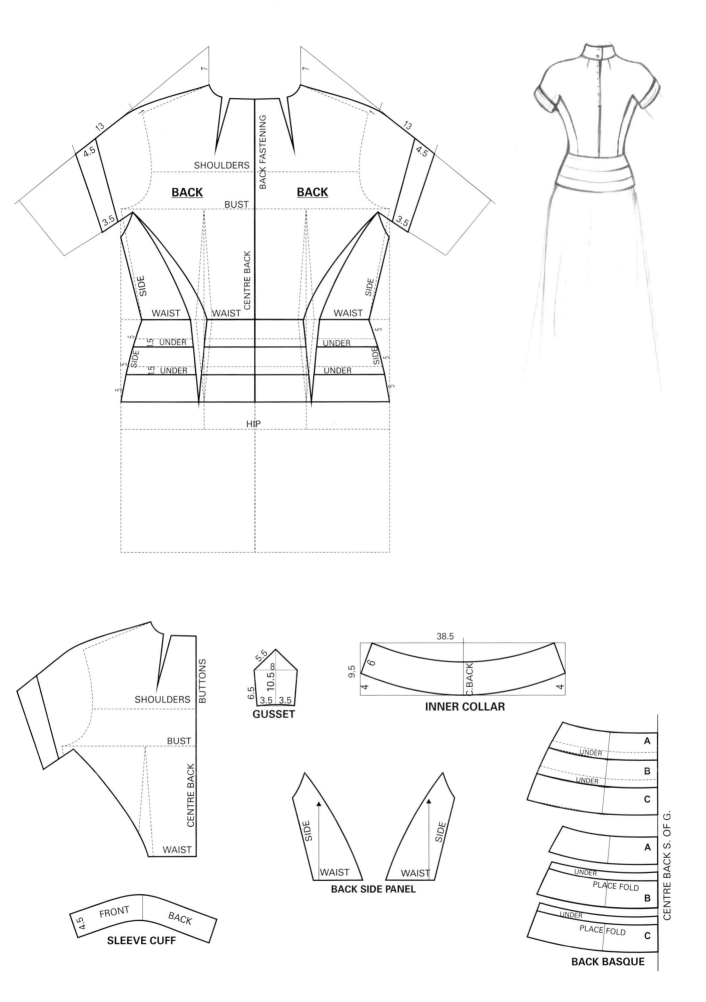

7

13

4.5

3.5

SHOULDERS

BACK FASTENING

BACK

BACK

BUST

CENTRE BACK

SIDE

SIDE

WAIST

WAIST

WAIST

5

1.5 UNDER

5

SIDE

5

1.5 UNDER

5

SIDE

UNDER

UNDER

5

HIP

SHOULDERS

BUTTONS

BUST

CENTRE BACK

WAIST

4.5 FRONT BACK

SLEEVE CUFF

5.5

8

10.5

6.5

3.5 3.5

GUSSET

38.5

9.5

6

4

C.BACK

4

INNER COLLAR

SIDE

SIDE

WAIST

WAIST

BACK SIDE PANEL

A

UNDER

B

UNDER

C

A

UNDER

PLACE FOLD

B

UNDER

PLACE FOLD

C

CENTRE BACK S. OF G.

BACK BASQUE

BUSTIER DRESS WITH OVERLAPPING FRILLS

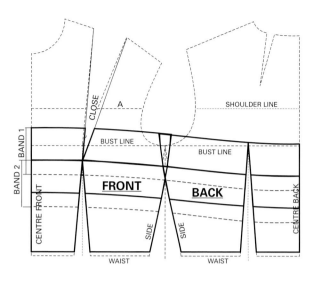

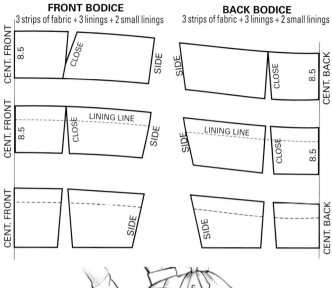

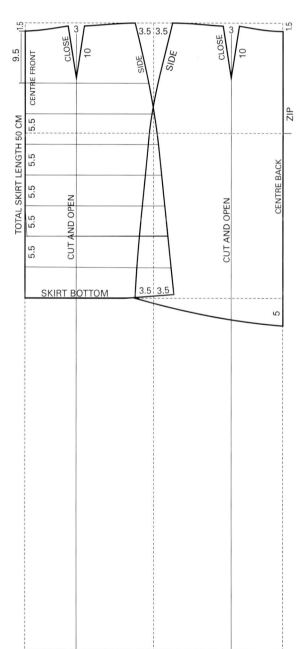

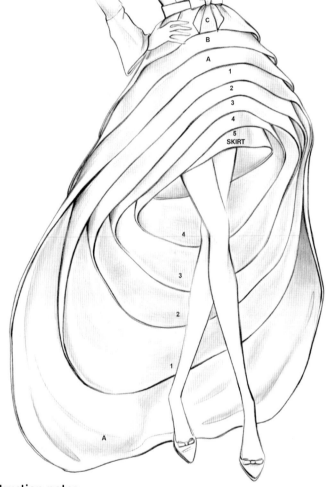

Construction notes

For this dress we recommend using a lightweight material which is still a bit rigid, such as taffeta. The layers are doubled with the seams on the inside, except the straight skirt underneath, close to the legs.

Layers 1, 2, and 3 are to be sewn into the waist along with the bodice and the skirt underneath. The other 4 are to be sewn to a lining sewn into the waist, which is quite short (20 cm / 7.87") as it shouldn't be visible). Layers 4 and 5 are to be sewn to the lining 10 cm / 3.94" from the waist, and layers 6 and 7 on the hem of the lining.

We also recommend inserting a nylon cord in the seams of the petals to create a perfect oval.

BUSTIER DRESS WITH OVERLAPPING FRILLS

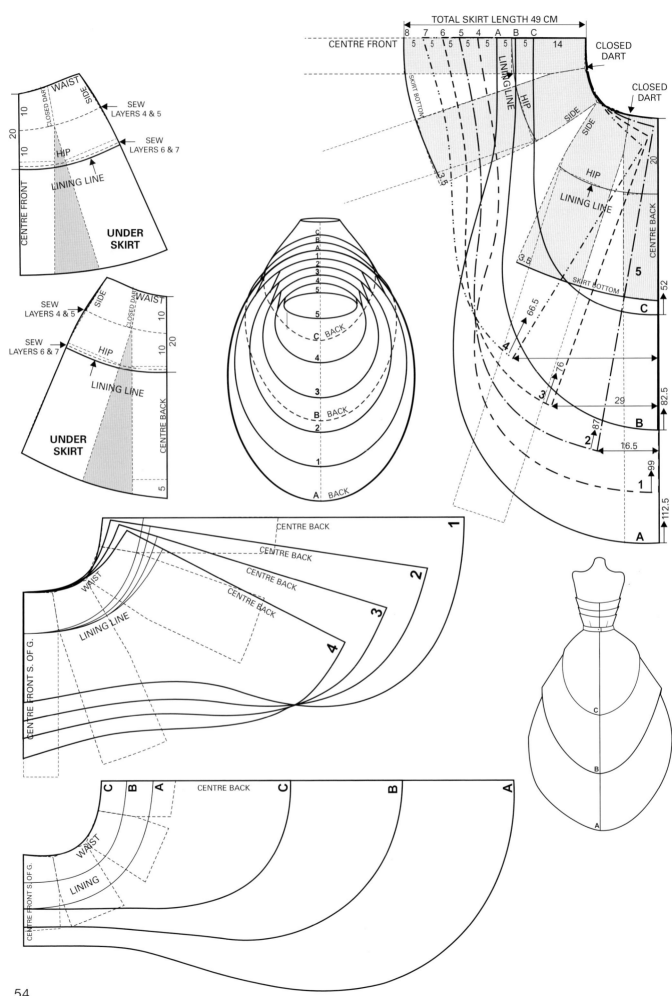

FITTED JACKET WITH OVERLAPPING FRILLS ON THE SLEEVES

DOUBLE SKIRT IN THE FRONT

FITTED JACKET WITH OVERLAPPING FRILLS ON THE SLEEVES

JOIN WITH THE BACK

FRONT

BACK

CENTRE FRONT

BUST

WAIST

SIDE

HIP

CENTRE BACK

SHOULDER LINE

BUST

WAIST

SIDE

HIP LINE

FRONT

BACK

CENTRE FRONT

WAIST

HIP

SHOULDER

BUST

BACK

SIDE

SIDE

HIP

SHOULDER

BUST

SIDE

CENTRE BACK

HIP

CLOSED DART

C. FRONT

BUST

BUST

DOUBLE

FRONT STRAP

BASE FRONT SLEEVE FOR FOLDS

SHOULDER

BUST

CENTRE BACK

BASE BACK SLEEVE FOR FOLDS

CONSTRUCTION

Construct the base of the kimono dress with darts and a tube skirt, transforming it as illustrated here.

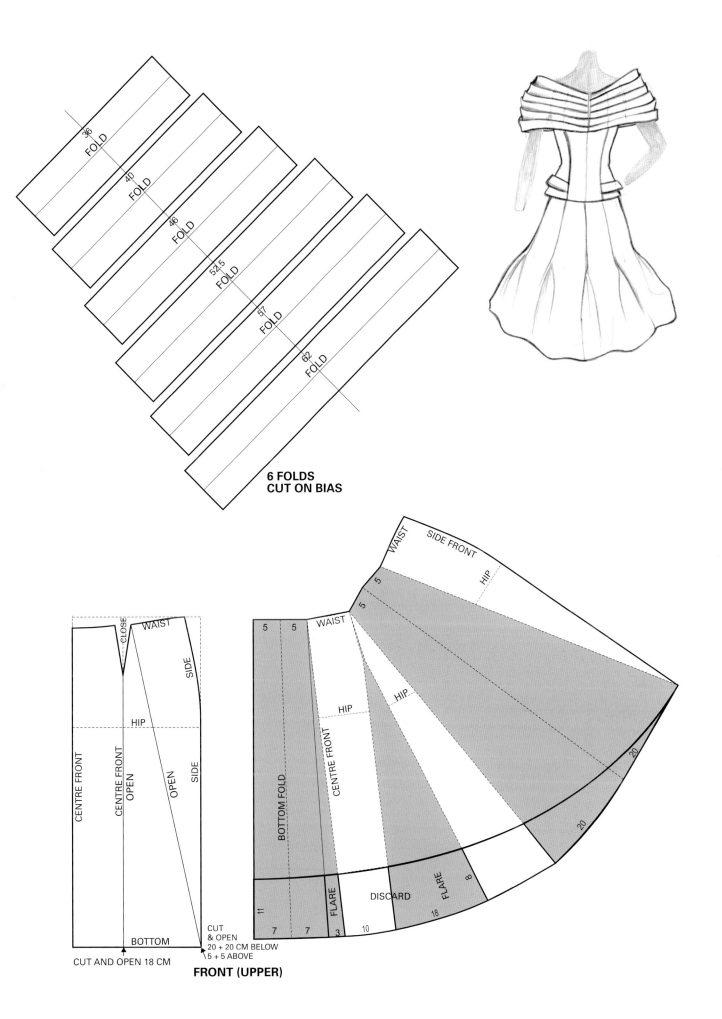

**6 FOLDS
CUT ON BIAS**

36 FOLD
40 FOLD
46 FOLD
52.5 FOLD
57 FOLD
62 FOLD

WAIST
SIDE FRONT
HIP
5
5
WAIST
5 5
HIP
HIP
BOTTOM FOLD
CENTRE FRONT
20
20
FLARE
DISCARD
FLARE
8
11
18
7 7 3 10

CLOSE
WAIST
SIDE
CENTRE FRONT
CENTRE FRONT
OPEN
OPEN
SIDE
HIP
BOTTOM
CUT
& OPEN
20 + 20 CM BELOW
5 + 5 ABOVE
CUT AND OPEN 18 CM

FRONT (UPPER)

57

FITTED JACKET WITH OVERLAPPING FRILLS ON THE SLEEVES

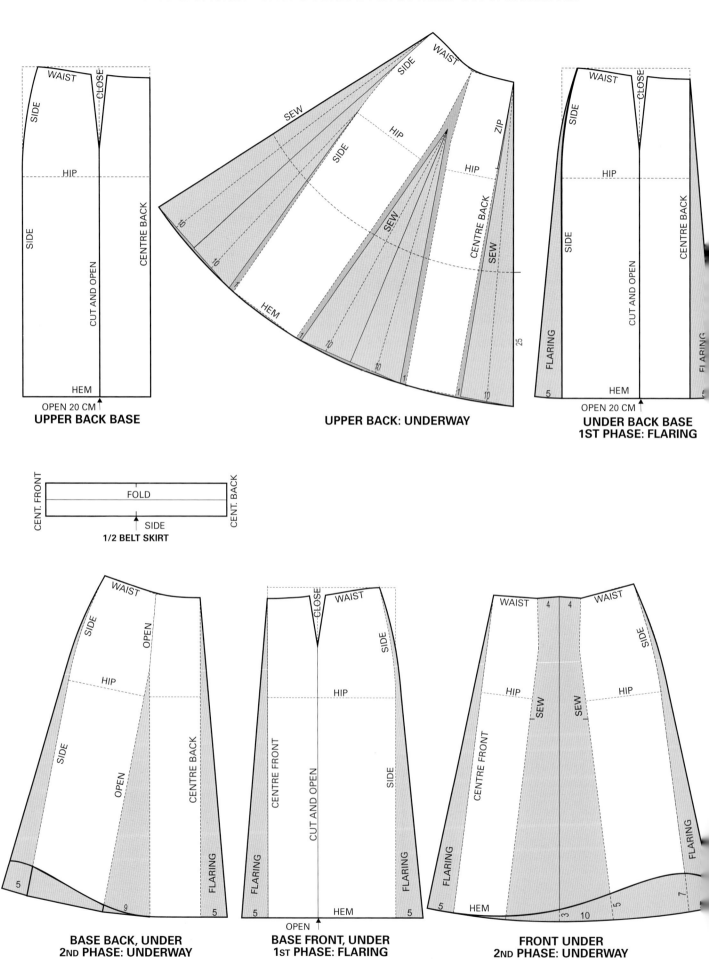

UPPER BACK BASE

UPPER BACK: UNDERWAY

UNDER BACK BASE
1ST PHASE: FLARING

1/2 BELT SKIRT

BASE BACK, UNDER
2ND PHASE: UNDERWAY

BASE FRONT, UNDER
1ST PHASE: FLARING

FRONT UNDER
2ND PHASE: UNDERWAY

DRESS WITH OVERLAPPING, PLEATED PUFF SLEEVES

AND CRISS-CROSS BANDS ON THE FRONT

DRESS WITH OVERLAPPING PUFF SLEEVES

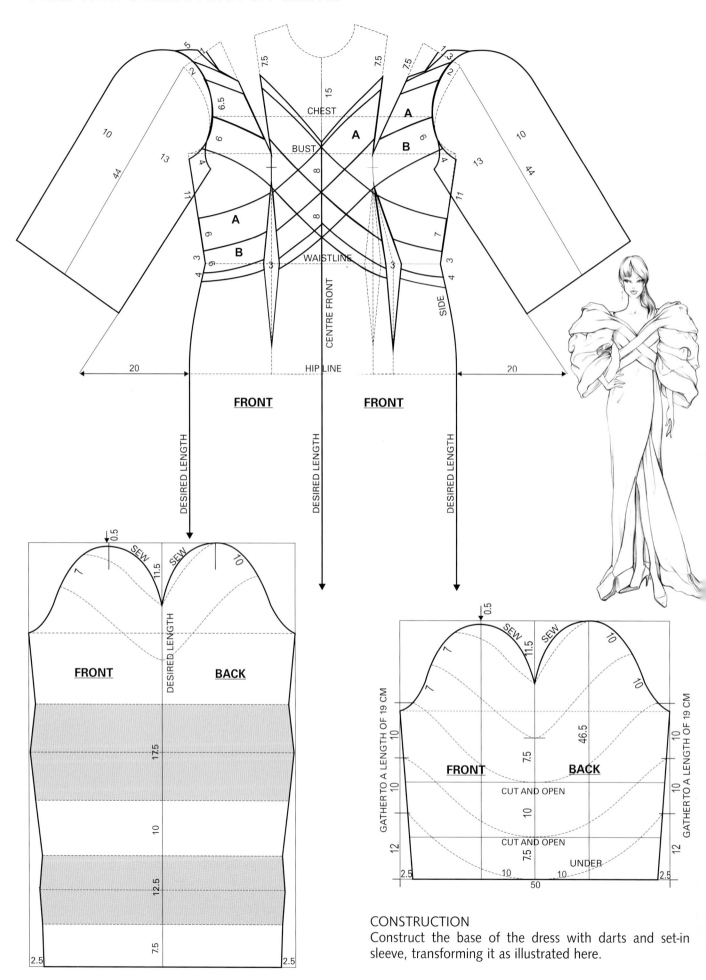

CONSTRUCTION
Construct the base of the dress with darts and set-in sleeve, transforming it as illustrated here.

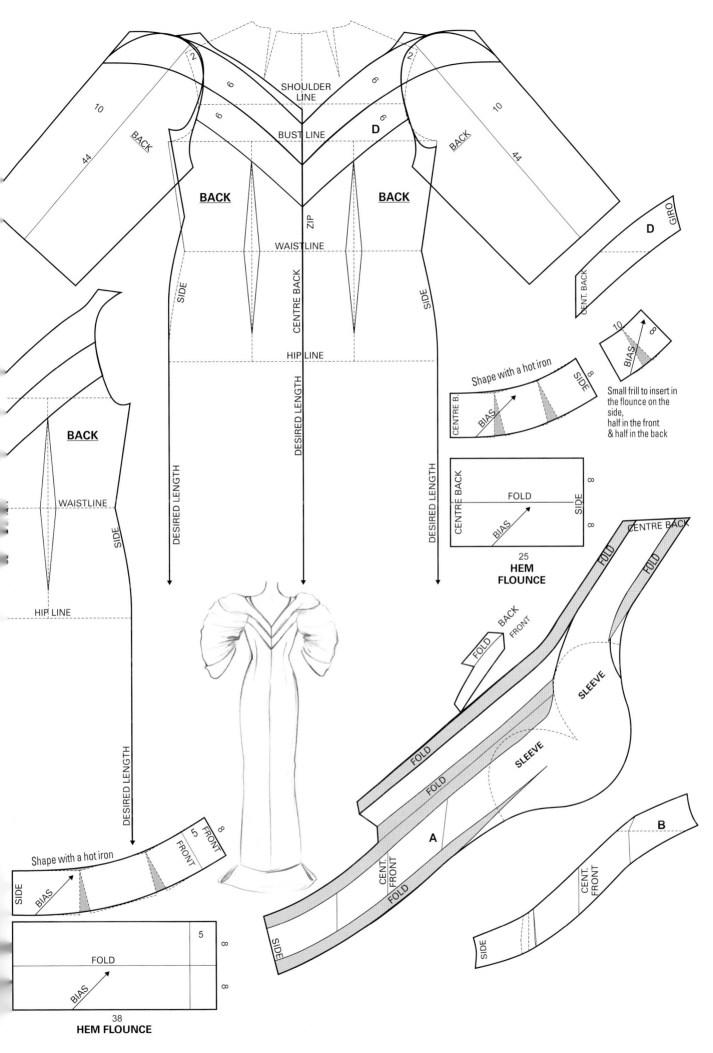

SHOULDER LINE

BUST LINE

D

BACK

BACK

BACK

2

6

6

6

6

10

10

44

44

ZIP

WAISTLINE

CENTRE BACK

SIDE

SIDE

HIP LINE

DESIRED LENGTH

DESIRED LENGTH

DESIRED LENGTH

BACK

WAISTLINE

SIDE

HIP LINE

DESIRED LENGTH

D

GIRO

CENT. BACK

10

8

BIAS

Small frill to insert in the flounce on the side, half in the front & half in the back

Shape with a hot iron

CENTRE B.

BIAS

SIDE

8

8

CENTRE BACK

FOLD

BIAS

SIDE

8

8

25

HEM FLOUNCE

CENTRE BACK

FOLD

FOLD

FOLD

FOLD

FOLD

BACK

FRONT

SLEEVE

SLEEVE

A

B

CENT. FRONT

CENT. FRONT

SIDE

SIDE

Shape with a hot iron

SIDE

BIAS

FRONT

FRONT

5

8

5

8

FOLD

BIAS

8

38

HEM FLOUNCE

DRESS WITH A PLEATED STAND-UP COLLAR
FLOWING BELOW THE KNEE WITH A SPIRAL AT THE CENTRE

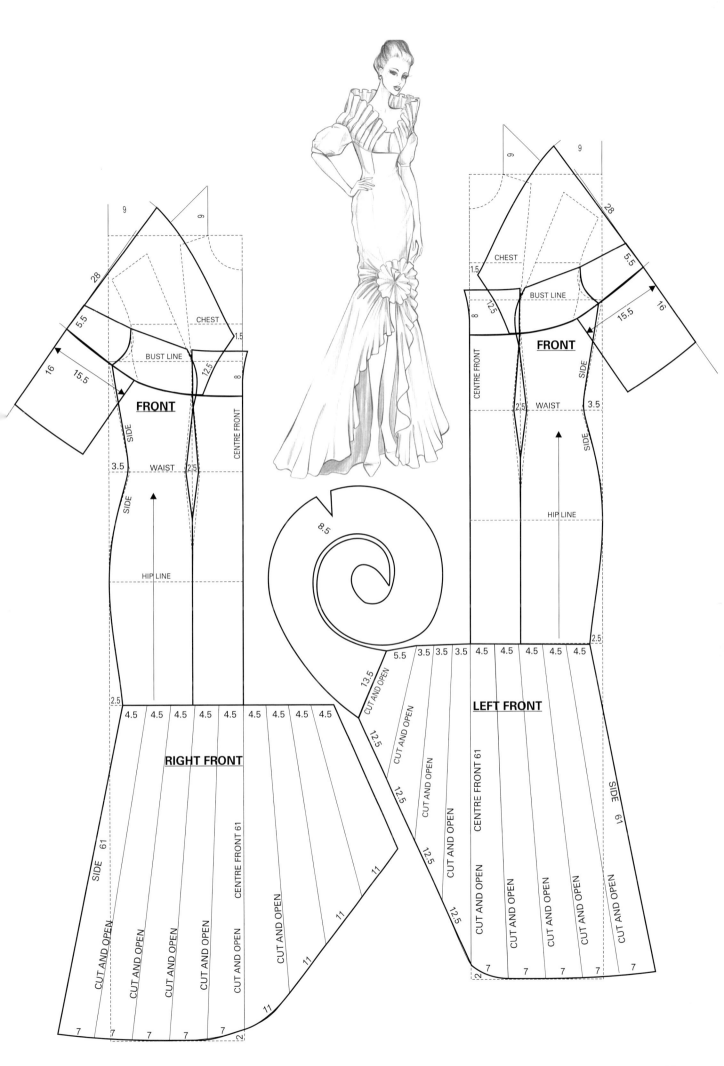

FRONT

FRONT

RIGHT FRONT

LEFT FRONT

DRESS WITH A PLEATED STAND-UP COLLAR

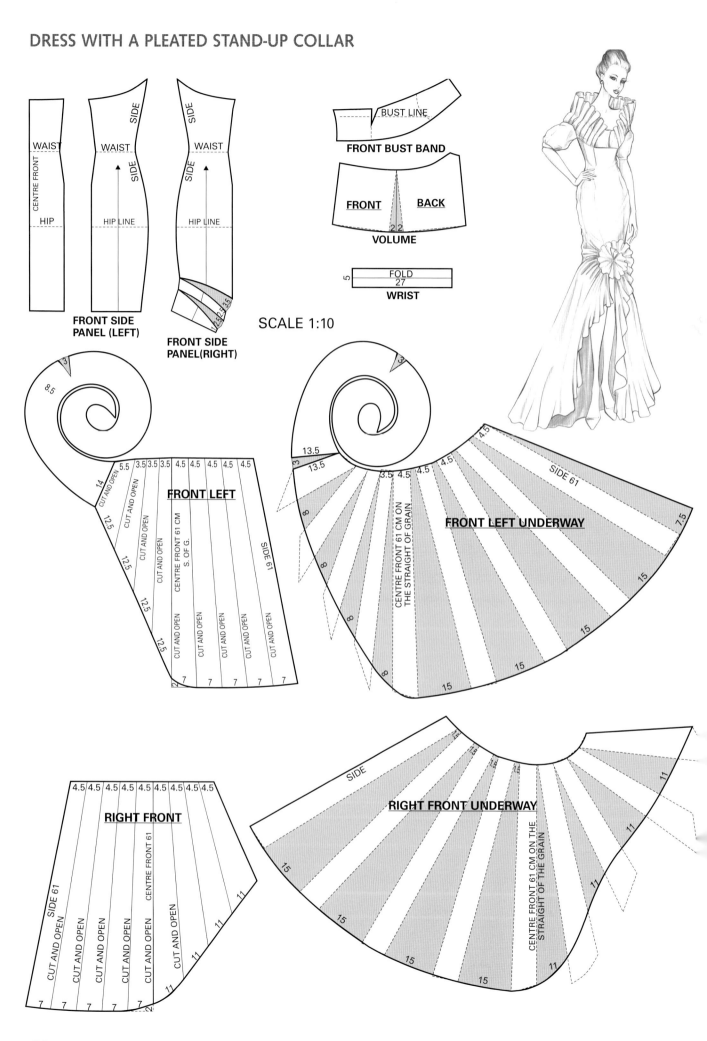

FRONT SIDE PANEL (LEFT)

FRONT SIDE PANEL(RIGHT)

SCALE 1:10

FRONT BUST BAND

BUST LINE

FRONT **BACK**

VOLUME

FOLD
27
WRIST

FRONT LEFT

CENTRE FRONT 61 CM
S. OF G.

SIDE 61

CUT AND OPEN

FRONT LEFT UNDERWAY

SIDE 61

CENTRE FRONT 61 CM ON
THE STRAIGHT OF GRAIN

RIGHT FRONT

SIDE 61

CENTRE FRONT 61

CUT AND OPEN

RIGHT FRONT UNDERWAY

SIDE

CENTRE FRONT 61 CM ON THE
STRAIGHT OF THE GRAIN

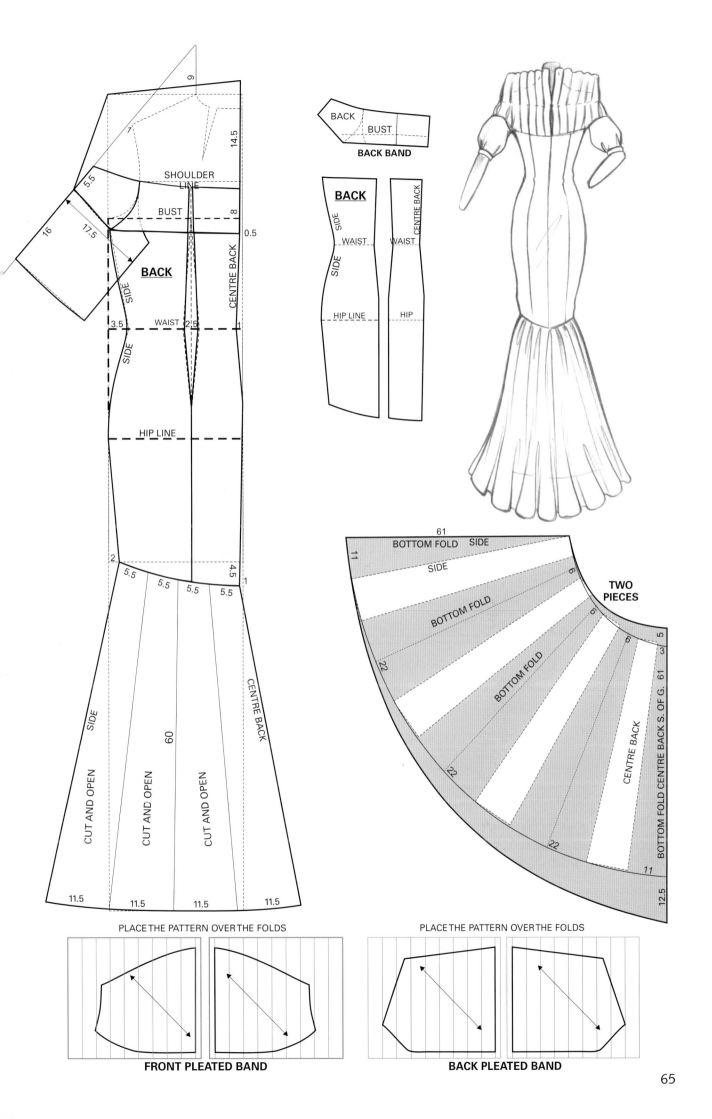

BACK

BACK BAND

BACK

SHOULDER LINE

BUST

CENTRE BACK

WAIST

SIDE

SIDE

HIP LINE

CUT AND OPEN

CUT AND OPEN

CUT AND OPEN

SIDE

CENTRE BACK

60

BACK

SIDE

WAIST

HIP LINE

CENTRE BACK

WAIST

HIP

BOTTOM FOLD   SIDE

SIDE

BOTTOM FOLD

BOTTOM FOLD

TWO PIECES

CENTRE BACK

BOTTOM FOLD CENTRE BACK S. OF G. 61

PLACE THE PATTERN OVER THE FOLDS

FRONT PLEATED BAND

PLACE THE PATTERN OVER THE FOLDS

BACK PLEATED BAND

65

TROUSERS AND MATCHING JACKET
JACKET AND TROUSERS WITH FAN-SHAPED INSERTS

JACKET WITH FAN-SHAPED INSERTS AND PLEATS

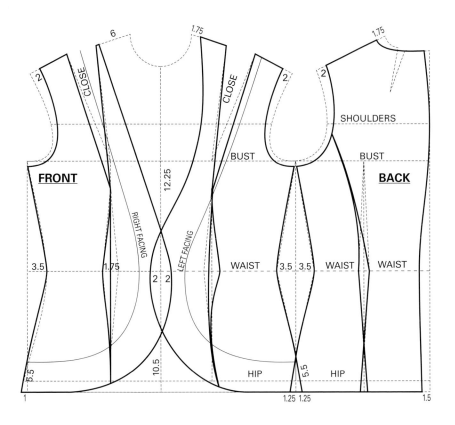

Pattern created using the jacket base with darts, with set-in sleeves and appropriate ease, transforming them as illustrated here.

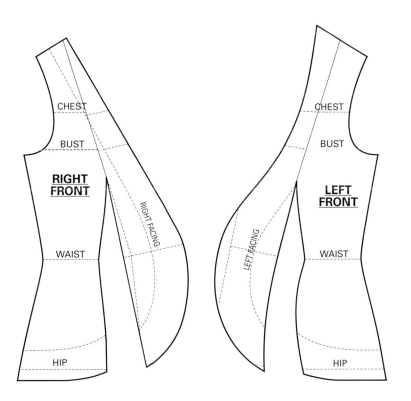

TROUSERS WITH FAN-SHAPED INSERTS AND PLEATS

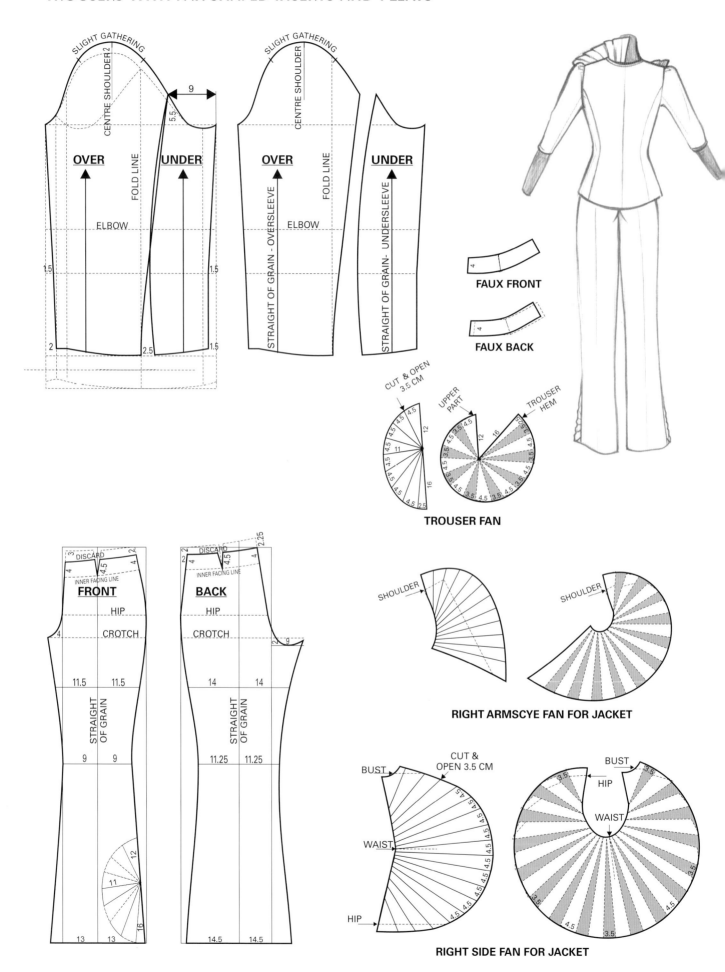

SLIGHT GATHERING

CENTRE SHOULDER 2

OVER FOLD LINE **UNDER**

ELBOW

9

5.5

1.5 1.5

1.5

2 2.5 1.5

SLIGHT GATHERING

CENTRE SHOULDER

OVER FOLD LINE **UNDER**

ELBOW

STRAIGHT OF GRAIN - OVERSLEEVE

STRAIGHT OF GRAIN - UNDERSLEEVE

4 **FAUX FRONT**

4 **FAUX BACK**

CUT & OPEN 3.5 CM

UPPER PART

TROUSER HEM

12 16

11 4.5 4.5

16 4.5

2.5

TROUSER FAN

SHOULDER

SHOULDER

RIGHT ARMSCYE FAN FOR JACKET

DISCARD 3 2

4 4.5 4

INNER FACING LINE

FRONT

HIP

CROTCH

4

11.5 11.5

STRAIGHT OF GRAIN

9 9

12

11

16

13 13

2.25

DISCARD 2

2 4 4.5 4

INNER FACING LINE

BACK

HIP

CROTCH

2 9

14 14

STRAIGHT OF GRAIN

11.25 11.25

14.5 14.5

CUT & OPEN 3.5 CM

BUST

WAIST

HIP

BUST 3.5

HIP

WAIST

3.5

RIGHT SIDE FAN FOR JACKET

68

TROUSERS AND CREATIVE-SLEEVE JACKET

WITH CREATIVE SLEEVES AND WING-PEAKS AT THE SHOULDER

TROUSER-JACKET SET

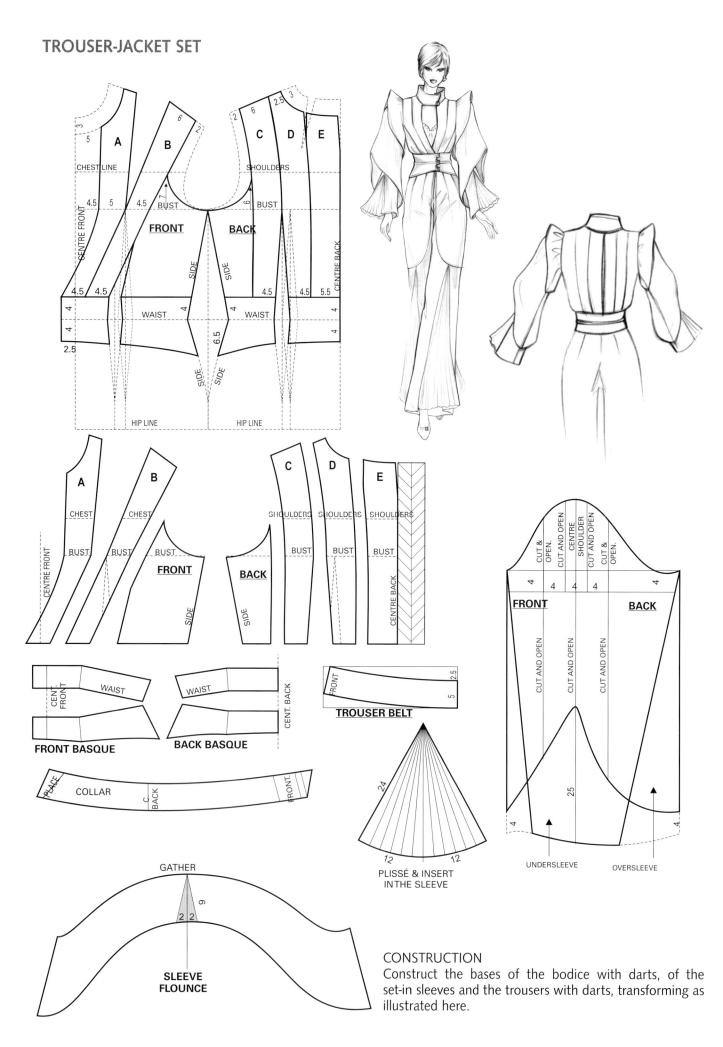

FRONT   **BACK**

CHESTLINE · SHOULDERS · BUST · WAIST · HIP LINE · CENTRE FRONT · CENTRE BACK · SIDE

3 · 5 · A · B · 6 · 2 · 2 · 6 · 2.5 · 3 · C · D · E
4.5 · 5 · 4.5 · 6 · 4.5 · 4.5 · 5.5
4 · 4 · 4 · 4 · 4
2.5 · 6.5 · 4

A · B · C · D · E
CHEST · BUST · SHOULDERS · CENTRE FRONT · CENTRE BACK · SIDE · FRONT · BACK

FRONT BASQUE · BACK BASQUE
CENT. FRONT · WAIST · CENT. BACK

TROUSER BELT
FRONT · 2.5 · 5

COLLAR
PLACE · C. BACK · FRONT

PLISSÉ & INSERT IN THE SLEEVE
24 · 12 · 12

FRONT · BACK
CUT & OPEN · CUT AND OPEN · CENTRE SHOULDER · CUT AND OPEN · CUT & OPEN
4 · 4 · 4 · 4 · 4
CUT AND OPEN · CUT AND OPEN · CUT AND OPEN
25
4 · 4
UNDERSLEEVE · OVERSLEEVE

GATHER
9 · 2 · 2
SLEEVE FLOUNCE

CONSTRUCTION
Construct the bases of the bodice with darts, of the set-in sleeves and the trousers with darts, transforming as illustrated here.

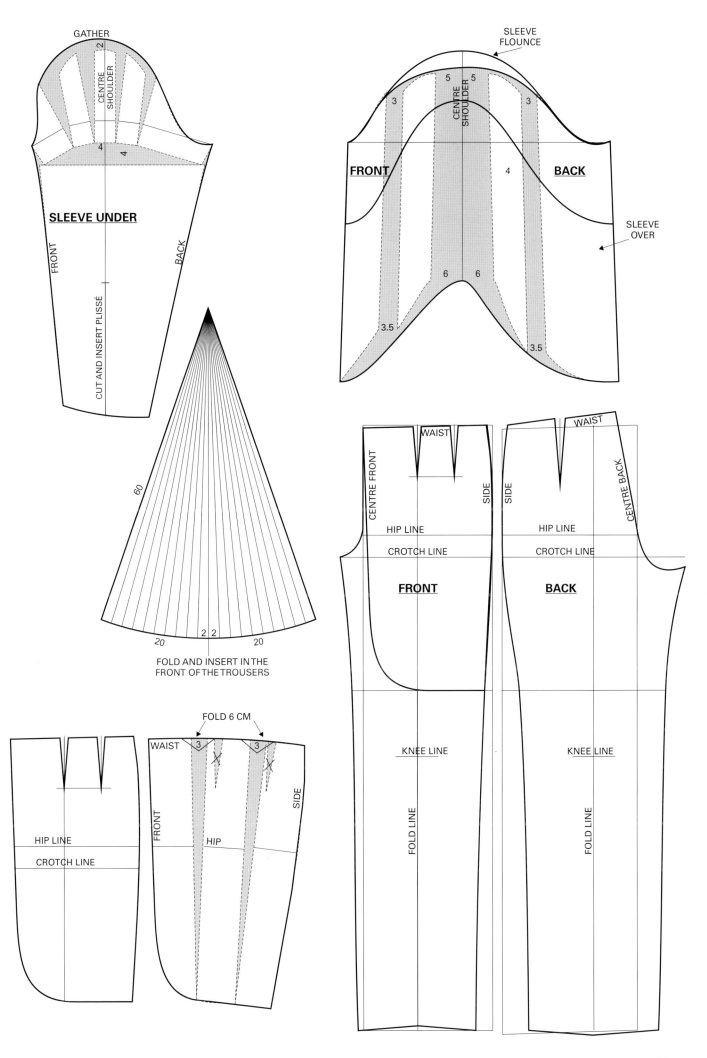

GATHER

2

CENTRE SHOULDER

4　4

SLEEVE UNDER

FRONT

BACK

CUT AND INSERT PLISSÉ

SLEEVE FLOUNCE

5　5

3　CENTRE SHOULDER　3

FRONT　4　**BACK**

SLEEVE OVER

6　6

3.5　3.5

60

20　2　2　20

FOLD AND INSERT IN THE
FRONT OF THE TROUSERS

CENTRE FRONT

WAIST

SIDE

SIDE

WAIST

CENTRE BACK

HIP LINE

CROTCH LINE

HIP LINE

CROTCH LINE

FRONT　**BACK**

KNEE LINE　KNEE LINE

FOLD LINE　FOLD LINE

HIP LINE

CROTCH LINE

FOLD 6 CM

WAIST　3　3

FRONT

HIP

SIDE

71

1950s STYLE DRESS

WITH FOLDS AT THE WAIST AND FLARED HEMLINE

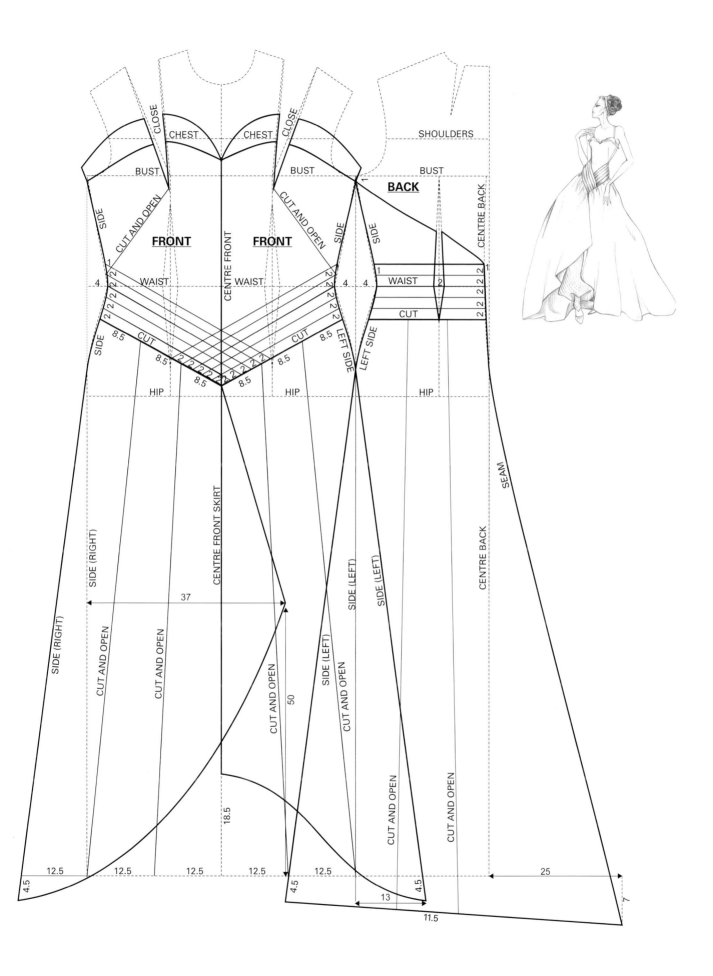

CLOSE

CHEST CHEST

CLOSE

SHOULDERS

BUST BUST BUST

BACK

SIDE SIDE CUT AND OPEN **FRONT** CENTRE FRONT **FRONT** CUT AND OPEN SIDE SIDE SIDE CENTRE BACK

1 1
2 2 2 2 2 1 WAIST 2 2 2 2 1
4 WAIST WAIST 4 4

CUT

SIDE 8.5 CUT CUT 8.5 LEFT SIDE LEFT SIDE

8.5 2 2 2 2 8.5

8.5 8.5

HIP HIP HIP

SIDE (RIGHT) CENTRE FRONT SKIRT SIDE (LEFT) SIDE (LEFT) CENTRE BACK SEAM

SIDE (RIGHT) CUT AND OPEN CUT AND OPEN

37

CUT AND OPEN 50 SIDE (LEFT)

CUT AND OPEN CUT AND OPEN CUT AND OPEN

18.5

12.5 12.5 12.5 12.5 12.5

4.5 4.5 4.5

13

11.5

25

7

73

1950s STYLE DRESS

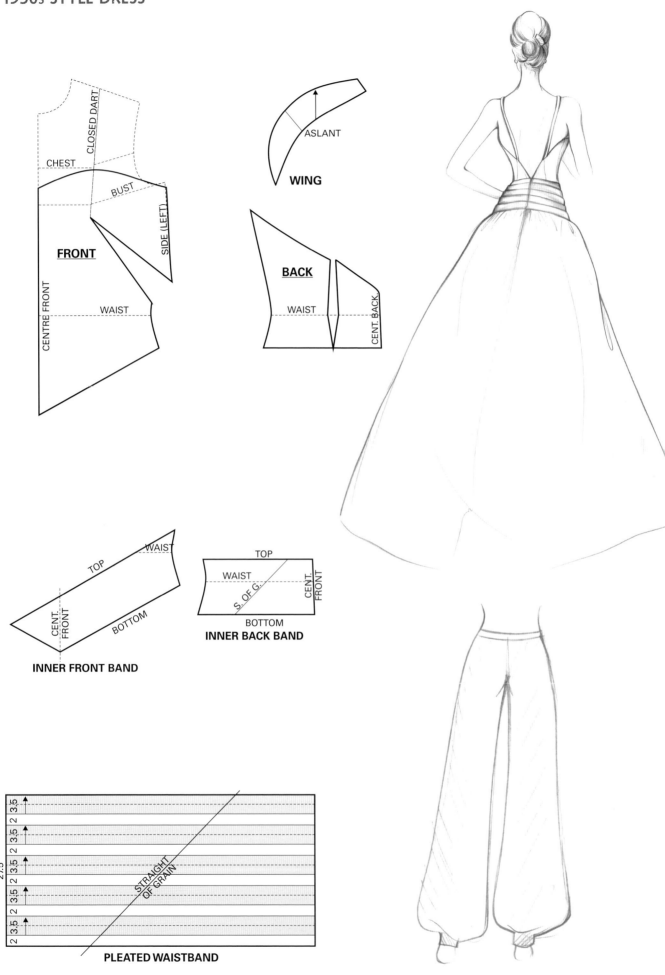

CLOSED DART

CHEST

BUST

SIDE (LEFT)

FRONT

CENTRE FRONT

WAIST

ASLANT

WING

BACK

WAIST

CENT. BACK.

TOP

WAIST

CENT. FRONT

BOTTOM

INNER FRONT BAND

TOP

WAIST

S. OF G.

CENT. FRONT

BOTTOM

INNER BACK BAND

27.5

3.5 2 3.5 2 3.5 2 3.5 2 3.5 2

STRAIGHT OF GRAIN

PLEATED WAISTBAND

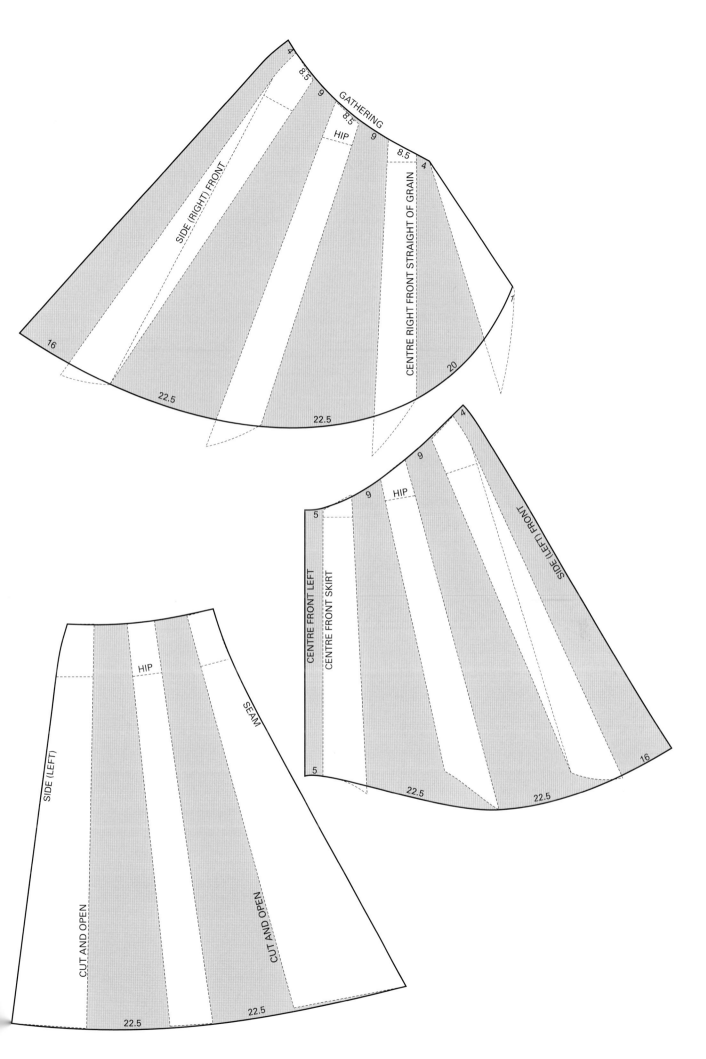

SIDE (RIGHT) FRONT

GATHERING

4
8.5
9
8.5
HIP
9
8.5
4

CENTRE RIGHT FRONT STRAIGHT OF GRAIN

16

22.5

22.5

20

4
9
9
HIP
5
CENTRE FRONT LEFT
CENTRE FRONT SKIRT
SIDE (LEFT) FRONT
16
5
22.5
22.5

HIP

SEAM

SIDE (LEFT)

CUT AND OPEN

CUT AND OPEN

22.5

22.5

DRESS WITH A WIDE, COROLLA-SHAPED COLLAR

WHICH MAKES A SMALL CAPE ON THE BACK

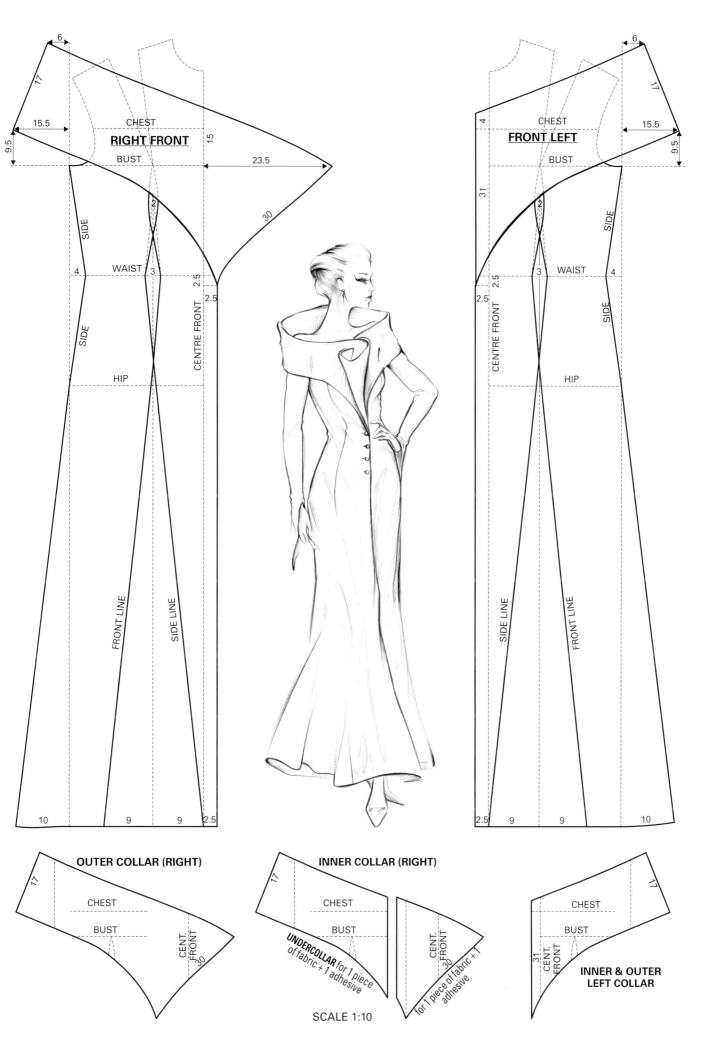

RIGHT FRONT

6
17
15.5
9.5
CHEST
15
BUST
23.5
30
SIDE
WAIST
4
3
2.5
2.5
CENTRE FRONT
SIDE
HIP
FRONT LINE
SIDE LINE
10
9
9
2.5

FRONT LEFT

6
17
15.5
9.5
4
CHEST
BUST
31
SIDE
2
WAIST
3
4
2.5
2.5
CENTRE FRONT
SIDE
HIP
SIDE LINE
FRONT LINE
2.5
9
9
10

OUTER COLLAR (RIGHT)

17
CHEST
BUST
CENT. FRONT
30

INNER COLLAR (RIGHT)

17
CHEST
BUST
UNDERCOLLAR for 1 piece of fabric + 1 adhesive
CENT. FRONT
30
for 1 piece of fabric + 1 adhesive

SCALE 1:10

INNER & OUTER LEFT COLLAR

17
CHEST
BUST
31
CENT. FRONT

77

DRESS WITH A WIDE, COROLLA-SHAPED COLLAR

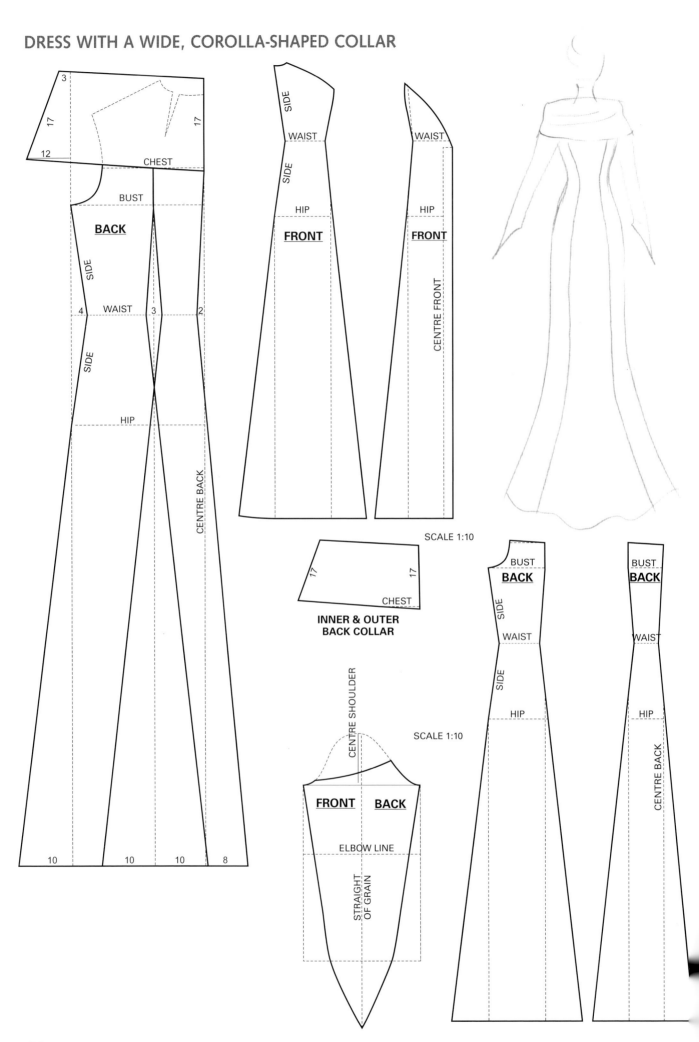

3

17

12

CHEST

BACK

BUST

SIDE

4 WAIST 3 2

SIDE

HIP

CENTRE BACK

10 10 10 8

SIDE

WAIST

SIDE

HIP

FRONT

WAIST

HIP

FRONT

CENTRE FRONT

SCALE 1:10

17 17

CHEST

**INNER & OUTER
BACK COLLAR**

CENTRE SHOULDER

SCALE 1:10

FRONT   BACK

ELBOW LINE

STRAIGHT
OF GRAIN

BUST

BACK

SIDE

WAIST

SIDE

HIP

BUST

BACK

WAIST

HIP

CENTRE BACK

3. RUFFLES, FLOUNCES AND JABOT

RUFFLES, FLOUNCES AND JABOT

Even if used interchangeably, from a technical point a view "ruffles" and "flounces" are quite different. Both are wavy pieces of fabric which sinuously fall on the body, a favourite of women who love to highlight their femininity.

RUFFLES

Ruffles are decorative applications of fabric which are attached to the main garment fabric by a central seam, making them curl on both sides. Ruffles are used to decorate and trim hems and edges. They can be sewn under skirts, at the edges of shirt sleeves, along the chest of a blouse or dress, and even on curtains or pillows.

FLOUNCES

Flounces, on the other hand, are applied with a single seam, edge to edge, which makes them curled only along one side. To create the flounce, you must measure the edge or the seam of the garment where it is to be applied. They may be either:

1. Gathered (Fig.1) along the part which is to be sewn to the garment. In this case, the length must be one and a half times the measurement of the hem, or as otherwise desired. The cut can be either on the bias or straight. Trace a rectangle, the height of which is equal to the applied piece to be made plus a centimetre for the seam, and the length equal to one and a half times the measurement of the edge of the garment to be decorated. If you want a very curly flounce, the length of the rectangle should be double that of the edge. The curliness depends on how long the piece of fabric is. Once the rectangle is cut, you'll need to finish the edges of the fabric. Flounces can be single or double layer.

If you'd like to make a double-curled flounce, bias-cut a rectangle of fabric which is double the measurement needed and fold it in half. Baste stitch it to the fabric, put face-to-face, machine sew and then turn over.

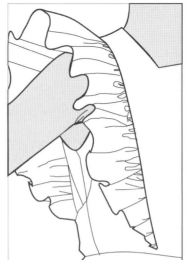 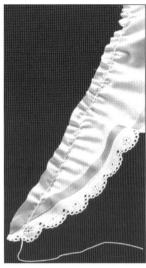

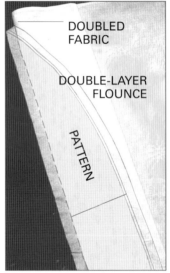 

DOUBLED FABRIC

DOUBLE-LAYER FLOUNCE

PATTERN

FLOUNCE GATHERED ALONG THE EDGE TO BE SEWN
To gather a long piece of fabric, sew a zig-zag stitch over a thick piece of string or pearl cotton, which won't break apart when pulled. Pull the thick string, evenly distributing the gathering, and pin it at the ends to hold it in place. Sew the flounce to the "right" side of the garment and remove the thick string. Single layer flounces should be made in dense fabric or in fabric which is slightly transparent, such as brodierie anglaise or see-through prints.

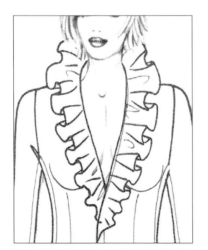

SPIRAL FLOUNCE MADE WITH NOTCHES
Collars trimmed with flounces are made by creating a more or less upright shawl collar, as desired:
- Measure the collar of the garment.

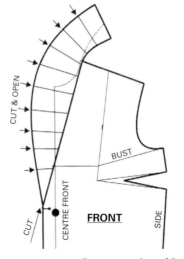

CUT & OPEN

BUST

CENTRE FRONT

CUT

FRONT

SIDE

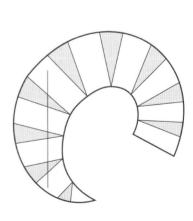

- Draw a number of lines according to the curliness desired.
- Cut along these lines and open as illustrated, leaving a more or less wide space, as desired.
- Smoothly wrap the spiral created around the neckline.

CIRCULAR FLOUNCES

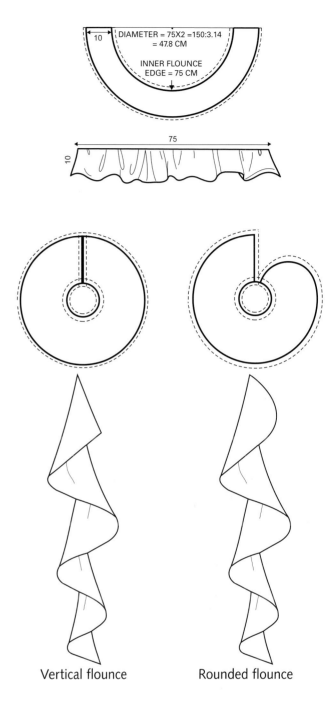

SEAM MARGIN

COMPASS

FLOUNCE WIDTH 14 CM

11

OPENING

DIAMETER = 75:3.14 = 23.9 CM

INNER FLOUNCE EDGE = 75 CM

10

CUT

Upward curving flounce

Straight flounce

Downward curving flounce

SEMI-CIRCULAR FLOUNCES

DIAMETER = 75X2 =150:3.14 = 47.8 CM

10

INNER FLOUNCE EDGE = 75 CM

75

10

Vertical flounce

Rounded flounce

2. Constructed flounces are those created by making cuts on the base model and, opening the outer side, adding volume to create the waves along the outer edge, leaving the measurements where it's sewn unchanged (Fig. 2).

3. Circular flounces may be made in full circle, half circle or spiral shapes.

Circular flounces are made by creating two circles, one of which (the inner circle) has a circumference equal to the length of where it will be inserted. The second, outer, circle has a circumference equal to the height desired for the flounce. Then make a crosswise cut to establish the two sides of the flounce.

Semi-circular flounces are less curly than full circle flounces. In fact, if its measurement is equal to half of the circles constructed (both inner and outer), the waves will be much less evident.

CONSTRUCTING FLOUNCES FROM ONE PIECE OF FABRIC

The measurement of the length of the part where the flounce is to be applied is used as the measurement of the perimeter (P) of a circle. From that, calculate the diameter (D) of the circle by using the following formula: D = P:3.14 (e.g. 75:3.14 = 23.885 cm). For half circle flounces, the circumference is twice the length of the flounce.

FLOUNCES MADE FROM MULTIPLE PIECES

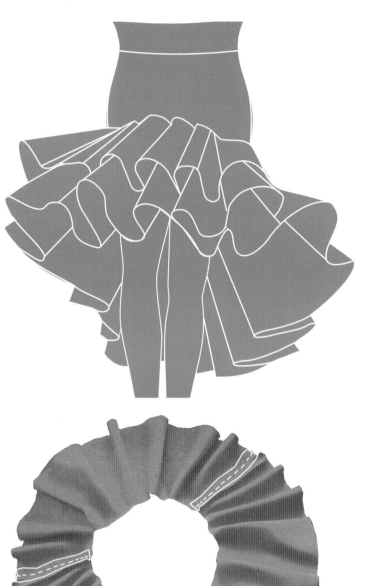

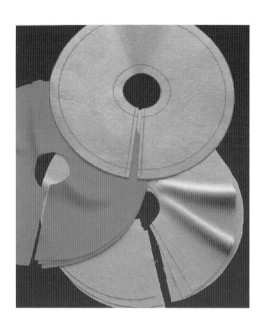

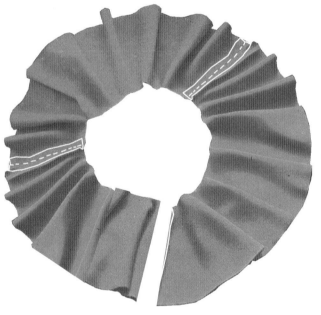

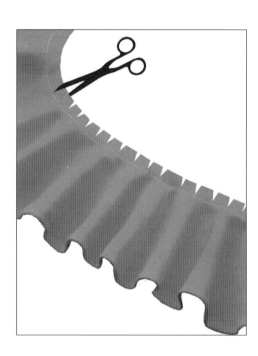

MAKING FLOUNCES FROM MULTIPLE PIECES

When required by the pattern, you can construct multiple flounces with a smaller inner circle to create more waves and curls. The circle may be of any size but the smaller the inner circle is, the fuller the flounce will be. On the other hand, if the inner circle is larger, the flounce will be more subtle.

Because of the way this flounce is cut, there is no gathering along the seam line. To precisely determine how many circular pieces are needed, you must first measure the in-

ner seamline of the circle's pattern, less 1 cm/0.39" which is left for the seam margin. Compare this with the length of the area where the finished flounce will be applied.

Sew the cut pieces of fabric together, right side to right side, and open the seam with an iron. Repeat with the lining (even if it is of the same fabric). Create evenly-spaced, small notches in the seam allowance, creating larger or smaller notches according to the depth of the curve, then apply the flounce to the garment.

SPIRAL FLOUNCES

The spiral is a geometric figure essentially formed by a curved line which rotates around a central point without ever returning to the starting point and continuing on infinitely. This central point may be made up of two or four centres. Making a spiral may seem complicated, but it's actually one of the easiest figures to carry out through a few steps which are repeated in a given sequence, until you've created the spiral size desired.

REGULAR SPIRAL FLOUNCE CONSTRUCTION WITH TWO CENTRES

- Draw a straight line (r) on a white piece of paper with a sharp pencil.
In the centre of the line, mark a segment with two points, A-B, the appropriate distance apart (e.g. 8 cm/3.15"). These points are the two "centres" around which to make the spiral. The distance between the two points is ½ the "step" of the spiral.

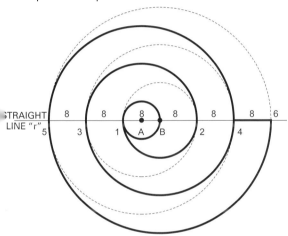

-With the compass opened to half of the "step", put the point on A and draw the semicircle B-1.
- With the compass opened to the length equal to B-1, put the point on B and draw the semicircle 1-2
- With the compass opened to the length equal to A-2, put the point on A and draw the semicircle 2-3.
- With the compass opened to the length equal to B-3, put the point on B and draw the semicircle 3-4.
- With the compass opened to the length equal to A-4, put the point on A and draw the semicircle 4-5.
- With the compass opened to the length equal to B-5, put the point on B and draw the semicircle 5-6.

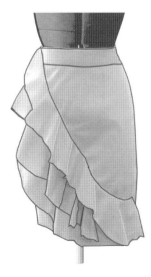

At the end, after a certain number of openings, semicircles and new points, you'll have created a spiral with two centres, as illustrated.

REGULAR SPIRAL FLOUNCE CONSTRUCTION WITH FOUR CENTRES

1) Draw a square with the sides equal to ¼ of the "step" - the width desired for the spiral. If the given step is to be 8 cm (3.15"), each side of the square will be 2 cm (0.79"); if you want a 16 cm (6.30") width, each side will be 4 cm (1.57"), and so on. Mark the corners of the square with the numbers 1-2-3-4, counter-clockwise, starting from the top left corner. Extend the sides as follows:
1 upwards, 2 to the left, 3 downwards, 4 to the right.
These are the lines upon which you'll create the figure. The longer they are, the greater the size of the spiral will be; there are no limits, the size depends on the length of the flounce or ruffles.
- With the compass opened to the length equal to 1-4, put the point on corner 1 and draw the arch from A-4 (mark A).
- With the compass opened the length equal to 2-A, put the point on corner 2 and draw the arch from A-B (mark B).
- With the compass opened to a length equal to 3-B, put the point on corner 3 and draw the arch B-C (mark C).
- With the compass opened to a length equal to 4-C, put the point on the corner.

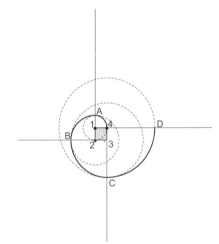

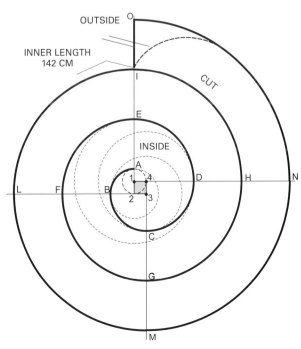

83

Repeat the sequence in the same way, starting again from number 1, continuing on. As noted, there are no limits to making a spiral. With this method, you can create small or quite large spirals, according to the measurement of the "step".

Draw the outer and inner sides with the contour desired, according to the figure.

Today, making a spiral flounce on a computer (using a CAD programme), is quick and easy.

The important thing to know is the length where the flounce will be sewn and the "step" measurement, i.e. its width.

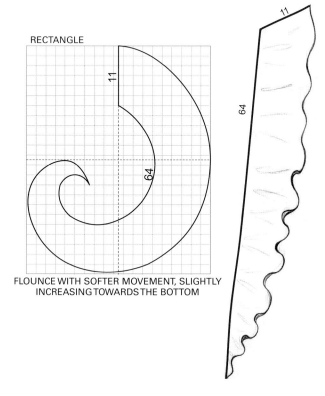

REGULAR SPIRAL
WITH SEAM EASES

LENGTH 142 CM

FLOUNCE WITH MORE MOVEMENT ON THE INSIDE AND
SOFTER MOVEMENT ON THE OUTSIDE

IRREGULAR SPIRAL FLOUNCE

Irregular spiral flounces are those that don't have a uniform width along their entire length. Patterns for these flounces are created by keeping two things in mind: first, the length where they are to be sewn, and second, the outer shape and movement, which may be tightly curled or softer, equal along its length or tightly curled in one part and softly wavy on another, according to the pattern.

RECTANGLE

FLOUNCE WITH SOFTER MOVEMENT, SLIGHTLY
INCREASING TOWARDS THE BOTTOM

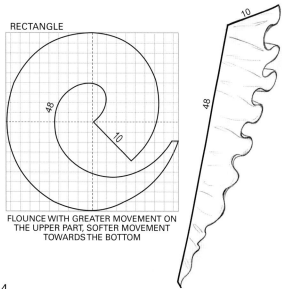

FLOUNCE WITH GREATER MOVEMENT ON
THE UPPER PART, SOFTER MOVEMENT
TOWARDS THE BOTTOM

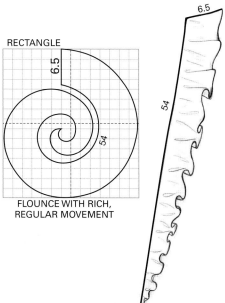

FLOUNCE WITH RICH,
REGULAR MOVEMENT

IRREGULAR SPIRAL FLOUNCES (LOGARITHMIC)

A spiral that is irregular (also called logarithmic or equiangular) can be distinguished from another well-known spiral, a regular one (that of Archimedes), because the distance between the arms of a logarithmic spiral increase according to a geometric progression while regular spirals maintain an even distance. This spiral is constructed through a series of progressive squares in the size desired.

1. With a square ABCD, where AB=1, draw square ABEF on the AB side. Centred around A, draw the arch BF.

2. On the side FE=DA+AF=1+1=2, create the square FGHD and, centred on D, draw the circumference arch EH.

3. On the side CH=CD+DH=1+2=3, create the square CHIL and, centred on C, draw the circumference arch HL as shown in step 3.

4. On the side EL=EC+CL=2+3=5, create the square ELMN, centred on E, draw the circumference arch LN.

5. On the side GN=GE+EN=3+5=8, create the square GNOP and, centred on G, draw the circumference arch PN.

6. On the side PI=PG+GI=5+8=13, create the square PQRI and, centred on H, draw the circumference arch RP. These steps can be repeated to continue the spiral indefinitely.

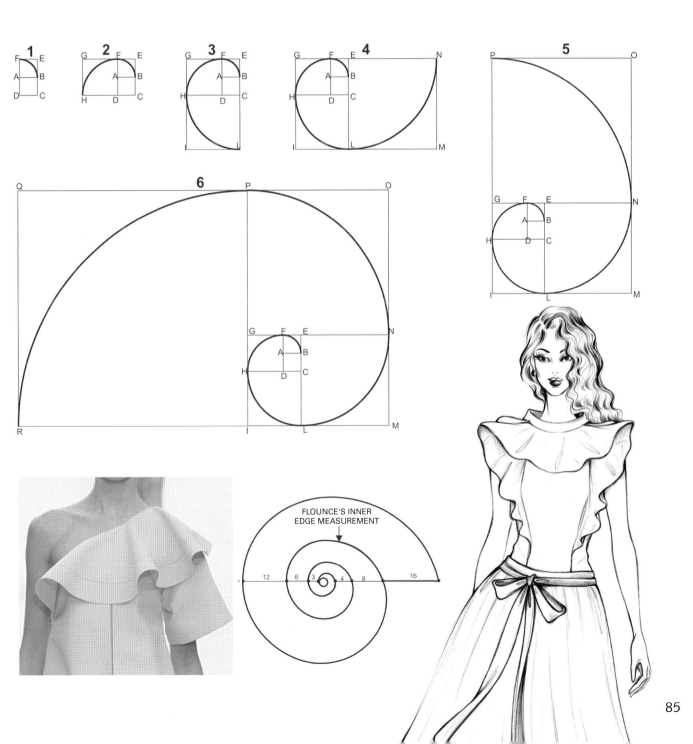

FLOUNCE'S INNER EDGE MEASUREMENT

RUFFLES

To have the necessary length, often it's necessary to join various pieces of fabric which have been cut in the same way (along the same grain) and following the direction of the print, if any. When making ruffles with checked or striped fabric, it's important to pay close attention to make sure the lower edge perfectly matches along the same line or square.

Ruffles can be made in various widths and shapes: simple ruffles, ruffles with protruding edges, zig-zag ruffles, rosette shaped ruffles, heart shaped ruffles, Tyrol-style ruffles.

The various possible shapes depend on the way the fabric is folded and how the strips are sewn.

Simple ruffles are made by sewing the lower edge of the garment, or by compressing ruffles into the folded pieces of fabric on the edge, such as on a seam, a collar or a neckline.

Ruffles with a protruding edge are applied after having sewn a light seam along the edges or a rolled hem. The curls are created by making two gather stitches along the height of the protruding edge.

Zig-zag ruffles are made with a soft ribbon or with a strip of soft fabric cut on the bias. This type of ruffle must be three times longer than the part where it is to be applied and be affixed with double thread, carrying out small gather stitches in a zig-zag pattern on the strip.

Rosette shaped ruffles are made with a double-face ribbon three times the length of where they are to be applied, such as box pleats. Topstitch along the centre of the ribbon and join the edges with a stitch in the middle of the ribbon.

Heart shaped ruffles are made with a ribbon one and a half times the length of where it is to be applied.

Mark three points on the back: one in the middle of the ribbon and the other two on the edges at the desired distance. Begin by inserting the needle at the centre, then insert it in the two points on the edges and pull the thread, affixing it with a backstitch.

Tyrol-style ruffles are made mostly for traditional costumes using velvet or satin ribbon or gold-thread trimming, with the appropriate length and width for the ruffle chosen.

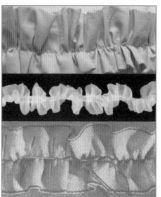

Cotton ruffles   *Ruffles on a shirt*

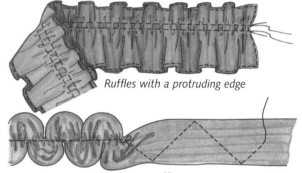

Simple ruffles

Ruffles with a protruding edge

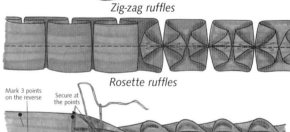

Zig-zag ruffles

Rosette ruffles

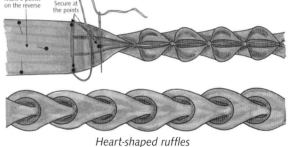

Mark 3 points on the reverse   Secure at the points

Heart-shaped ruffles

Ruffles on an umbrella

DRESS WITH FRONT AND BACK FLOUNCES

WITH A LOOSE, SPIRAL SKIRT

DRESS WITH FRONT AND BACK FLOUNCES

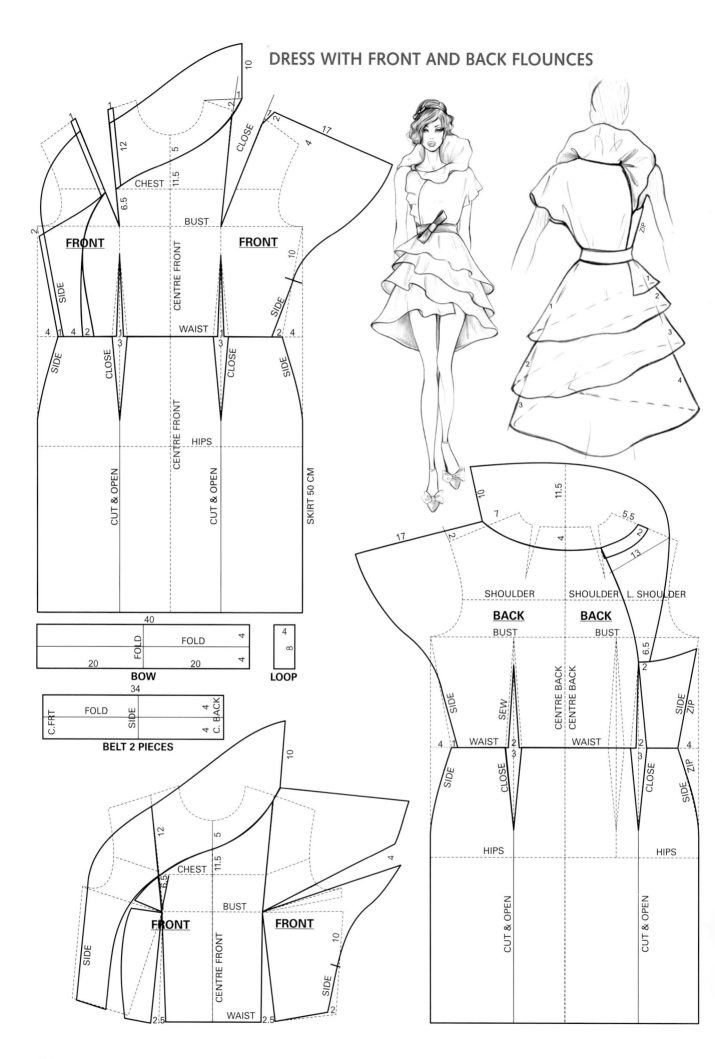

FRONT

FRONT

CHEST

BUST

CENTRE FRONT

SIDE

SIDE

WAIST

CLOSE

CLOSE

SIDE

SIDE

CLOSE

CLOSE

SIDE

SIDE

HIPS

CENTRE FRONT

CUT & OPEN

CUT & OPEN

SKIRT 50 CM

12

5

11.5

6.5

10

2

2

1

2

4

17

10

4

1

4

2

1

3

1

3

1

2

4

2

10

40

FOLD

FOLD

4

4

20

20

BOW

4

8

LOOP

34

C.FRT

FOLD

SIDE

4

4

C. BACK

BELT 2 PIECES

FRONT

FRONT

CHEST

BUST

SIDE

SIDE

CENTRE FRONT

SIDE

WAIST

12

5

11.5

6.5

10

4

10

2.5

2.5

2

SHOULDER

SHOULDER   L. SHOULDER

BACK

BACK

BUST

BUST

SIDE

SIDE

SEW

CENTRE BACK

CENTRE BACK

SIDE
ZIP

WAIST

WAIST

CLOSE

CLOSE

SIDE

ZIP

HIPS

HIPS

CUT & OPEN

CUT & OPEN

10

7

17

2

11.5

4

5.5

2

13

6.5

2

4

2
3

2
3

4

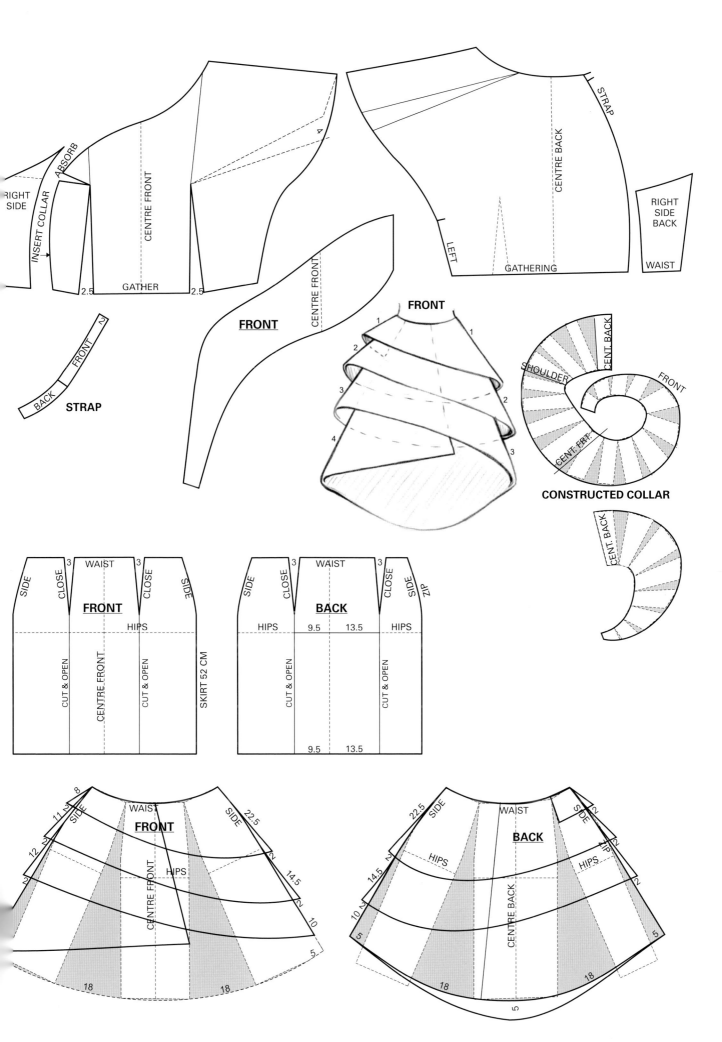

RIGHT SIDE

INSERT COLLAR

ABSORB

CENTRE FRONT

GATHER

2.5

2.5

4

CENTRE BACK

STRAP

LEFT

GATHERING

RIGHT SIDE BACK

WAIST

CENTRE FRONT

FRONT

FRONT

2

BACK

STRAP

FRONT

1

2

3

4

1

2

3

SHOULDER

CENT. BACK

FRONT

CENT. FRT.

CONSTRUCTED COLLAR

CENT. BACK

SIDE

CLOSE

3

WAIST

3

CLOSE

SIDE

FRONT

HIPS

CUT & OPEN

CENTRE FRONT

CUT & OPEN

SKIRT 52 CM

SIDE

CLOSE

3

WAIST

3

CLOSE

SIDE

ZIP

BACK

HIPS

9.5

13.5

HIPS

CUT & OPEN

CUT & OPEN

9.5

13.5

8

11

12

2

2

2

SIDE

WAIST

FRONT

SIDE

22.5

2

14.5

HIPS

CENTRE FRONT

HIPS

10

2

5

18

18

22.5

SIDE

WAIST

SIDE

2

ZIP

BACK

14.5

2

HIPS

HIPS

2

10

2

CENTRE BACK

5

5

18

18

5

DRESS WITH FLOUNCES ON THE COLLAR AND BUST

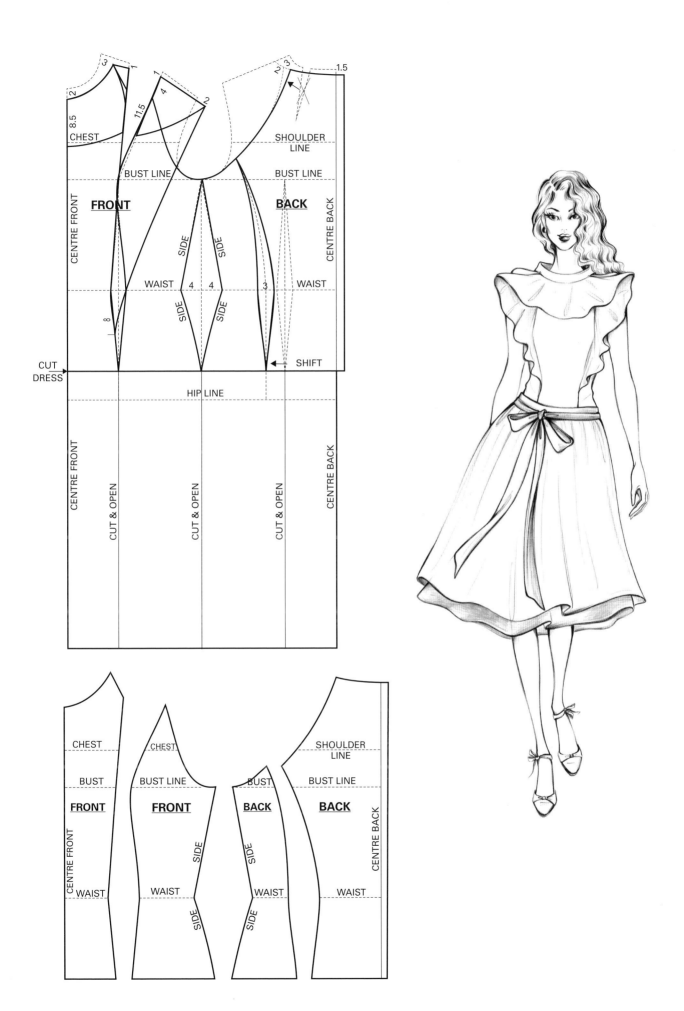

FRONT

BACK

CENTRE FRONT

CENTRE BACK

CHEST

8.5

11.5

3

1

1

4

2

2

3

2

3

1.5

SHOULDER LINE

BUST LINE

BUST LINE

SIDE

SIDE

WAIST

4

4

3

WAIST

SIDE

SIDE

8

CUT DRESS

SHIFT

HIP LINE

CENTRE FRONT

CUT & OPEN

CUT & OPEN

CUT & OPEN

CENTRE BACK

CHEST

BUST

FRONT

CENTRE FRONT

WAIST

CHEST

BUST LINE

FRONT

SIDE

WAIST

SIDE

BUST

BACK

SIDE

WAIST

SIDE

SHOULDER LINE

BUST LINE

BACK

CENTRE BACK

WAIST

DRESS WITH FLOUNCES ON THE COLLAR AND BUST

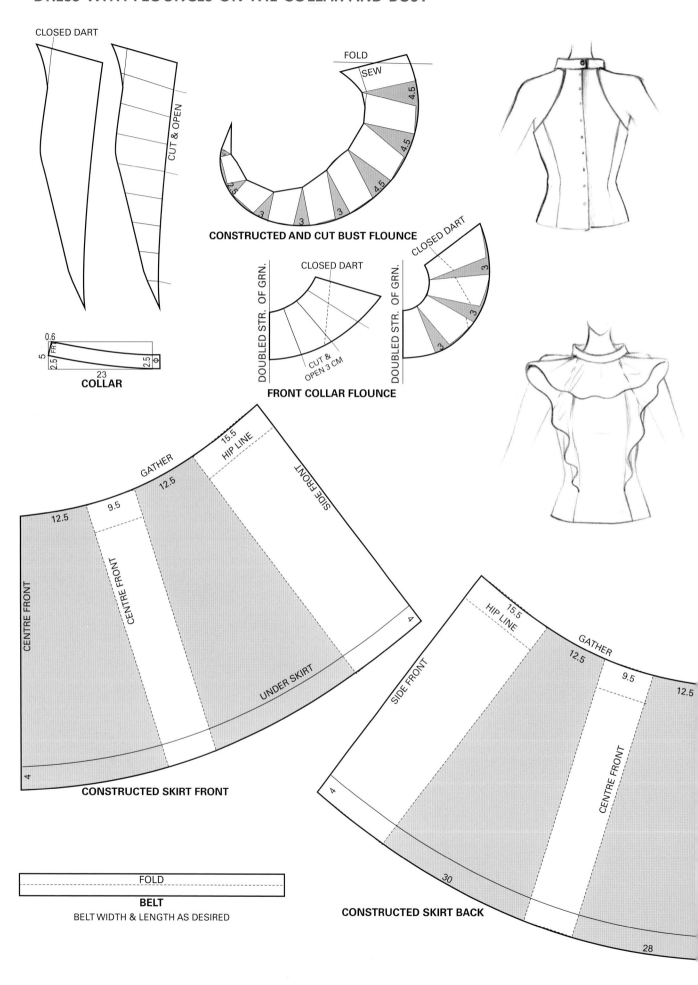

CLOSED DART

CUT & OPEN

CONSTRUCTED AND CUT BUST FLOUNCE

FOLD

SEW

4.5
4.5
4.5
3
3
3

0.6
FRT
5
2.5
2.5
23
COLLAR

DOUBLED STR. OF GRN.

CLOSED DART

CUT & OPEN 3 CM

DOUBLED STR. OF GRN.

CLOSED DART

3
3
3
3

FRONT COLLAR FLOUNCE

15.5
HIP LINE
GATHER
12.5
9.5
12.5
SIDE FRONT
CENTRE FRONT
CENTRE FRONT
UNDER SKIRT
12.5
4
4

CONSTRUCTED SKIRT FRONT

15.5
HIP LINE
GATHER
12.5
9.5
12.5
SIDE FRONT
CENTRE FRONT
4
30
28

CONSTRUCTED SKIRT BACK

FOLD
BELT
BELT WIDTH & LENGTH AS DESIRED

92

DRESS WITH COLLAR FLOUNCES AND SPIRALS ON THE SLEEVES

DRESS WITH COLLAR FLOUNCES AND SPIRALS ON THE SLEEVES

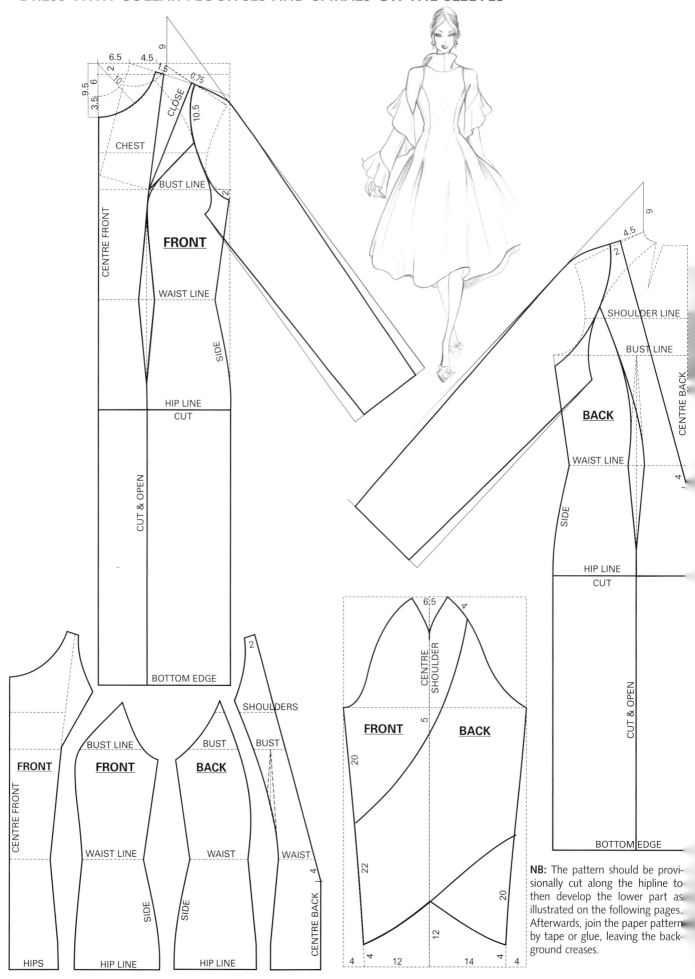

NB: The pattern should be provisionally cut along the hipline to then develop the lower part as illustrated on the following pages. Afterwards, join the paper pattern by tape or glue, leaving the background creases.

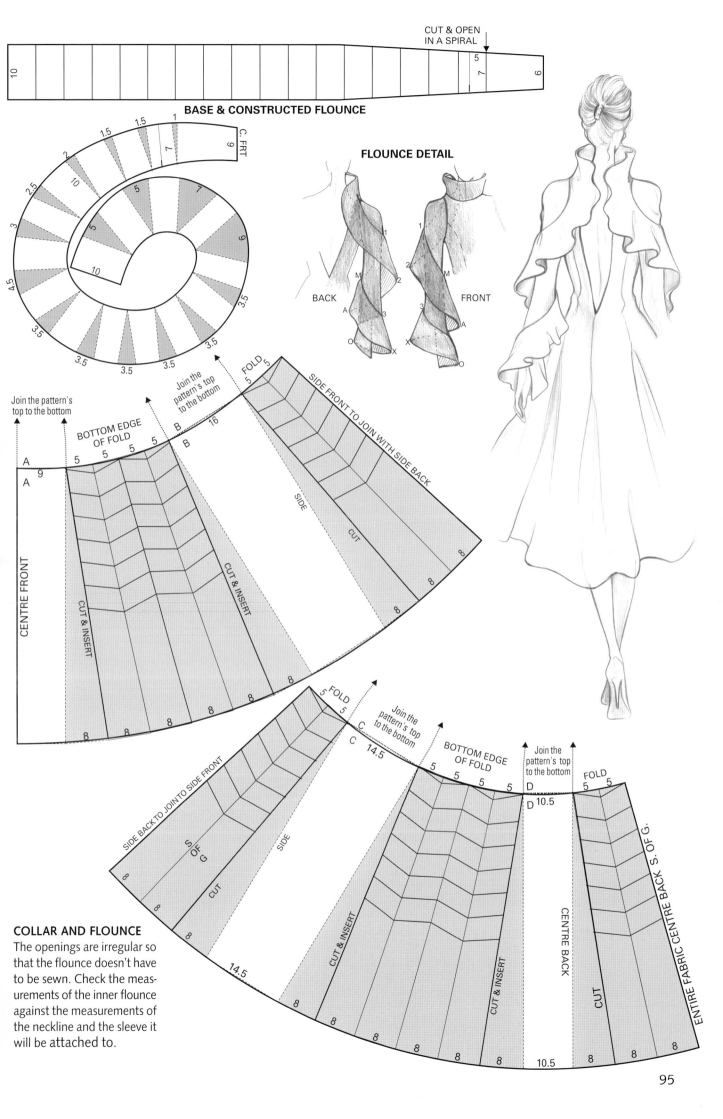

BASE & CONSTRUCTED FLOUNCE

CUT & OPEN IN A SPIRAL

10 ... 5 7 6

FLOUNCE DETAIL

BACK 1 2 M A O X FRONT 1 2 M A 3 O X

C. FRT 6 7 1 1.5 1.5 1.5 2 2.5 3 10 5 5 7 9 10 4.5 3.5 3.5 3.5 3.5 3.5 3.5 3.5

Join the pattern's top to the bottom

Join the pattern's top to the bottom

FOLD 5 5

BOTTOM EDGE OF FOLD

SIDE FRONT TO JOIN WITH SIDE BACK

A A 9 5 5 5 B B 16

CENTRE FRONT

SIDE

CUT

CUT & INSERT

CUT & INSERT

8 8 8 8 8 8 8 8 8

SIDE BACK TO JOIN TO SIDE FRONT

FOLD 5 C C 14.5

Join the pattern's top to the bottom

BOTTOM EDGE OF FOLD

Join the pattern's top to the bottom

FOLD 5 5

S OF G

SIDE

CUT

CUT & INSERT

CUT & INSERT

CENTRE BACK

CUT

ENTIRE FABRIC CENTRE BACK S. OF G.

D D 10.5

5 5 5

14.5 8 8 8 8 8 8 8 10.5 8 8

COLLAR AND FLOUNCE

The openings are irregular so that the flounce doesn't have to be sewn. Check the measurements of the inner flounce against the measurements of the neckline and the sleeve it will be attached to.

DRESS WITH DOUBLE FLOUNCES

ASYMMETRICAL ON THE SHOULDERS AND NECKLINE

SKIRT WITH DOUBLE FLOUNCES INSERTED IN
THE SIDE SEAMS

Create this pattern by using the base block of the dress
with darts, transforming it as illustrated here.

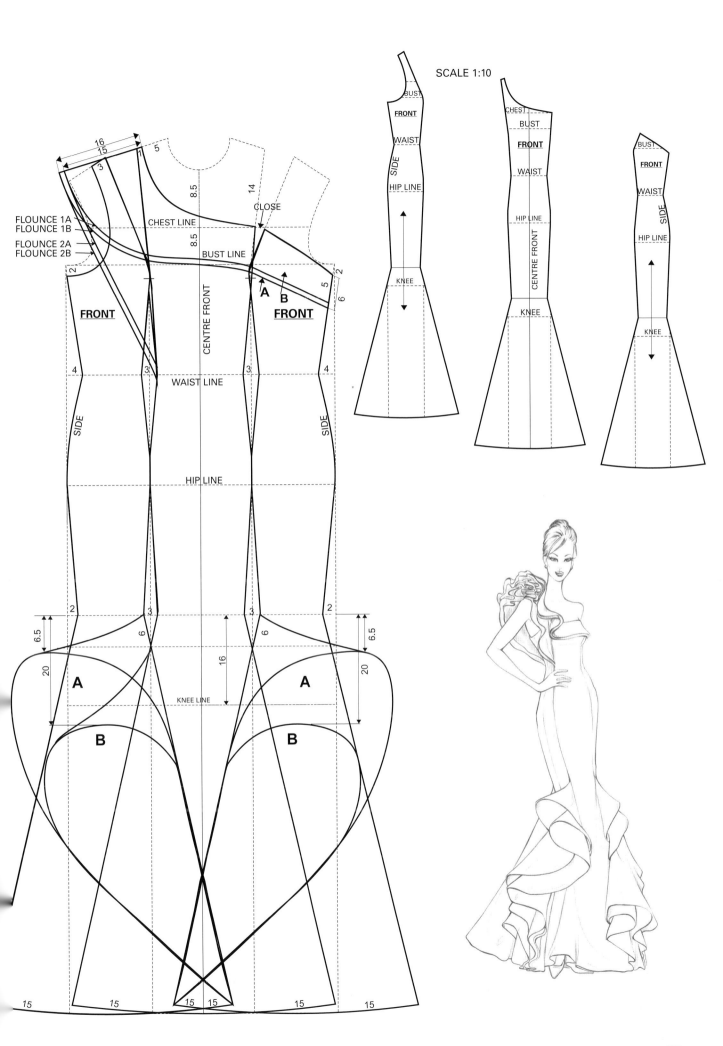

SCALE 1:10

FLOUNCE 1A
FLOUNCE 1B
FLOUNCE 2A
FLOUNCE 2B

CHEST LINE

BUST LINE

CLOSE

CENTRE FRONT

FRONT

A   B

FRONT

SIDE

SIDE

WAIST LINE

HIP LINE

A

A

KNEE LINE

B

B

16
15
3
5

8.5
14

8.5

2
2

4
3
3
4

2
3
3
2

6.5
6
16
6
6.5

20
20

5
6

15   15   15 15   15   15

BUST
FRONT
WAIST
SIDE
HIP LINE
KNEE

CHEST
BUST
FRONT
WAIST
HIP LINE
CENTRE FRONT
KNEE

BUST
FRONT
WAIST
SIDE
HIP LINE
KNEE

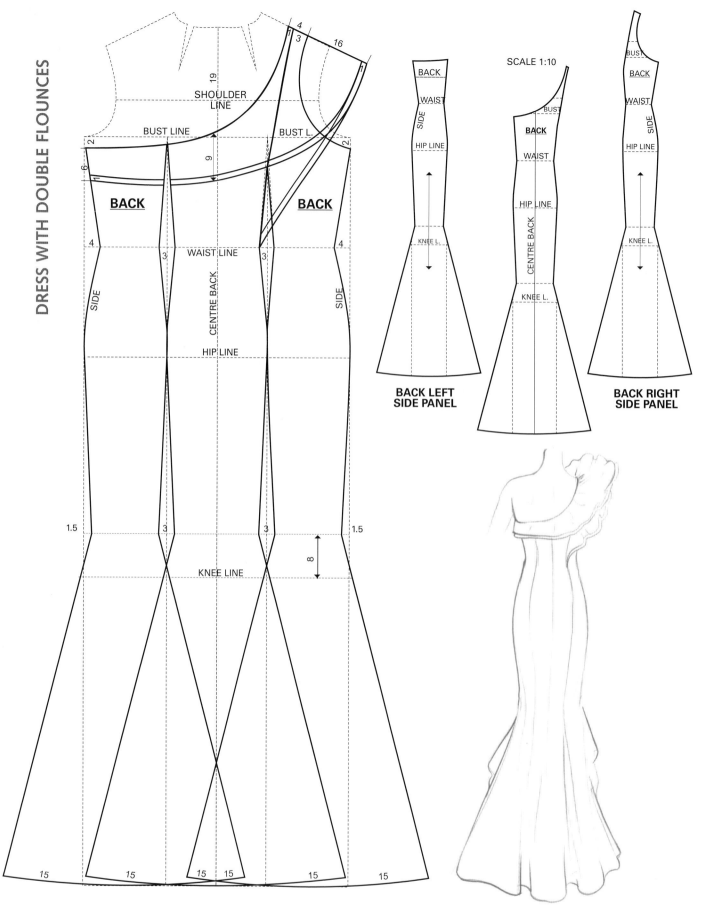

SCALE 1:10

**BACK LEFT
SIDE PANEL**

**BACK RIGHT
SIDE PANEL**

- Construct the base block of the dress with darts and extend the bottom to the desired length (to the floor).
- Separate the front from the back.
- Construct the entire front and the entire back.

FRONT

- Construct the three front panels as shown in the illustration.
- Draw the flounce, double the length of the neckline on the front bodice: 1A and 1B.

- Draw the double flounce on the front side: 2A and 2B.
- Draw flounce A and flounce B on the skirt as shown in the illustration.
- Divide flounces 1A and 1B on the neckline, cut and rotate, as shown in the figure.
- Smoothly draw the contours of flounces A and B and take them up again on tissue paper.

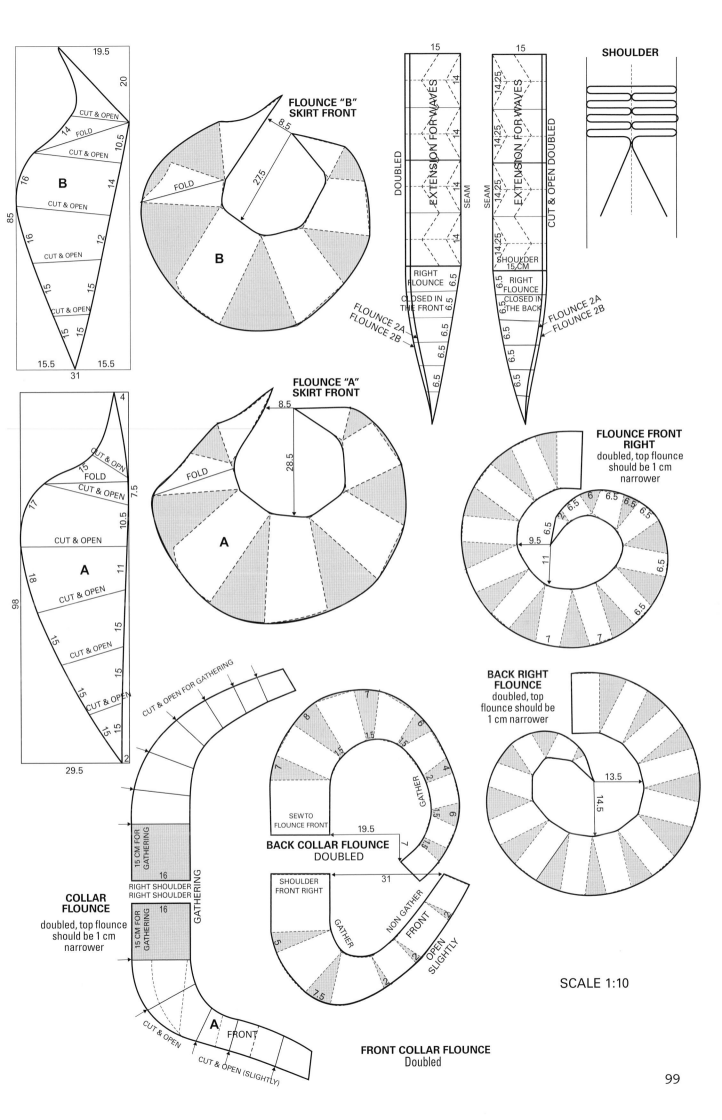

SHOULDER

FLOUNCE "B" SKIRT FRONT

FLOUNCE "A" SKIRT FRONT

FLOUNCE FRONT RIGHT
doubled, top flounce
should be 1 cm
narrower

BACK RIGHT FLOUNCE
doubled, top
flounce should be
1 cm narrower

COLLAR FLOUNCE
doubled, top flounce
should be 1 cm
narrower

BACK COLLAR FLOUNCE
DOUBLED

FRONT COLLAR FLOUNCE
Doubled

SCALE 1:10

99

DRESS WITH FLOUNCES ON THE COLLAR AND FRONT/BACK SIDES

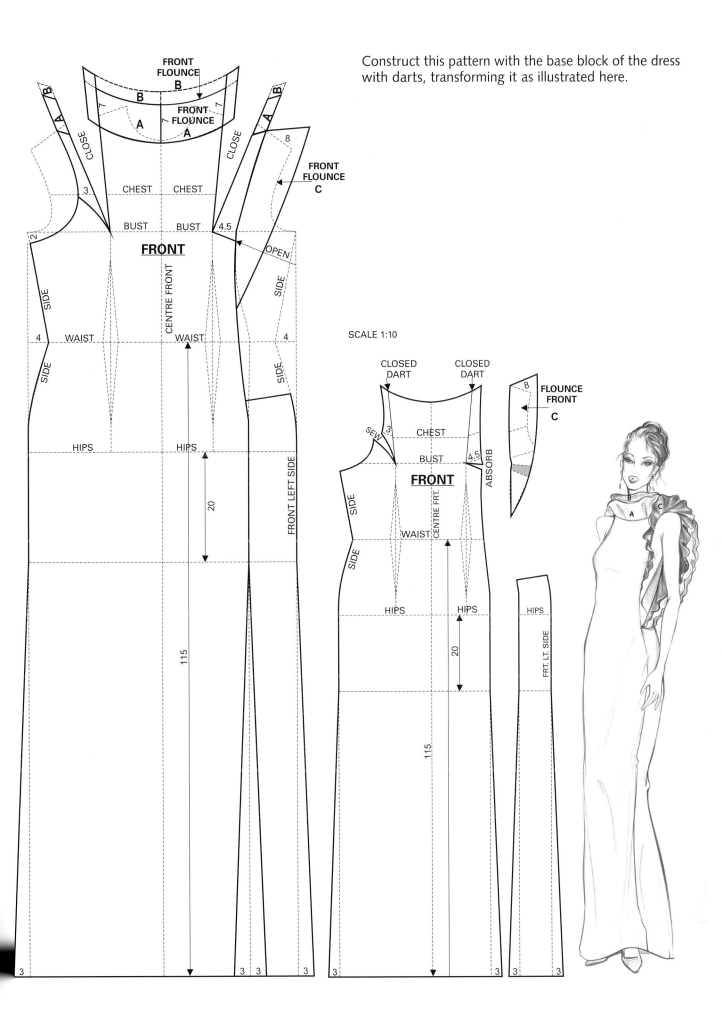

Construct this pattern with the base block of the dress with darts, transforming it as illustrated here.

FRONT FLOUNCE
B

FRONT FLOUNCE
A

FRONT FLOUNCE
C

CLOSE

CLOSE

CHEST CHEST

BUST BUST

FRONT

OPEN

CENTRE FRONT

SIDE

SIDE

SIDE

SIDE

WAIST WAIST

HIPS HIPS

FRONT LEFT SIDE

20

115

SCALE 1:10

CLOSED DART CLOSED DART

FLOUNCE FRONT
C

SEW

CHEST

BUST

FRONT

ABSORB

SIDE

SIDE

CENTRE FRT.

WAIST

HIPS HIPS

FRT. LT. SIDE

HIPS

20

115

101

DRESS WITH FLOUNCES ON THE COLLAR AND FRONT/BACK SIDES

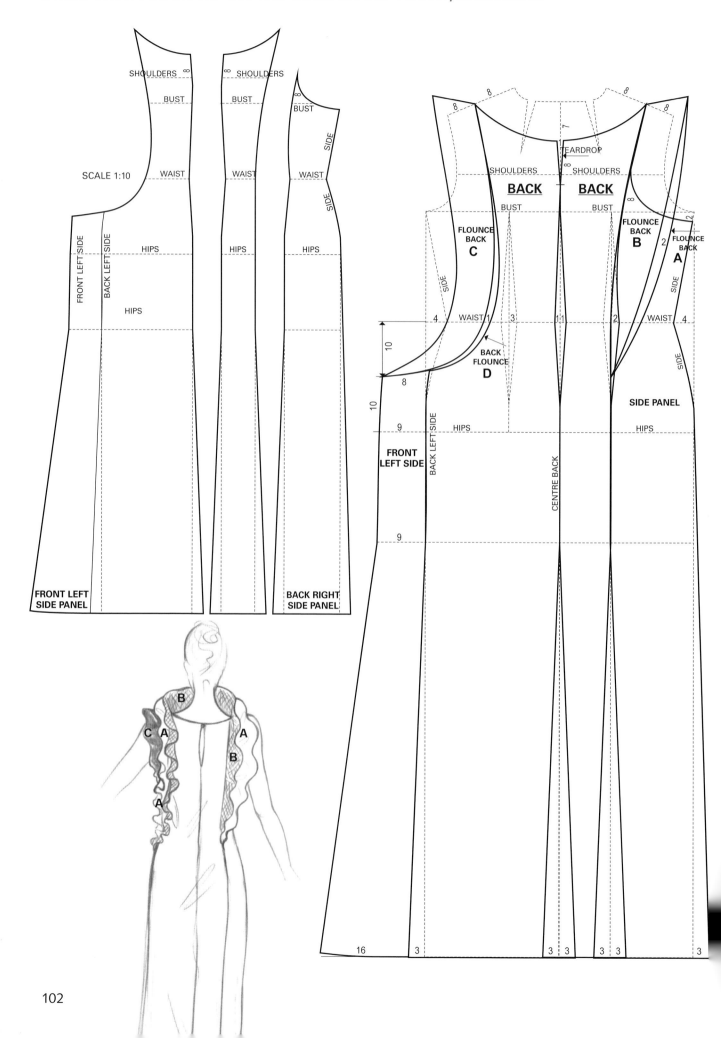

SCALE 1:10

SHOULDERS ∞   ∞ SHOULDERS   ∞
BUST   BUST   BUST
    SIDE
WAIST   WAIST   WAIST   SIDE
HIPS   HIPS   HIPS
FRONT LEFT SIDE   BACK LEFT SIDE   SIDE
HIPS

FRONT LEFT SIDE PANEL   BACK RIGHT SIDE PANEL

8   8   8   8
8   8
TEARDROP   7   ∞
SHOULDERS   ∞   SHOULDERS
BACK   **BACK**
BUST   BUST   ∞
FLOUNCE BACK **C**   FLOUNCE BACK **B**   2 FLOUNCE BACK **A**
SIDE   SIDE   2
4   WAIST 1   3   11   2   WAIST   4
10   BACK FLOUNCE **D**   SIDE
10   8   SIDE PANEL
FRONT LEFT SIDE   BACK LEFT SIDE   CENTRE BACK
9   HIPS   HIPS
9

16   3   3   3   3   3   3

102

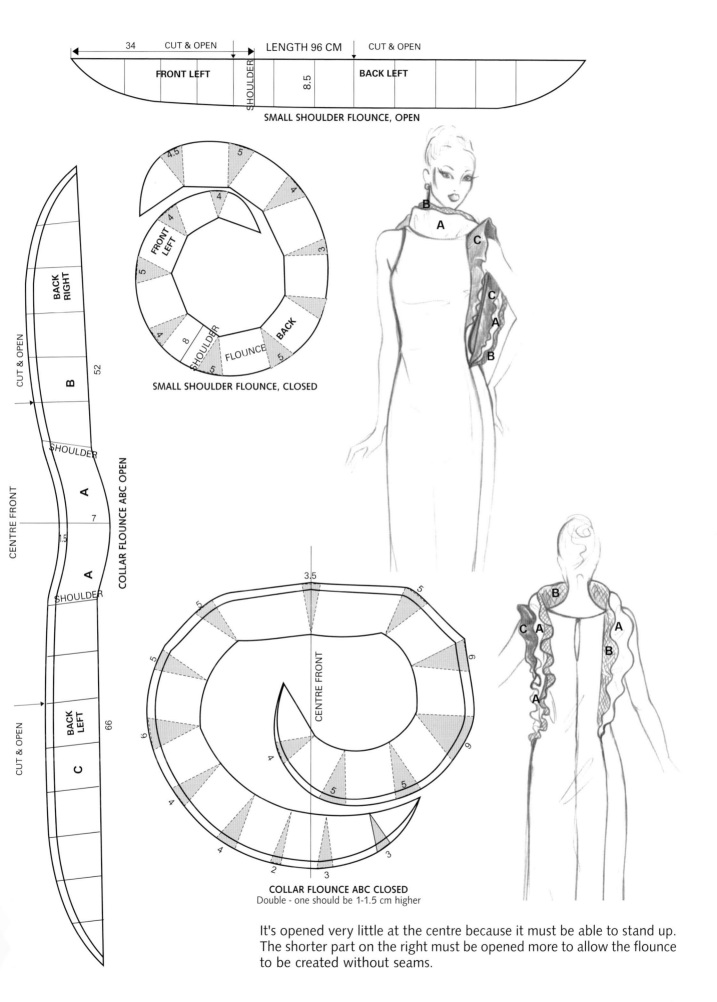

SMALL SHOULDER FLOUNCE, OPEN

34 | CUT & OPEN | LENGTH 96 CM | CUT & OPEN
FRONT LEFT | SHOULDER | 8.5 | BACK LEFT

SMALL SHOULDER FLOUNCE, CLOSED

FRONT LEFT — 4.5 — 5 — 4 — 4 — 3 — 5 — 5 — FLOUNCE — BACK — 8 — 4 — SHOULDER

COLLAR FLOUNCE ABC OPEN

CENTRE FRONT

BACK RIGHT — 52 — B — SHOULDER — A — 7 — 1.5 — A — SHOULDER — BACK LEFT — 66 — C — CUT & OPEN — CUT & OPEN

COLLAR FLOUNCE ABC CLOSED
Double - one should be 1-1.5 cm higher

CENTRE FRONT — 3.5 — 5 — 5 — 5 — 9 — 9 — 5 — 5 — 4 — 4 — 4 — 2 — 3 — 3

It's opened very little at the centre because it must be able to stand up.
The shorter part on the right must be opened more to allow the flounce
to be created without seams.

TUNIC WITH FLOUNCES ON THE FRONT AND COLLAR

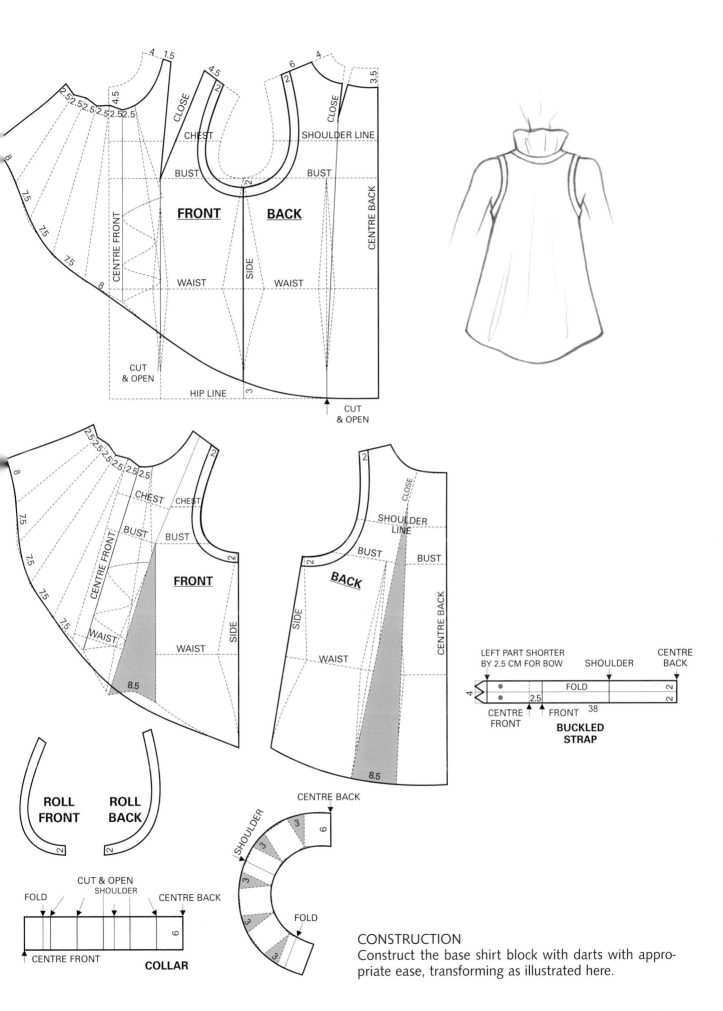

FRONT

BACK

CLOSE

CHEST

BUST

SHOULDER LINE

CENTRE FRONT

CENTRE BACK

WAIST

SIDE

WAIST

CUT & OPEN

HIP LINE

CUT & OPEN

FRONT

BACK

CHEST

CHEST

BUST

BUST

CLOSE

SHOULDER LINE

BUST

BUST

CENTRE FRONT

WAIST

WAIST

SIDE

SIDE

WAIST

CENTRE BACK

8.5

8.5

ROLL FRONT

ROLL BACK

CENTRE BACK

SHOULDER

3

6

3

3

FOLD

3

3

FOLD

CUT & OPEN

FOLD

SHOULDER

CENTRE BACK

6

CENTRE FRONT

COLLAR

LEFT PART SHORTER BY 2.5 CM FOR BOW

SHOULDER

CENTRE BACK

FOLD

4

2.5

CENTRE FRONT

FRONT

38

2 2

2 2

BUCKLED STRAP

CONSTRUCTION
Construct the base shirt block with darts with appropriate ease, transforming as illustrated here.

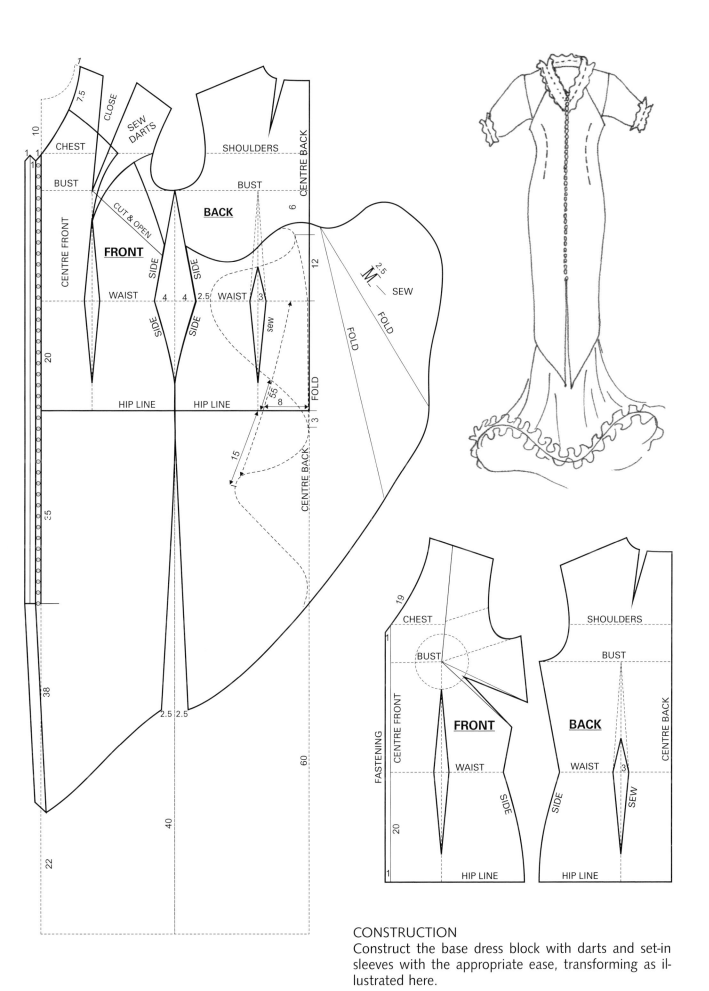

CONSTRUCTION
Construct the base dress block with darts and set-in sleeves with the appropriate ease, transforming as illustrated here.

LONG DRESS WITH A FLOUNCE ON THE BACK WHICH FORMS A MOTIF

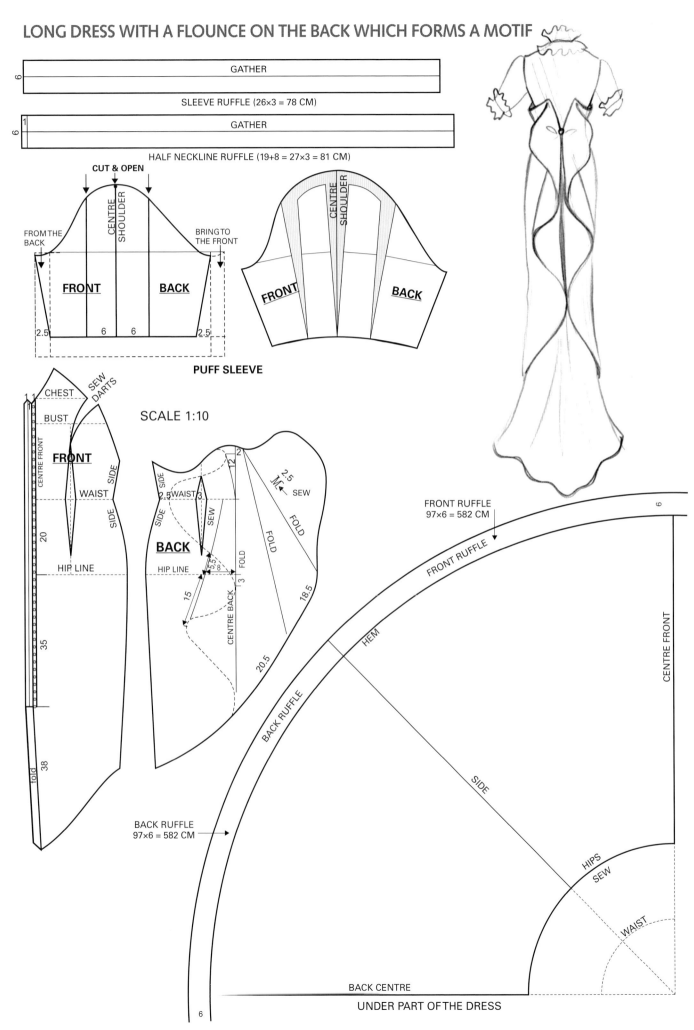

GATHER

SLEEVE RUFFLE (26×3 = 78 CM)

GATHER

HALF NECKLINE RUFFLE (19+8 = 27×3 = 81 CM)

CUT & OPEN

CENTRE SHOULDER

FROM THE BACK

BRING TO THE FRONT

FRONT   **BACK**

2.5   6   6   2.5

CENTRE SHOULDER

FRONT   **BACK**

PUFF SLEEVE

CHEST   SEW DARTS

BUST

SCALE 1:10

FRONT

CENTRE FRONT

WAIST

SIDE

SIDE

HIP LINE

20

35

fold

38

SIDE

2.5 SIDE

WAIST 3

SEW

BACK

HIP LINE

15

5.5

CENTRE BACK

FOLD

FOLD

FOLD

2

12

2.5

SEW

18.5

20.5

3

FRONT RUFFLE
97×6 = 582 CM

FRONT RUFFLE

HEM

BACK RUFFLE

SIDE

CENTRE FRONT

6

BACK RUFFLE
97×6 = 582 CM

HIPS

SEW

WAIST

BACK CENTRE

UNDER PART OF THE DRESS

6

MERMAID DRESS

WITH AN OPEN BACK

MERMAID DRESS

CHEST **CHEST**

14

BUST **BUST**

FRONT **FRONT**

SIDE

CENTRE FRONT

SIDE

3

1.5 3

3

WAIST 2 2 **WAIST** 3

HIPS **HIPS**

2 1.5 1.5 2

9 5 5 5 5 9

EMBROIDERED
STRAP

APPLIED
MOTIF

MOTIF
CONTINUES ON
THE BACK

RIGHT
SIDE

EMBROIDERED EDGE

EMBROIDERED
EDGE

CENTRE FRONT

LEFT SIDE

EMBROIDERED EDGE

CENT. FRT.

BUST BUST

RIGHT SIDE

UNDER-CUP BASE (BUST)
The cups at the bust should
be left shaped (as illustrated).

CUT & OPEN
FOR FASTENING

CENT. FRT.

BUST BUST

RIGHT SIDE

RIGHT CUP (BUST COVERING)
For the fabric which covers the bust, draw the cup
with closed dart. Open for the gathering.

PLACE
EMBROIDERED
STRAP

CENT. FRT.

BUST BUST

GATHER

RIGHT SIDE

CONSTRUCTION
Construct the base dress block with darts and set-in
sleeves with the appropriate ease, transforming as illustrated here.

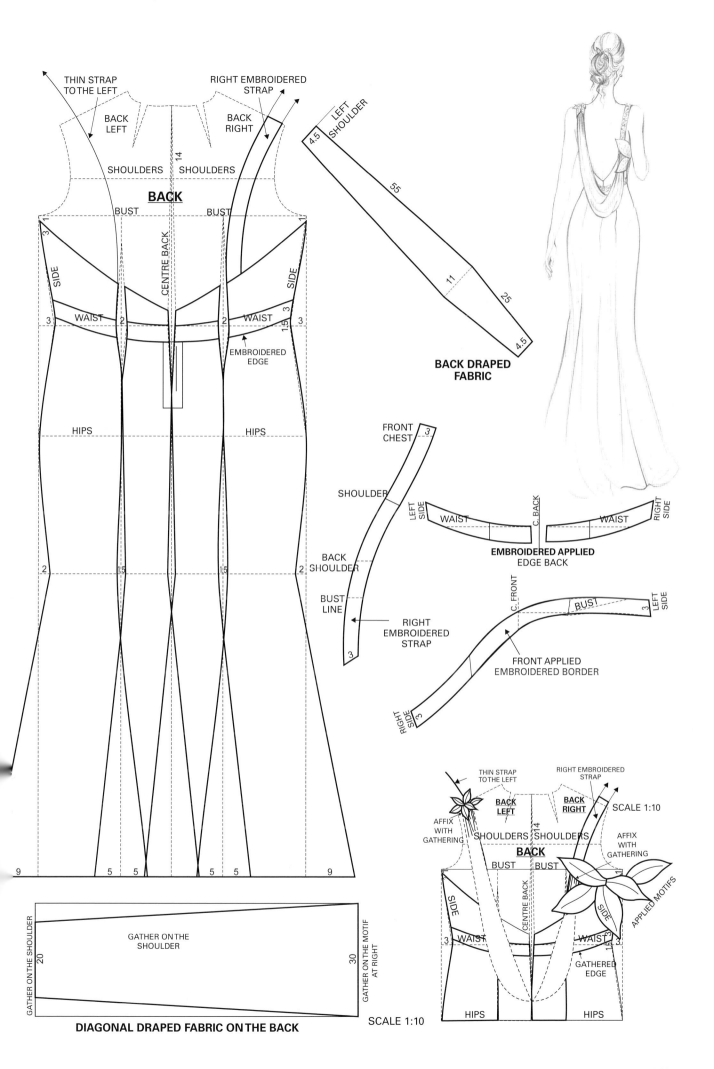

THIN STRAP TO THE LEFT

RIGHT EMBROIDERED STRAP

BACK LEFT

BACK RIGHT

SHOULDERS SHOULDERS

BACK

14

BUST BUST

CENTRE BACK

3

1 1

SIDE SIDE

WAIST WAIST

3 2 2 1.5 3

3

EMBROIDERED EDGE

HIPS HIPS

2 15 15 2

9 5 5 5 5 9

LEFT SHOULDER

4.5

55

11

25

4.5

BACK DRAPED FABRIC

FRONT CHEST 3

SHOULDER

BACK SHOULDER

BUST LINE

3

RIGHT EMBROIDERED STRAP

LEFT SIDE

WAIST

C. BACK

WAIST

RIGHT SIDE

EMBROIDERED APPLIED
EDGE BACK

C. FRONT

BUST

LEFT SIDE 3

FRONT APPLIED EMBROIDERED BORDER

RIGHT SIDE 3

GATHER ON THE SHOULDER

GATHER ON THE SHOULDER

20

GATHER ON THE MOTIF AT RIGHT

30

DIAGONAL DRAPED FABRIC ON THE BACK

THIN STRAP TO THE LEFT

RIGHT EMBROIDERED STRAP

BACK LEFT

BACK RIGHT

SCALE 1:10

AFFIX WITH GATHERING

AFFIX WITH GATHERING

SHOULDERS 14 SHOULDERS

BACK

BUST BUST

CENTRE BACK

SIDE SIDE

APPLIED MOTIFS

3 WAIST WAIST 15 3

GATHERED EDGE

HIPS HIPS

SCALE 1:10

MERMAID DRESS

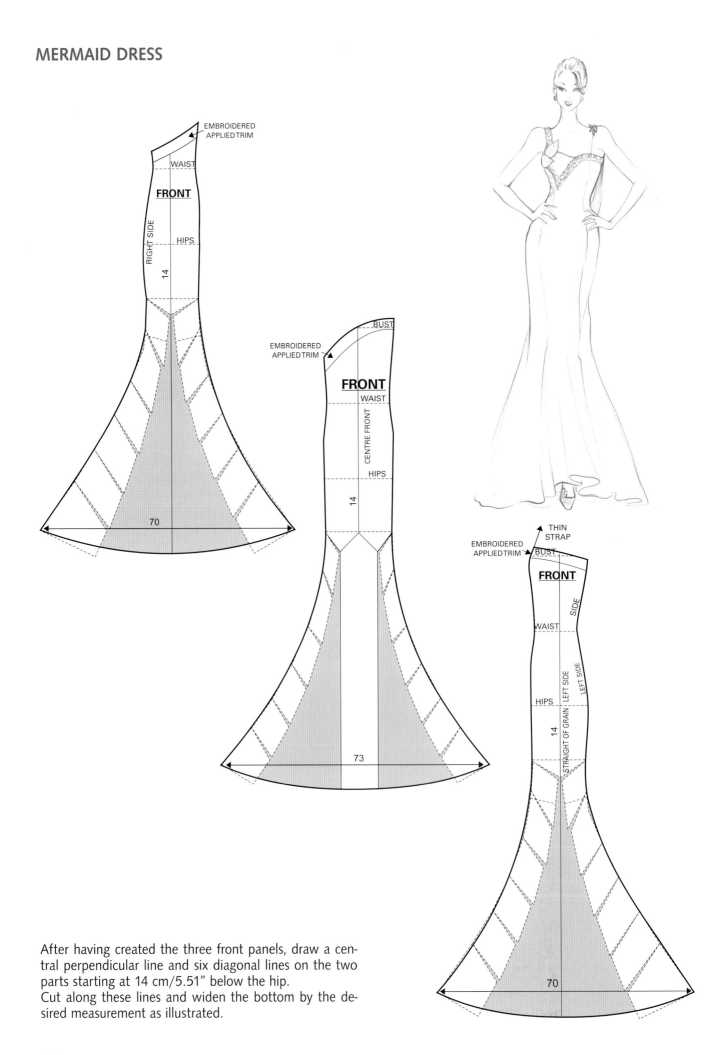

After having created the three front panels, draw a central perpendicular line and six diagonal lines on the two parts starting at 14 cm/5.51" below the hip.
Cut along these lines and widen the bottom by the desired measurement as illustrated.

CREATING THE BACK PANELS

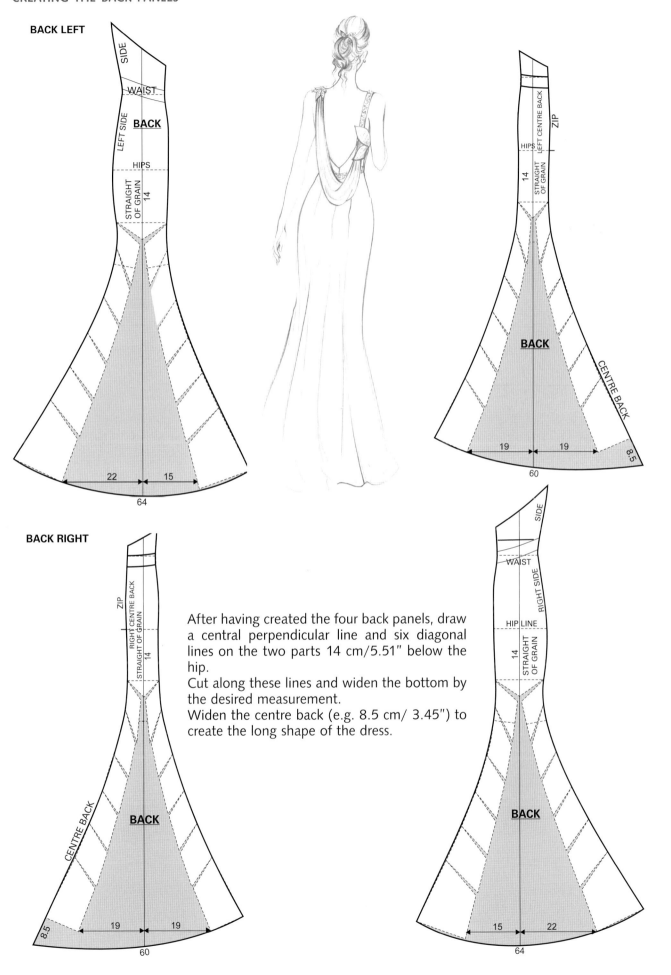

BACK LEFT

SIDE
WAIST
LEFT SIDE
BACK
HIPS
STRAIGHT OF GRAIN
14
BACK
22   15
64

ZIP
LEFT CENTRE BACK
HIPS
14
STRAIGHT OF GRAIN
BACK
CENTRE BACK
19   19
8.5
60

BACK RIGHT

ZIP
RIGHT CENTRE BACK
STRAIGHT OF GRAIN
14
BACK
CENTRE BACK
8.5
19   19
60

SIDE
WAIST
RIGHT SIDE
HIP LINE
14
STRAIGHT OF GRAIN
BACK
15   22
64

After having created the four back panels, draw a central perpendicular line and six diagonal lines on the two parts 14 cm/5.51″ below the hip.
Cut along these lines and widen the bottom by the desired measurement.
Widen the centre back (e.g. 8.5 cm/ 3.45″) to create the long shape of the dress.

OUTFITS - PRACTICE EXERCISES

Complete the patterns for these sets in a cut and size and test them out on some practice fabric.

4. RAGLAN SLEEVE GARMENTS

DRESS WITH DRAPED SLEEVES
ROSE-SHAPED WITH FOLDS

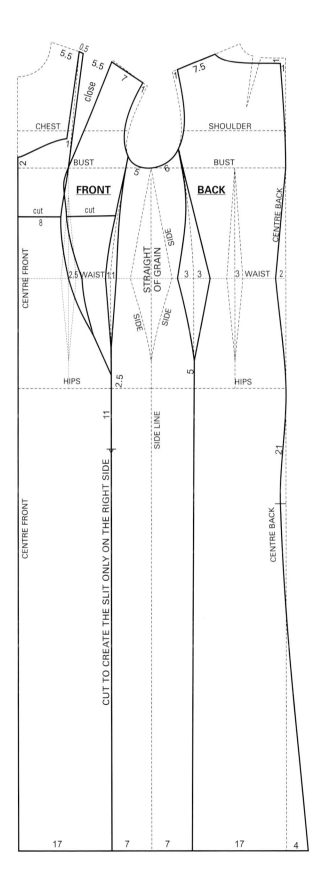

CONSTRUCTION
Construct the base dress block with darts and set-in sleeves, with the appropriate ease, transforming as illustrated here.

DRESS WITH DRAPED SLEEVES

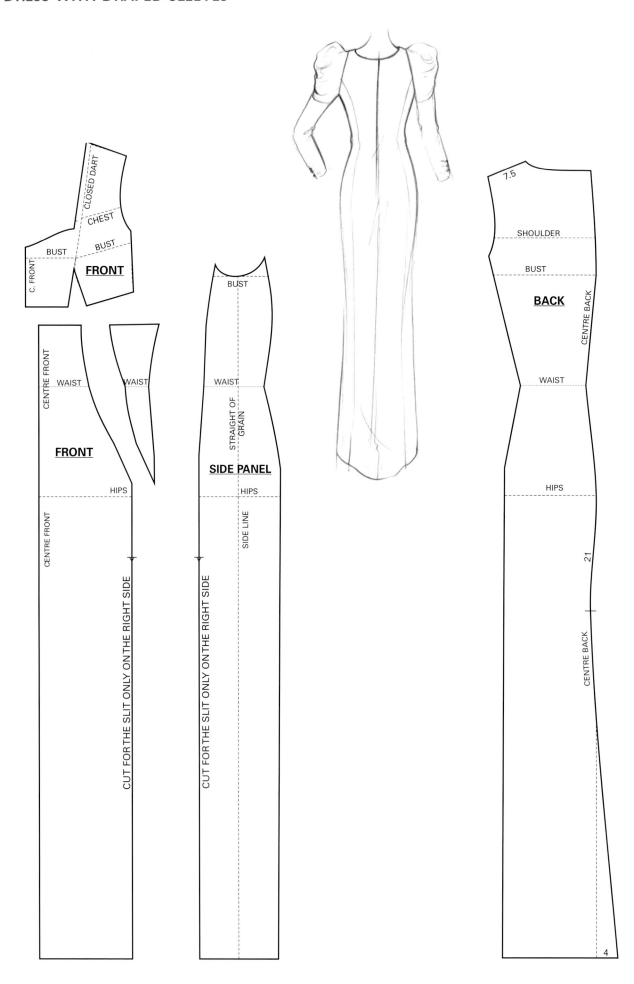

CLOSED DART

CHEST

BUST

BUST

C. FRONT

FRONT

CENTRE FRONT

WAIST

WAIST

FRONT

CENTRE FRONT

HIPS

CUT FOR THE SLIT ONLY ON THE RIGHT SIDE

BUST

WAIST

STRAIGHT OF GRAIN

SIDE PANEL

HIPS

SIDE LINE

CUT FOR THE SLIT ONLY ON THE RIGHT SIDE

7.5

SHOULDER

BUST

BACK

CENTRE BACK

WAIST

HIPS

21

CENTRE BACK

4

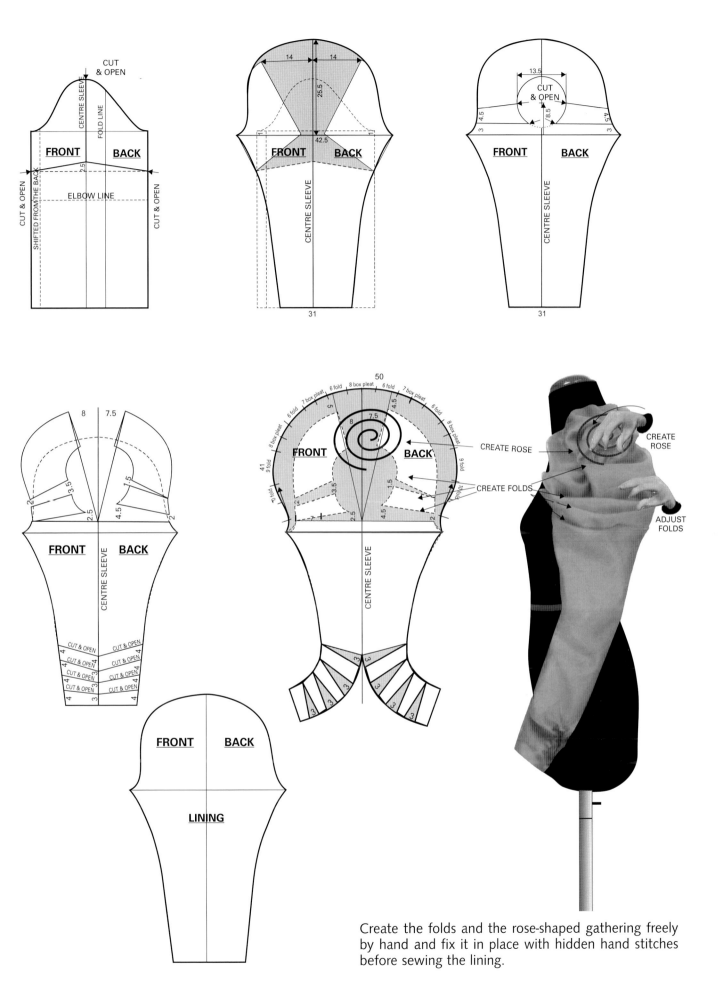

Create the folds and the rose-shaped gathering freely by hand and fix it in place with hidden hand stitches before sewing the lining.

DRESS WITH STAND UP COLLAR AND FRILLS
WHICH OVERLAP ON THE CAP SLEEVES AND FRONT

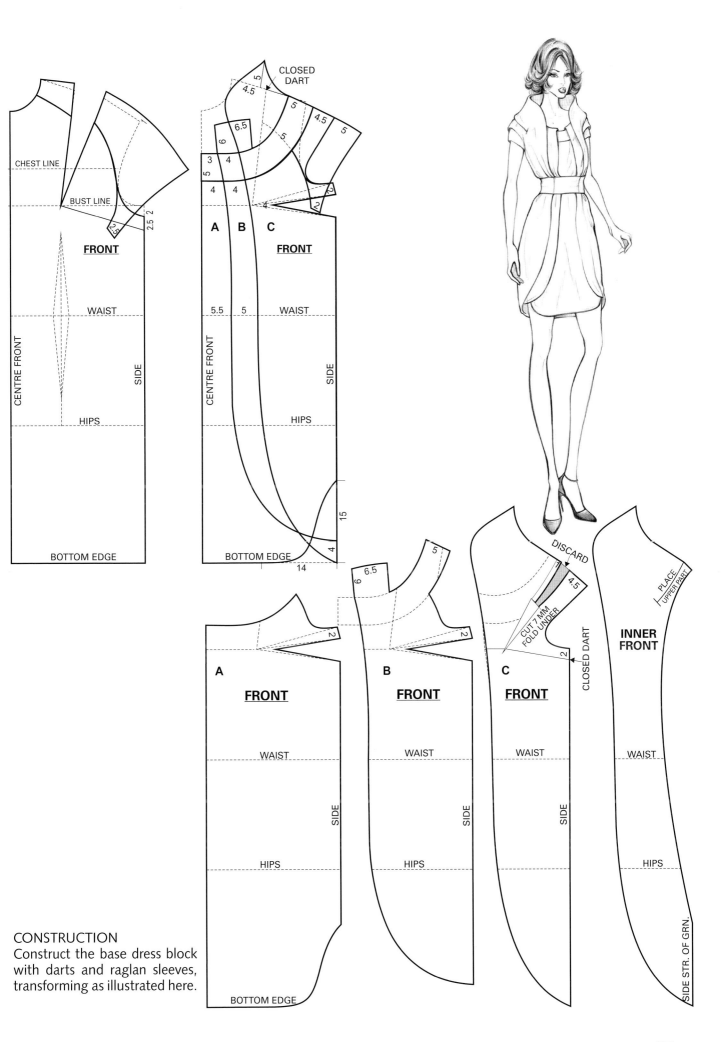

CHEST LINE

BUST LINE

FRONT

CENTRE FRONT

WAIST

SIDE

HIPS

BOTTOM EDGE

2.5 2

CLOSED DART

5
4.5
5
4.5
5
6.5
5
6
5
3 4
5
4 4
4
2
2

A B C

FRONT

CENTRE FRONT

5.5 5   WAIST

SIDE

HIPS

BOTTOM EDGE

15
4
14

6.5
6
5
2

A

FRONT

WAIST

SIDE

HIPS

BOTTOM EDGE

6.5
6
5
2

B

FRONT

WAIST

SIDE

HIPS

DISCARD

4.5

CUT 7 MM
FOLD UNDER

2

CLOSED DART

C

FRONT

WAIST

SIDE

HIPS

PLACE UPPER PART

INNER FRONT

WAIST

HIPS

SIDE STR. OF GRN.

CONSTRUCTION
Construct the base dress block
with darts and raglan sleeves,
transforming as illustrated here.

DRESS WITH STAND UP COLLAR AND FRILLS

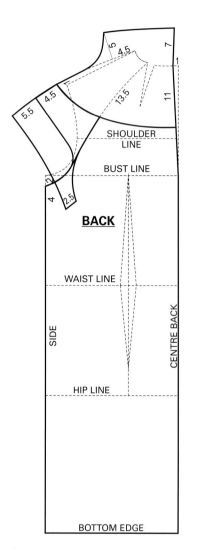

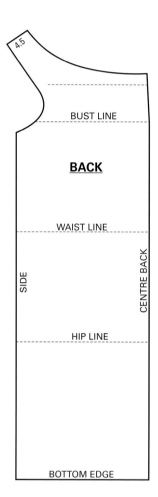

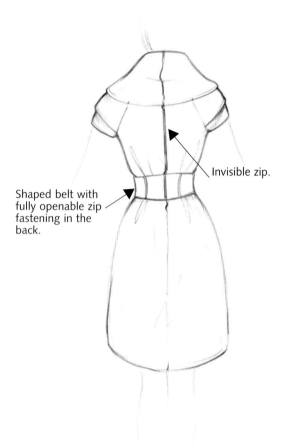

Invisible zip.

Shaped belt with fully openable zip fastening in the back.

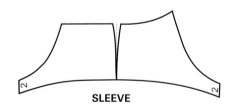

SLEEVE

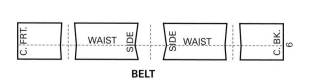

BELT

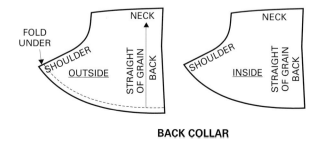

BACK COLLAR

DRESS WITH FRONT CAPE

LOOSE-FITTING AND ASYMMETRICAL ON THE BOTTOM

DRESS WITH FRONT CAPE

UNDER BODICE

NECK

SLEEVE

CAPE MOTIF

SHOULDER MOTIF

CONSTRUCTION

Construct the base of the bodice with darts and the base of the ½ circle skirt, transforming as illustrated here.

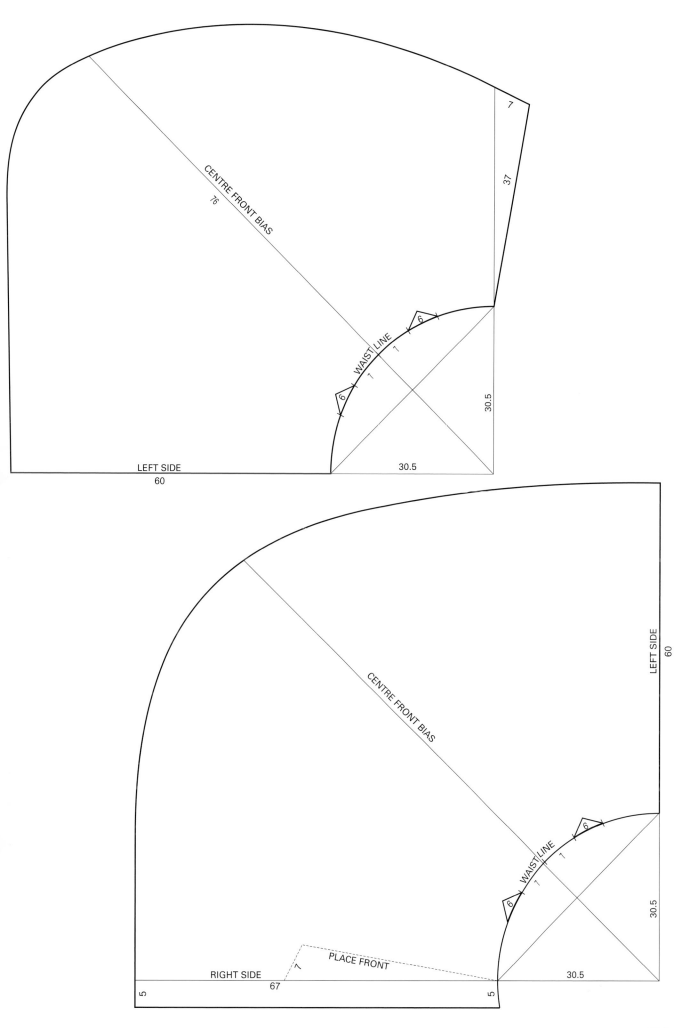

SPORTY SHORT-SLEEVE JACKET

WITH FOLDED RAGLAN SLEEVES

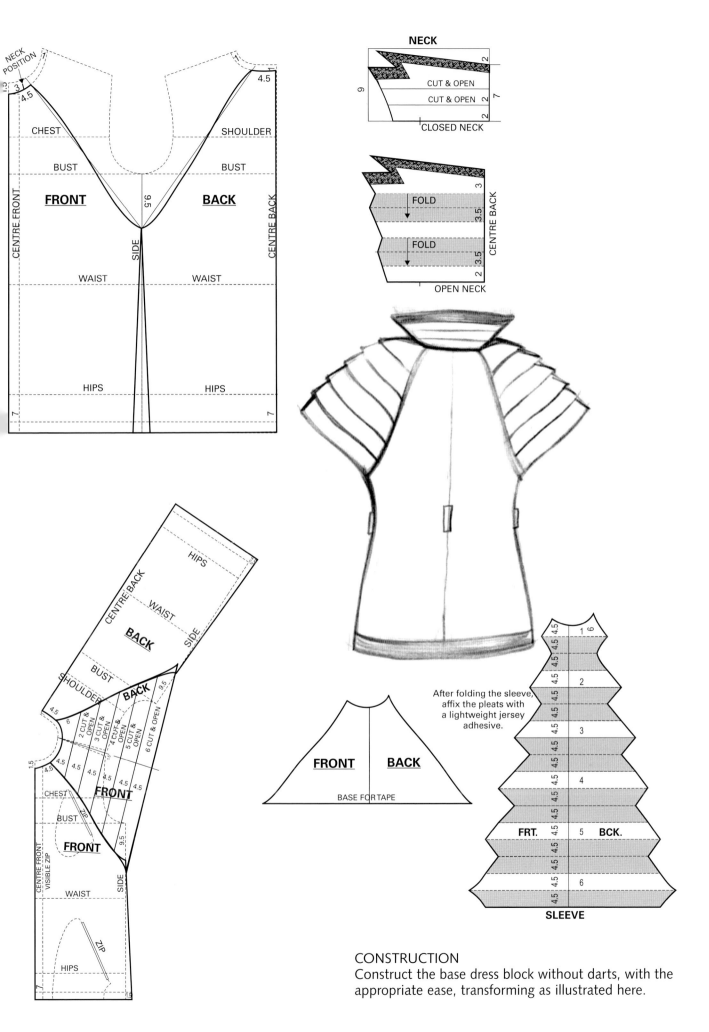

NECK

CUT & OPEN
CUT & OPEN
CLOSED NECK

FOLD
FOLD
OPEN NECK

NECK POSITION

CHEST
SHOULDER
BUST
BUST

FRONT
9.5
BACK

CENTRE FRONT
CENTRE BACK
SIDE

WAIST
WAIST

HIPS
HIPS

CENTRE BACK
WAIST
HIPS
BACK
BUST
SHOULDER
SIDE
BACK

2 CUT & OPEN
3 CUT & OPEN
4 CUT & OPEN
5 CUT & OPEN
6 CUT & OPEN

CHEST
BUST
FRONT
ZIP
FRONT

CENTRE FRONT
VISIBLE ZIP
WAIST
SIDE
ZIP
HIPS

FRONT   **BACK**

BASE FOR TAPE

After folding the sleeve, affix the pleats with a lightweight jersey adhesive.

1
2
3
4
FRT.   5   BCK.
6

SLEEVE

CONSTRUCTION
Construct the base dress block without darts, with the appropriate ease, transforming as illustrated here.

BLOUSE WITH SHORT WING-CAP SLEEVES

WITH RAISED COLLAR AND FOLDED-UP FRONT SLEEVES

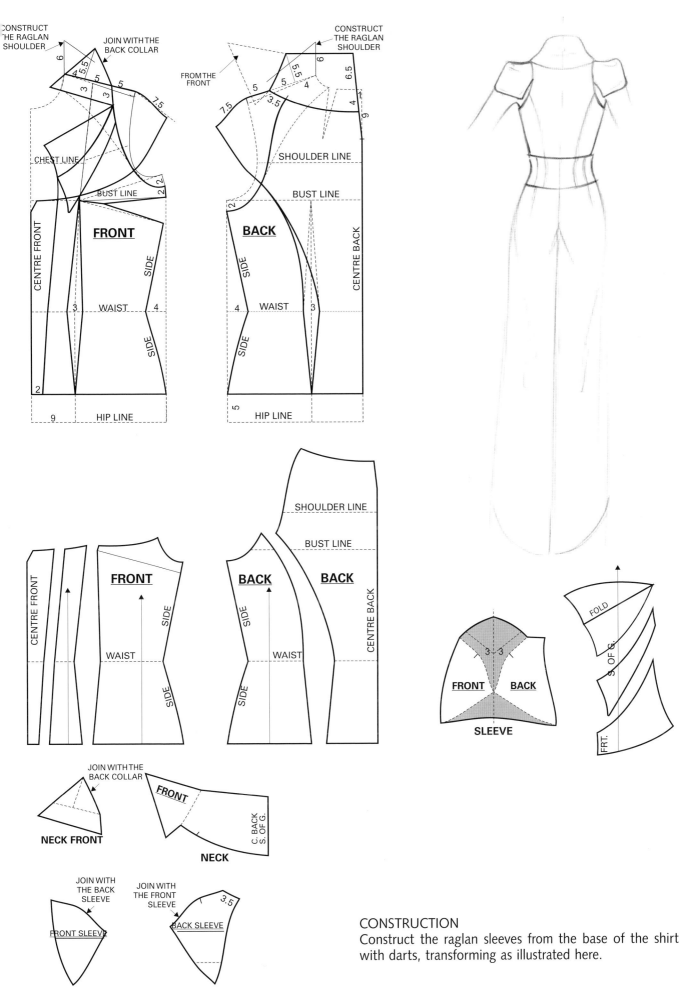

CONSTRUCTION

Construct the raglan sleeves from the base of the shirt with darts, transforming as illustrated here.

COCKTAIL DRESS

WITH DRAPING ON THE FRONT AND SIDE CUT-OUTS

CONSTRUCTION
Construct the raglan sleeves from the base of the shirt with darts, transforming as illustrated here.

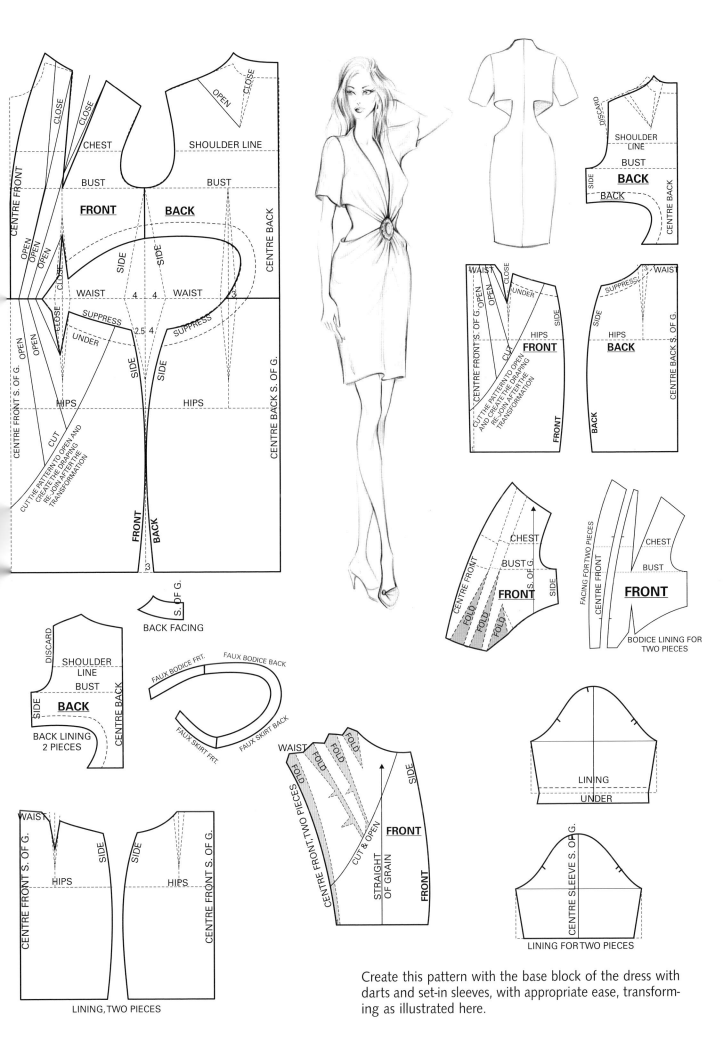

CLOSE
CLOSE
CLOSE
OPEN
CHEST
SHOULDER LINE
BUST
BUST
CENTRE FRONT
FRONT
BACK
CENTRE BACK
OPEN
OPEN
OPEN
SIDE
SIDE
CLOSE
CLOSE
WAIST
4   4
WAIST
3
CENTRE FRONT S. OF G.
OPEN
OPEN
SUPPRESS
UNDER
2.5   4
SUPPRESS
SIDE
SIDE
HIPS
HIPS
CENTRE BACK S. OF G.
CUT
CUT THE PATTERN TO OPEN AND CREATE THE DRAPING RE-JOIN AFTER THE TRANSFORMATION
FRONT
BACK
3

DISCARD
SHOULDER LINE
BUST
BACK
SIDE
CENTRE BACK
BACK

S. OF G.
BACK FACING

SHOULDER LINE
BUST
SIDE
BACK
CENTRE BACK
BACK LINING
2 PIECES

FAUX BODICE FRT.   FAUX BODICE BACK
FAUX SKIRT FRT.   FAUX SKIRT BACK

WAIST
CENTRE FRONT S. OF G.
SIDE
HIPS

SIDE
HIPS
CENTRE FRONT S. OF G.

LINING, TWO PIECES

WAIST
FOLD
FOLD
FOLD
CENTRE FRONT, TWO PIECES
SIDE
CUT & OPEN
STRAIGHT OF GRAIN
FRONT
FRONT

WAIST
'3'   WAIST
CENTRE FRONT S. OF G.   OPEN
UNDER
CLOSE
SUPPRESS
SIDE
SIDE
HIPS
FRONT
HIPS
BACK
CUT
CENTRE BACK S. OF G.
CUT THE PATTERN TO OPEN AND CREATE THE DRAPING RE-JOIN AFTER THE TRANSFORMATION
BACK

DISCARD
SHOULDER LINE
BUST
SIDE
BACK
BACK
CENTRE BACK

CHEST
BUST
S. OF G.
CENTRE FRONT
FRONT
SIDE
FOLD
FOLD
FOLD

FACING FOR TWO PIECES
CHEST
BUST
CENTRE FRONT
FRONT
BODICE LINING FOR TWO PIECES

LINING
UNDER

CENTRE SLEEVE S. OF G.
LINING FOR TWO PIECES

Create this pattern with the base block of the dress with darts and set-in sleeves, with appropriate ease, transforming as illustrated here.

5. KIMONO AND BATWING GARMENTS

KIMONO BASE BLOCK

USING THE BASE WITH DARTS

FRONT
- Draw the base of the bodice front with darts, with the appropriate ease.
- From U, draw a 3-12 cm/1.18-4.72" perpendicular line (according to the angle desired for the sleeve).
- Temporarily close the shoulder bust dart, opening it on the centre front.
- From A, passing through Z1 (1 cm/0.39" from Z), draw a straight line to Z2.
- From Q, drop down 8-16 cm/3.15-6.30" to E1.
- Draw the diagonal line from U-E1 to create the added volume.
- Draw E1-E2, parallel to Z1-Z2.
- Draw the base hem Z2-E2.
- Cut along the diagonal line E1-U and open as desired.

- Join the under sleeve and draw the bottom of the sleeve.
- Reopen the bust dart along the shoulder, restore and join all the lines.

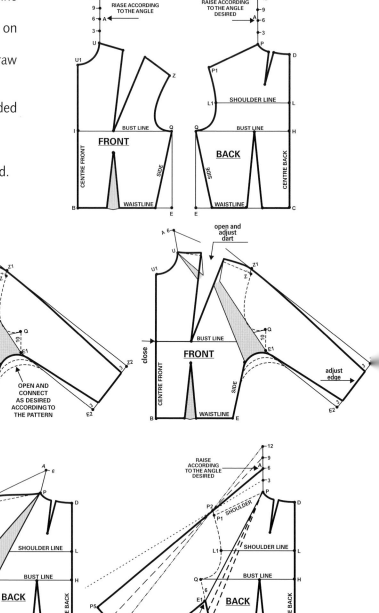

BACK
- Draw the base of the shirt or dress with darts, with the appropriate ease.
- Create the waist darts and discard the sides as needed; adjust the length as desired and separate the back from the front.
- From P, draw a 3-12 cm/1.18-4.72" perpendicular line according to the angle desired for the sleeve (e.g. 6 cm/2.36").
- From A, passing through P2 at 1 cm from P1, draw a straight line to P5.

- P2-P5 sleeve length from the point of the shoulder.
- From Q, drop down from 4-6 cm/1.57-2.36" according to the desired sleeve width (in this case, 6 cm/2.36") and draw point E1.
- Draw the diagonal line P-E1.
- Draw E1-E2, parallel to P2-P5.
- Draw the hem P5-E2 at a right angle to P2-P5, adjusting the width of the bottom of the sleeve to be 2 cm bigger than the front.
- Cut along the diagonal line E1-P, open as desired.

BLOUSE WITH FIT AND FLARE KIMONO SLEEVES

FLARED AT THE CUFF AND JOINED TO THE BROAD LOWER HALF OF THE BLOUSE

BLOUSE WITH FIT AND FLARE KIMONO SLEEVES

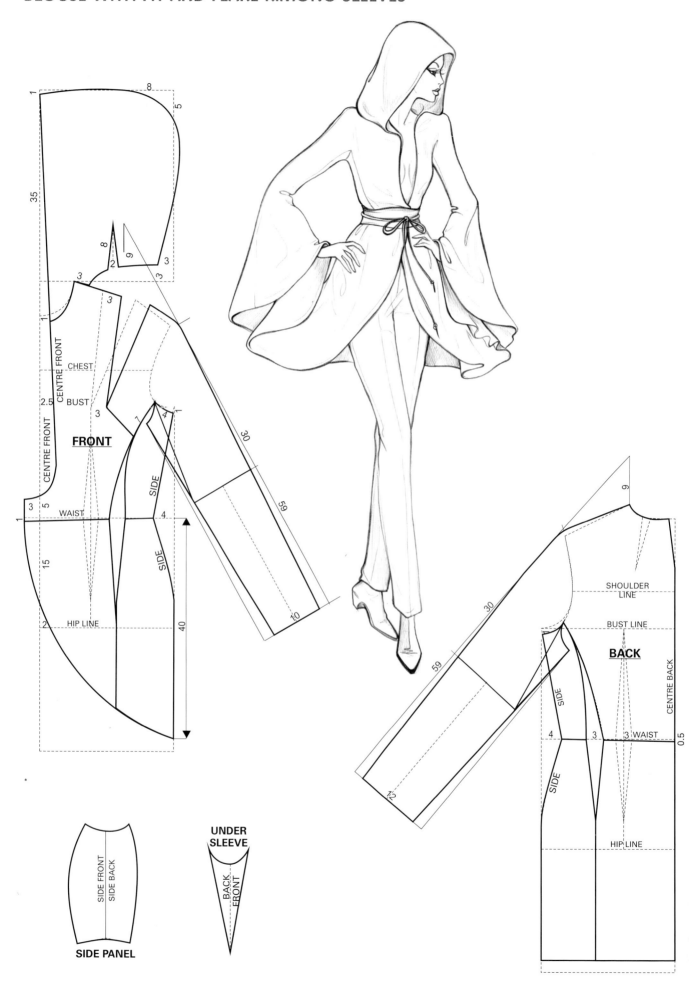

FRONT

CENTRE FRONT

CHEST

BUST

WAIST

HIP LINE

SIDE

UNDER
SLEEVE

SIDE FRONT / SIDE BACK

BACK / FRONT

SIDE PANEL

BACK

SHOULDER LINE

BUST LINE

CENTRE BACK

WAIST

HIP LINE

SIDE

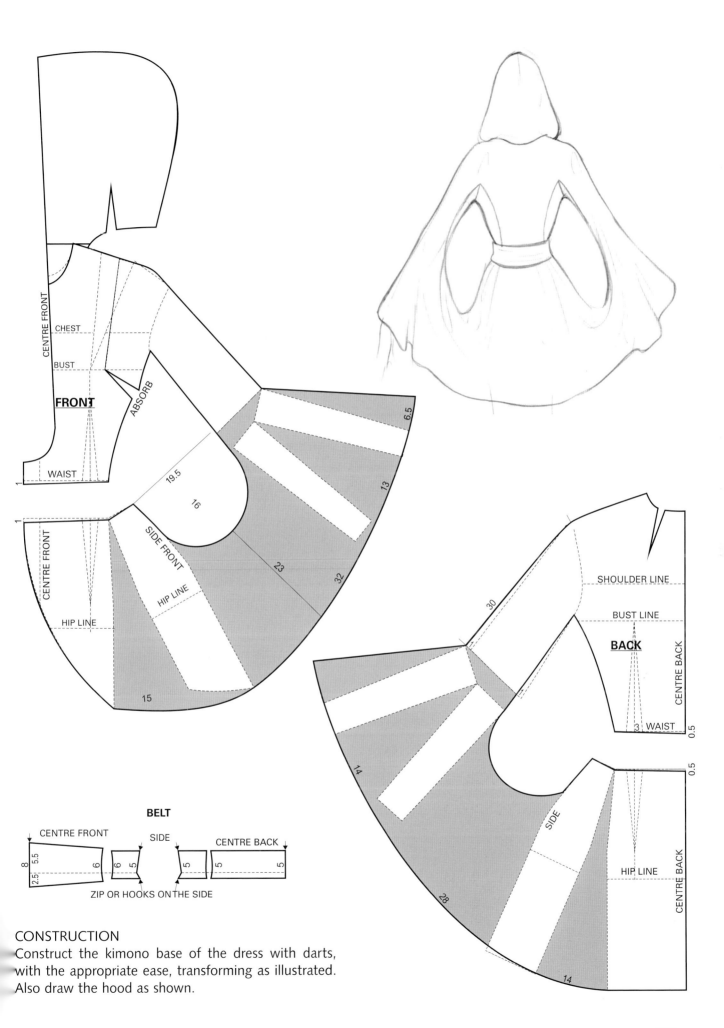

FRONT

CENTRE FRONT

CHEST

BUST

ABSORB

WAIST

CENTRE FRONT

SIDE FRONT

HIP LINE

HIP LINE

19.5

16

6.5

13

23

32

15

SHOULDER LINE

BUST LINE

BACK

CENTRE BACK

WAIST

3

0.5

0.5

SIDE

HIP LINE

CENTRE BACK

30

14

28

14

BELT

CENTRE FRONT

SIDE

CENTRE BACK

8

5.5

2.5

6

6

5

5

5

5

ZIP OR HOOKS ON THE SIDE

CONSTRUCTION

Construct the kimono base of the dress with darts, with the appropriate ease, transforming as illustrated. Also draw the hood as shown.

JACKET WITH INSERTS

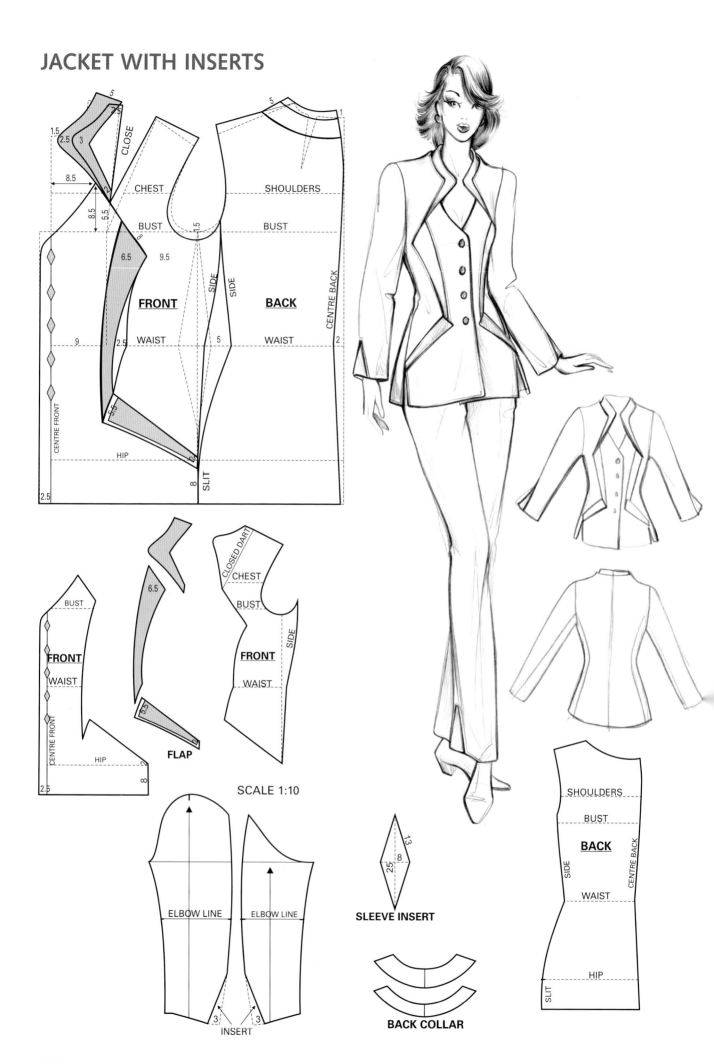

SCALE 1:10

CHEST
BUST
SHOULDERS
BUST
CLOSE
WAIST
WAIST
CENTRE FRONT
CENTRE BACK
SIDE
SIDE
HIP
SLIT

FRONT
BACK

FRONT
FLAP
FRONT
BACK

CLOSED DART
CHEST
BUST
SIDE
WAIST

ELBOW LINE
ELBOW LINE
INSERT

SLEEVE INSERT

BACK COLLAR

SHOULDERS
BUST
SIDE
CENTRE BACK
WAIST
HIP
SLIT

KIMONO JACKET WITH CREATIVE FASTENING

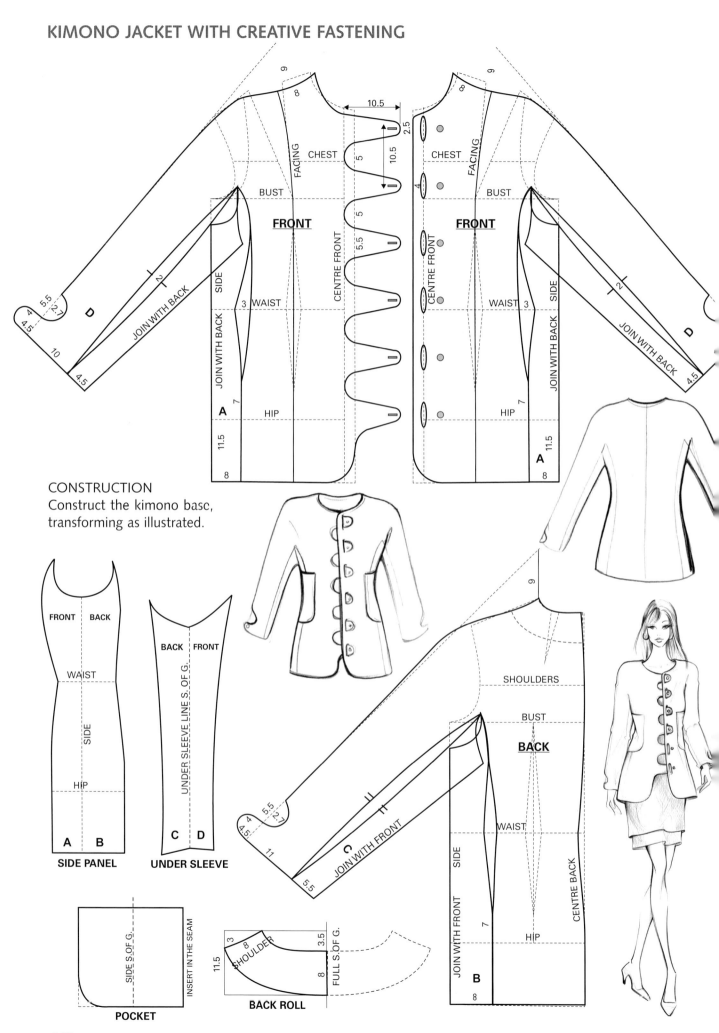

CONSTRUCTION
Construct the kimono basc,
transforming as illustrated.

FRONT

FRONT

BACK

SIDE PANEL

UNDER SLEEVE

POCKET

BACK ROLL

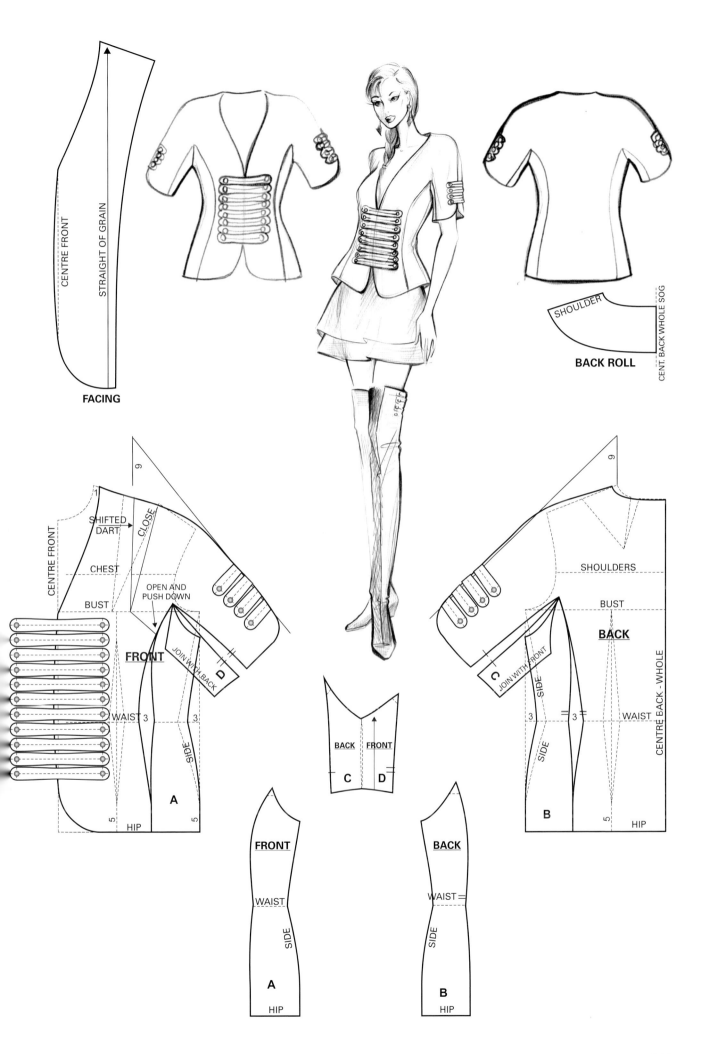

CENTRE FRONT

STRAIGHT OF GRAIN

FACING

SHOULDER

CENT. BACK WHOLE SOG

BACK ROLL

9

1

SHIFTED DART

CLOSE

CHEST

BUST

OPEN AND PUSH DOWN

CENTRE FRONT

FRONT

JOIN WITH BACK

D

WAIST 3   3

SIDE

A

5   5

HIP

9

SHOULDERS

BUST

BACK

JOIN WITH FRONT

C

SIDE

3   3   WAIST

CENTRE BACK - WHOLE

SIDE

B

5

HIP

BACK   FRONT

C   D

FRONT

WAIST

SIDE

A

HIP

BACK

WAIST

SIDE

B

HIP

DRESS WITH INSERTED TIE AND PANEL ABOVE THE SKIRT

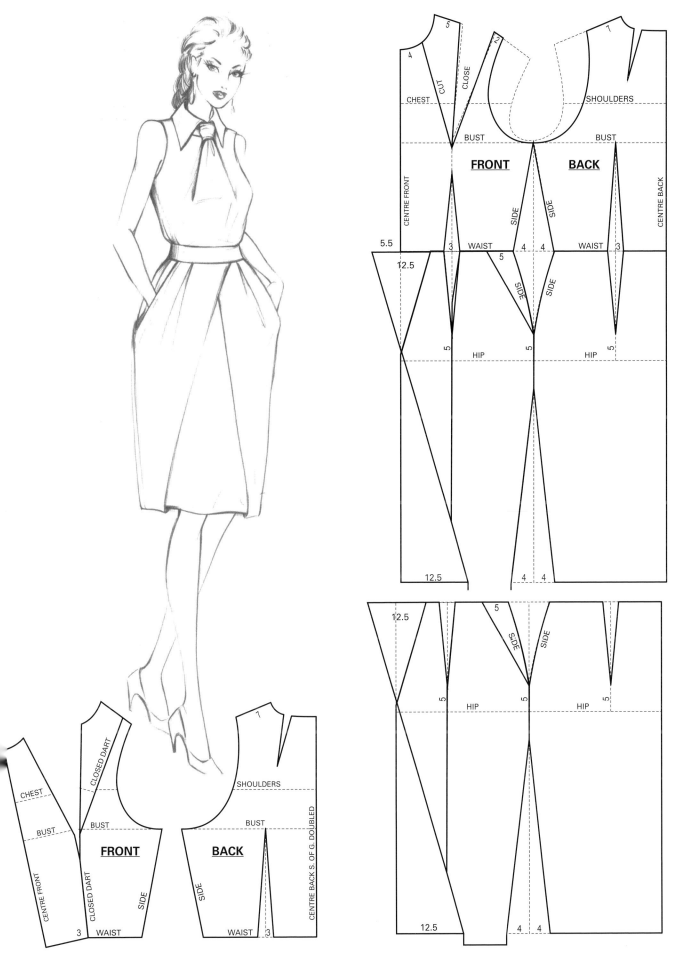

DRESS WITH INSERTED TIE AND PANEL ABOVE THE SKIRT

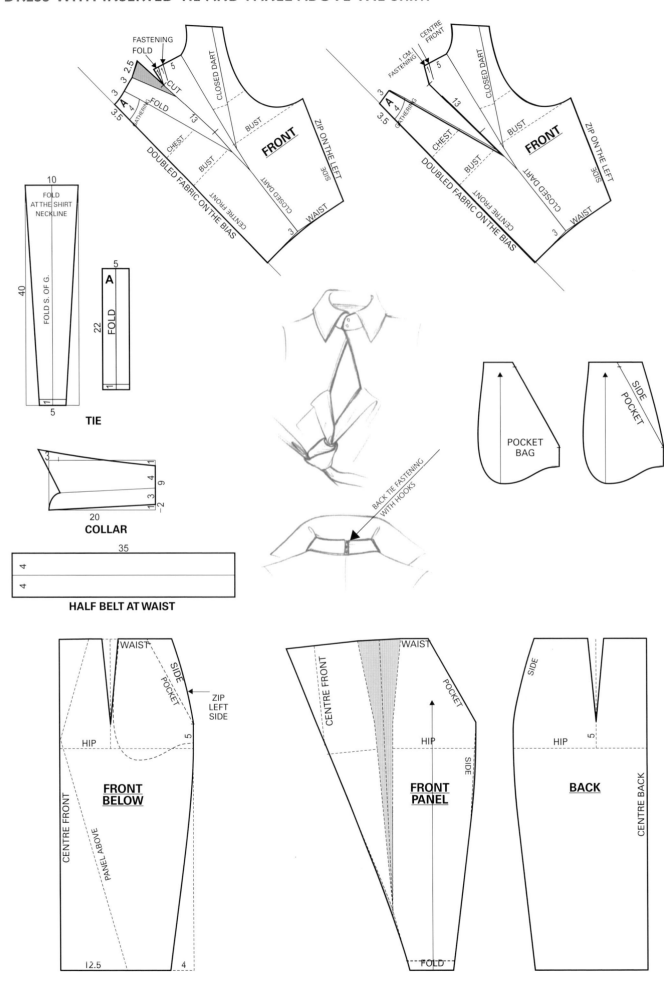

TIE

COLLAR

HALF BELT AT WAIST

POCKET BAG

SIDE POCKET

FRONT BELOW

FRONT PANEL

BACK

DRESS WITH CRISSCROSS SHAWL

DRESS WITH CRISSCROSS SHAWL

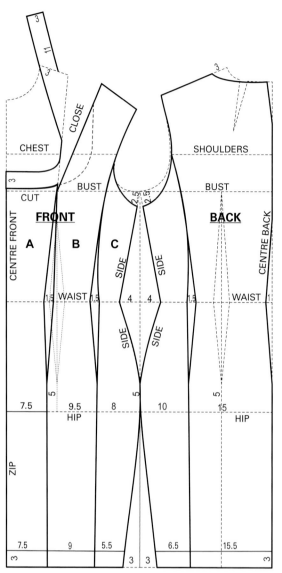

CONSTRUCTION
Construct the kimono base with darts, transforming as illustrated.

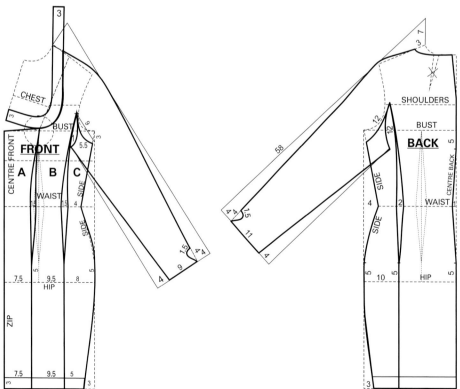

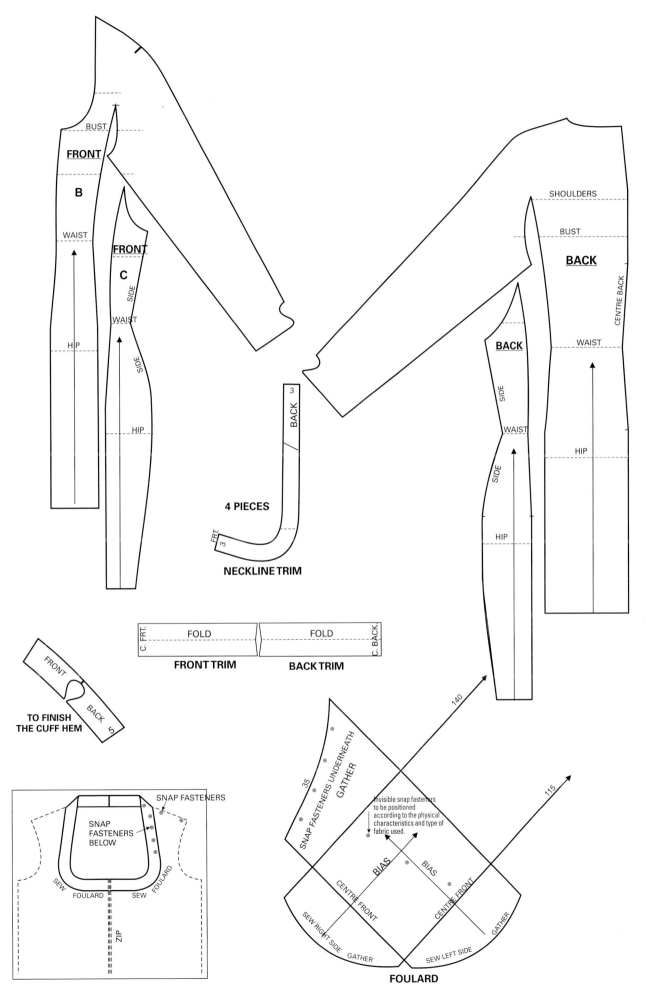

FRONT

B

BUST

WAIST

HIP

FRONT

C

SIDE

WAIST

SIDE

HIP

BACK

SHOULDERS

BUST

CENTRE BACK

WAIST

HIP

BACK

SIDE

WAIST

SIDE

HIP

4 PIECES

BACK

3

FRT.

3

NECKLINE TRIM

FOLD

C. FRT.

FOLD

C. BACK

FRONT TRIM

BACK TRIM

FRONT

BACK

**TO FINISH
THE CUFF HEM**

5

SNAP FASTENERS

SNAP
FASTENERS
BELOW

SEW

FOULARD

SEW

FOULARD

ZIP

140

35

SNAP FASTENERS UNDERNEATH

GATHER

Invisible snap fasteners
to be positioned
according to the physical
characteristics and type of
fabric used.

BIAS

BIAS

CENTRE FRONT

CENTRE FRONT

SEW RIGHT SIDE

GATHER

SEW LEFT SIDE

GATHER

115

FOULARD

DRESS WITH WIDE, STAND-UP, ASYMMETRICAL COLLAR

WITH KIMONO SLEEVES AND DRAPING ON THE FRONT

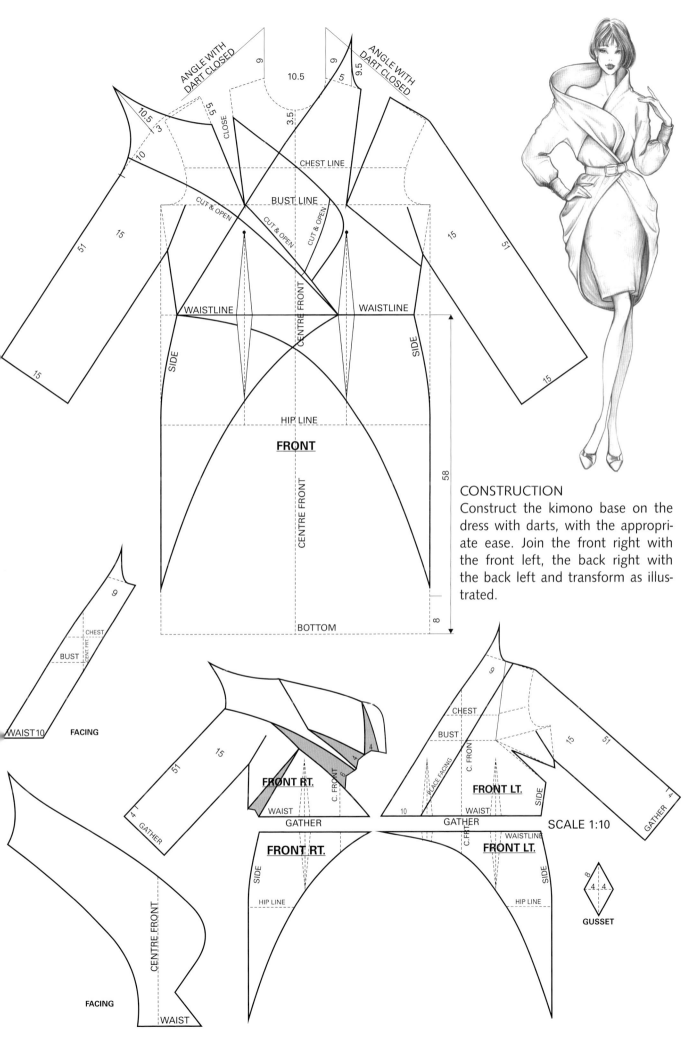

ANGLE WITH DART CLOSED

ANGLE WITH DART CLOSED

9

10.5

5

9.5

10.5

3

10

5.5

CLOSE

3.5

CHEST LINE

BUST LINE

CUT & OPEN

CUT & OPEN

CUT & OPEN

15

51

15

51

15

15

WAISTLINE

WAISTLINE

CENTRE FRONT

SIDE

SIDE

HIP LINE

FRONT

CENTRE FRONT

58

8

BOTTOM

CONSTRUCTION

Construct the kimono base on the dress with darts, with the appropriate ease. Join the front right with the front left, the back right with the back left and transform as illustrated.

9

CHEST

BUST

FRNT FRT

WAIST 10

FACING

15

51

4

GATHER

4

6

4

FRONT RT.

WAIST

GATHER

C. FRONT

9

CHEST

BUST

C. FRON

PLACE FACING

15

51

4

GATHER

FRONT LT.

SIDE

10

WAIST

GATHER

SCALE 1:10

SIDE

FRONT RT.

C. FRONT

HIP LINE

C. FRNT

FRONT LT.

SIDE

WAISTLINE

HIP LINE

8

4 4

GUSSET

CENTRE FRONT

FACING

WAIST

149

DRESS WITH WIDE, STAND-UP, ASYMMETRICAL COLLAR

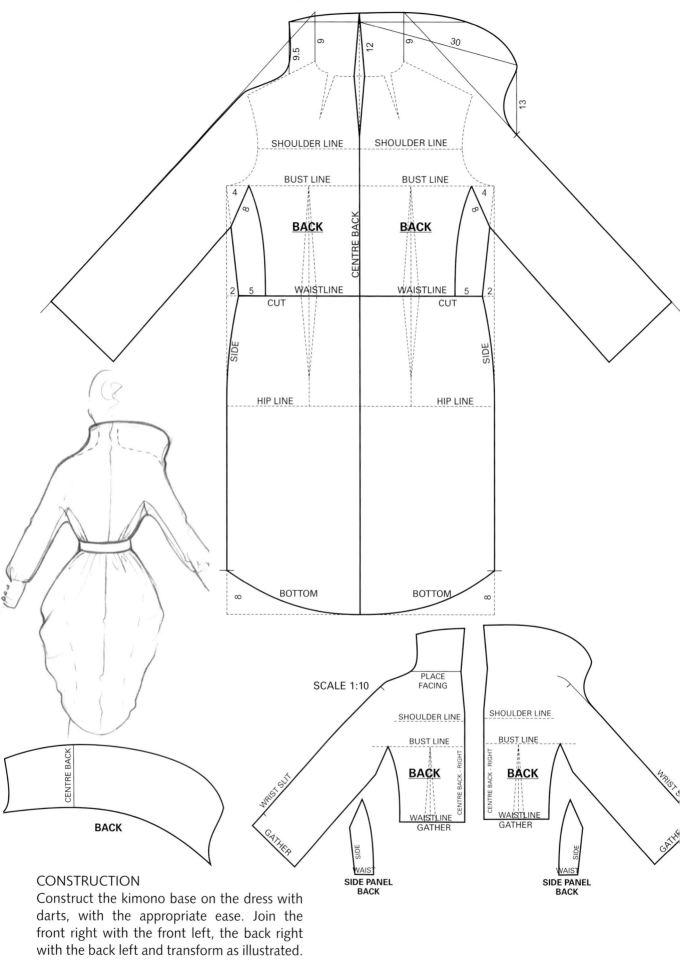

SCALE 1:10

CONSTRUCTION
Construct the kimono base on the dress with darts, with the appropriate ease. Join the front right with the front left, the back right with the back left and transform as illustrated.

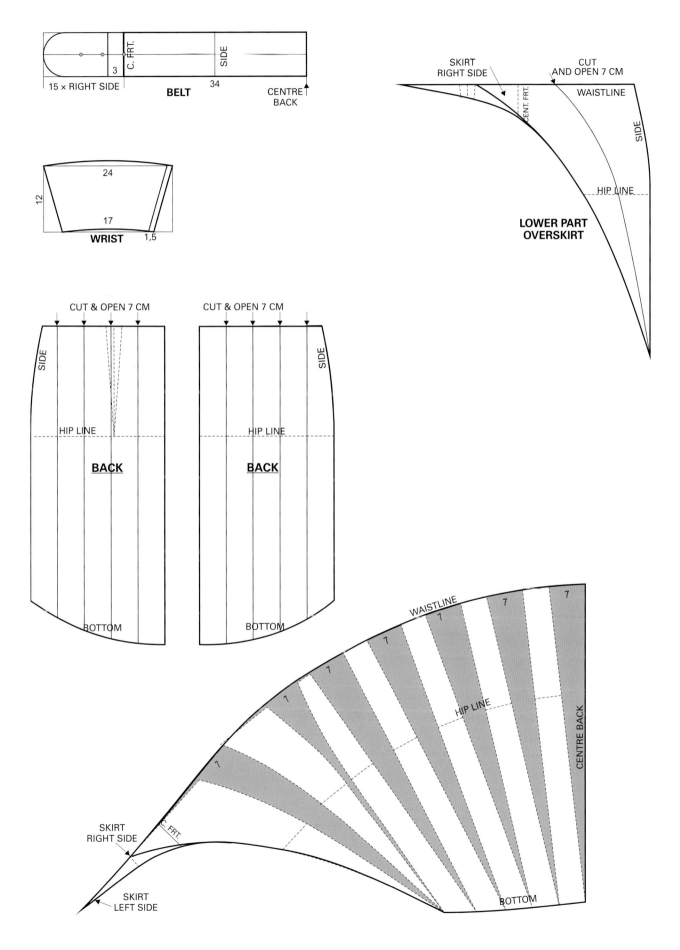

BELT

15 × RIGHT SIDE   3   C. FRT.   SIDE   34   CENTRE BACK

WRIST

12   24   17   1,5

CUT & OPEN 7 CM

SIDE   HIP LINE   BACK   BOTTOM

CUT & OPEN 7 CM

SIDE   HIP LINE   BACK   BOTTOM

SKIRT RIGHT SIDE   CUT AND OPEN 7 CM   WAISTLINE   CENT. FRT.   SIDE   HIP LINE

LOWER PART OVERSKIRT

WAISTLINE   7   7   7   7   HIP LINE   CENTRE BACK   BOTTOM

SKIRT RIGHT SIDE   C. FRT.   SKIRT LEFT SIDE

DRESS WITH SHAPED DROP SLEEVES

WITH A LOOSE SKATER SKIRT

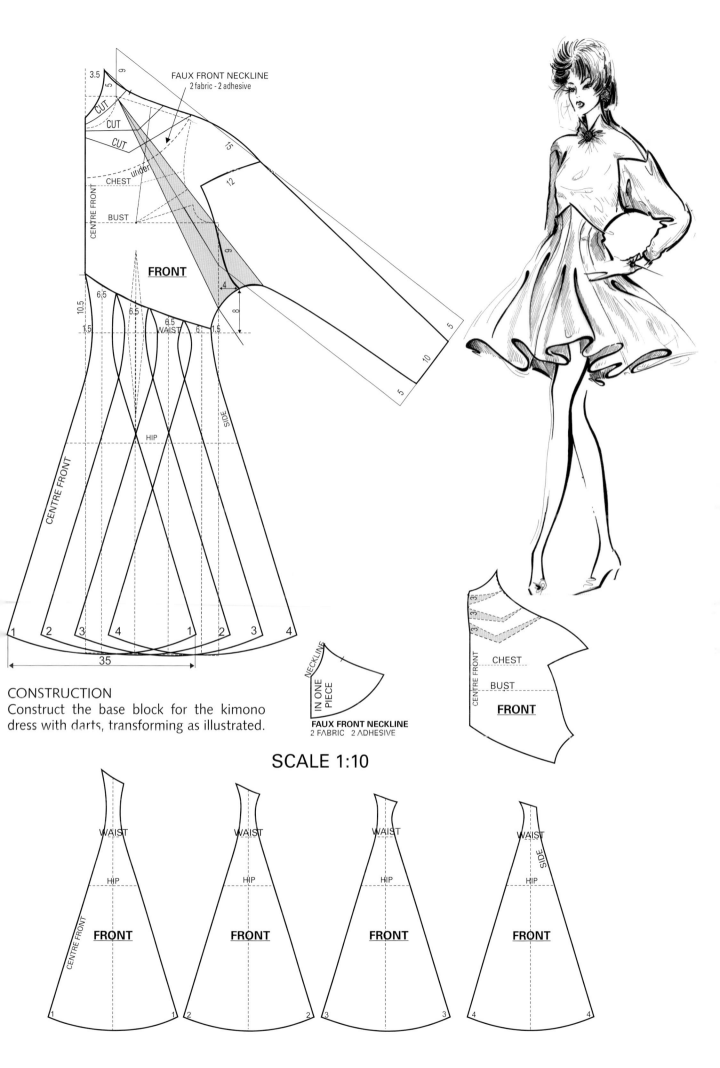

CONSTRUCTION
Construct the base block for the kimono dress with darts, transforming as illustrated.

FRONT

FAUX FRONT NECKLINE
2 fabric - 2 adhesive

IN ONE PIECE

FAUX FRONT NECKLINE
2 FABRIC 2 ADHESIVE

SCALE 1:10

DRESS WITH SHAPED DROP SLEEVES

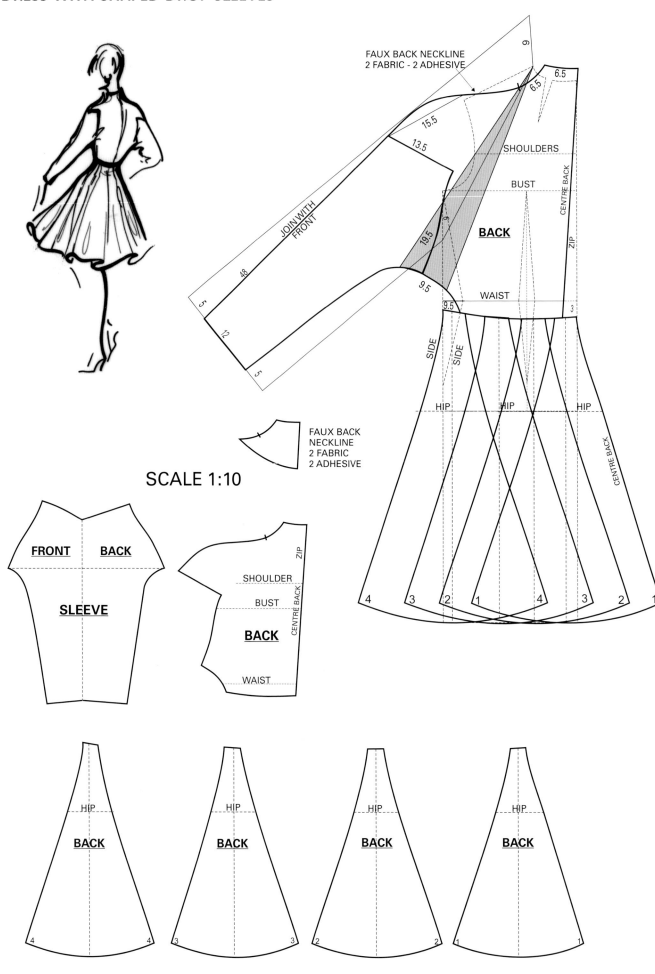

SCALE 1:10

FAUX BACK NECKLINE
2 FABRIC - 2 ADHESIVE

FAUX BACK
NECKLINE
2 FABRIC
2 ADHESIVE

BACK

FRONT   BACK

SLEEVE

BACK

SHOULDER

BUST

WAIST

CENTRE BACK

ZIP

JOIN WITH FRONT

SHOULDERS

BUST

WAIST

HIP

SIDE

CENTRE BACK

ZIP

15.5

13.5

48

5

12

5

9

6.5

6.5

19.5

9

9.5

9.5

3

HIP   HIP   HIP

4   3   2   1   4   3   2   1

HIP

BACK

HIP

BACK

HIP

BACK

HIP

BACK

4   4   3   3   2   2   1   1

LOOSE-FITTING OVERCOAT WITH DOUBLE COLLAR

WITH CREATIVE SLEEVES

LOOSE-FITTING OVERCOAT WITH DOUBLE COLLAR

FRONT

COLLAR

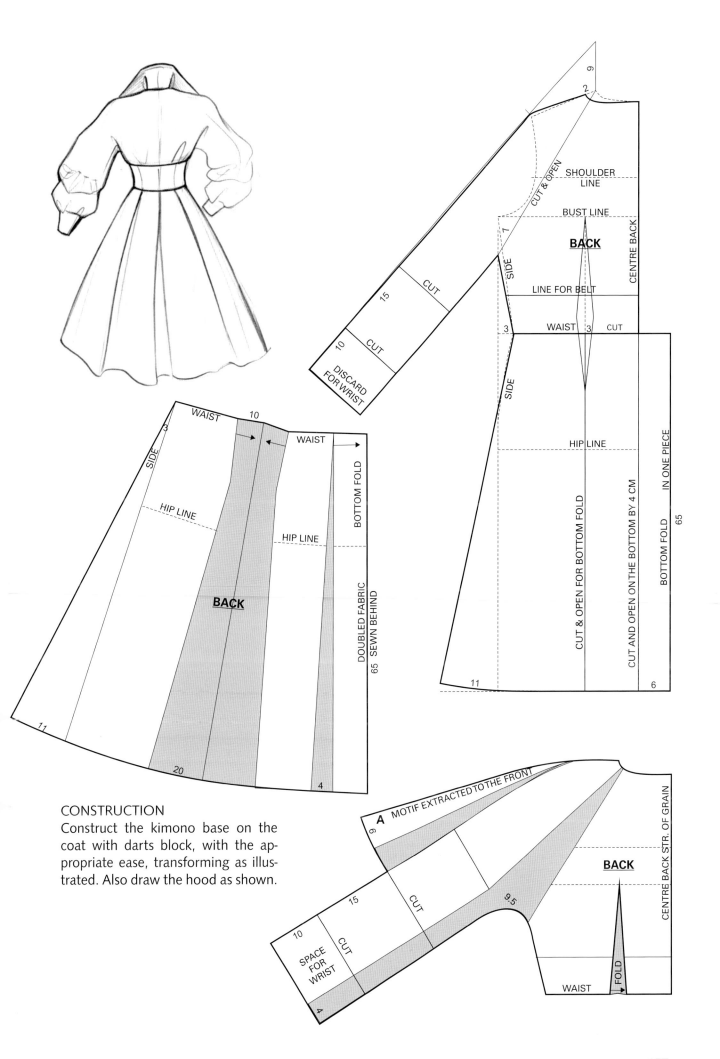

CONSTRUCTION

Construct the kimono base on the coat with darts block, with the appropriate ease, transforming as illustrated. Also draw the hood as shown.

Within the figure, the following labels appear:

SHOULDER LINE

BUST LINE

BACK

CENTRE BACK

LINE FOR BELT

WAIST — CUT

CUT & OPEN

SIDE

HIP LINE

IN ONE PIECE

CUT & OPEN FOR BOTTOM FOLD

CUT AND OPEN ON THE BOTTOM BY 4 CM

BOTTOM FOLD

15 CUT

10 CUT

DISCARD FOR WRIST

9

2

7

3

3

11

6

65

WAIST

10

3

SIDE

WAIST

BOTTOM FOLD

HIP LINE

HIP LINE

BACK

DOUBLED FABRIC

65 SEWN BEHIND

11

20

4

MOTIF EXTRACTED TO THE FRONT

A

9

15

CUT

10

SPACE FOR WRIST

CUT

4

9.5

BACK

CENTRE BACK STR. OF GRAIN

WAIST

FOLD

157

LOOSE-FITTING OVERCOAT WITH DOUBLE COLLAR

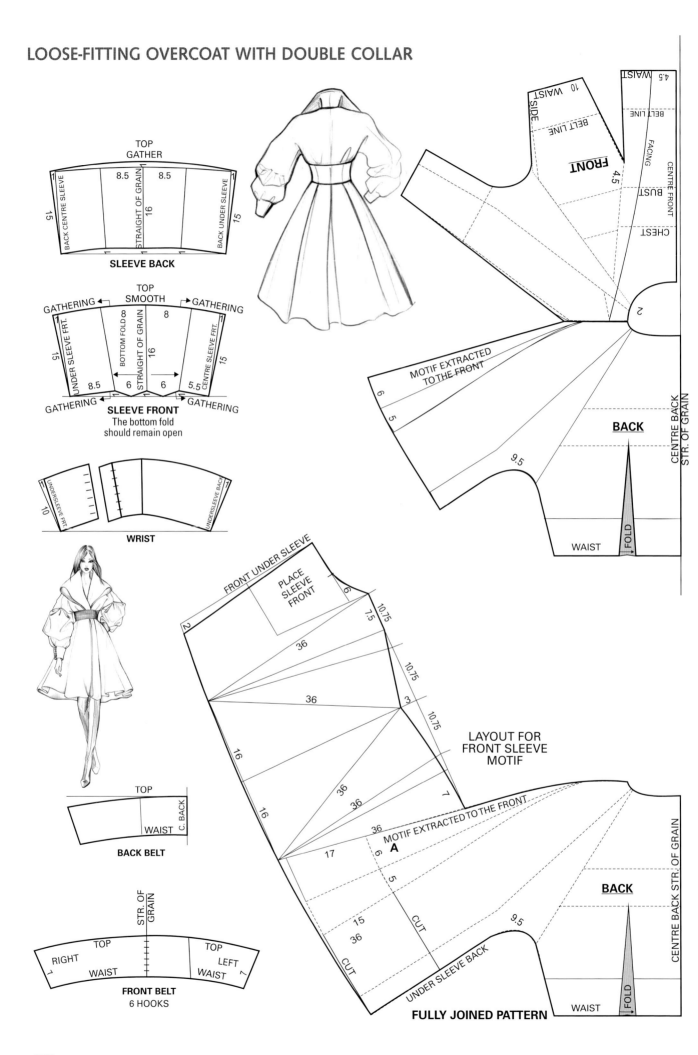

SLEEVE BACK

TOP GATHER

BACK CENTRE SLEEVE — 15
8.5
STRAIGHT OF GRAIN — 16
8.5
BACK UNDER SLEEVE — 15

SLEEVE FRONT
The bottom fold should remain open

TOP SMOOTH

GATHERING
UNDER SLEEVE FRT. — 15
BOTTOM FOLD 8
STRAIGHT OF GRAIN — 16
8
GATHERING
CENTRE SLEEVE FRT. — 15
GATHERING
8.5
6
6
5.5
GATHERING

WRIST

UNDERSLEEVE FRT. — 10
UNDERSLEEVE BACK

BACK BELT

TOP
WAIST
C. BACK

FRONT BELT
6 HOOKS

STR. OF GRAIN
RIGHT
TOP
WAIST — 7
TOP
LEFT
WAIST — 7

WAIST
10
BELT LINE
FRONT
4.5
WAIST
4.5
BELT LINE
FACING
CENTRE FRONT
BUST
CHEST
SIDE

MOTIF EXTRACTED TO THE FRONT
6
5
9.5

BACK
CENTRE BACK STR. OF GRAIN
WAIST
FOLD

FRONT UNDER SLEEVE
PLACE SLEEVE FRONT
2
6
7.5
10.75
36
36
3
10.75
16
10.75
16
36
36
7
17
36
6
A

LAYOUT FOR FRONT SLEEVE MOTIF

MOTIF EXTRACTED TO THE FRONT
5
15
36
CUT
9.5
UNDER SLEEVE BACK
CUT

BACK
CENTRE BACK STR. OF GRAIN
WAIST
FOLD

FULLY JOINED PATTERN

158

KIMONO DRESS WITH ASYMMETRICAL BATWING SLEEVES

AND LATERAL DRAPING

KIMONO DRESS WITH ASYMMETRICAL BATWING SLEEVES

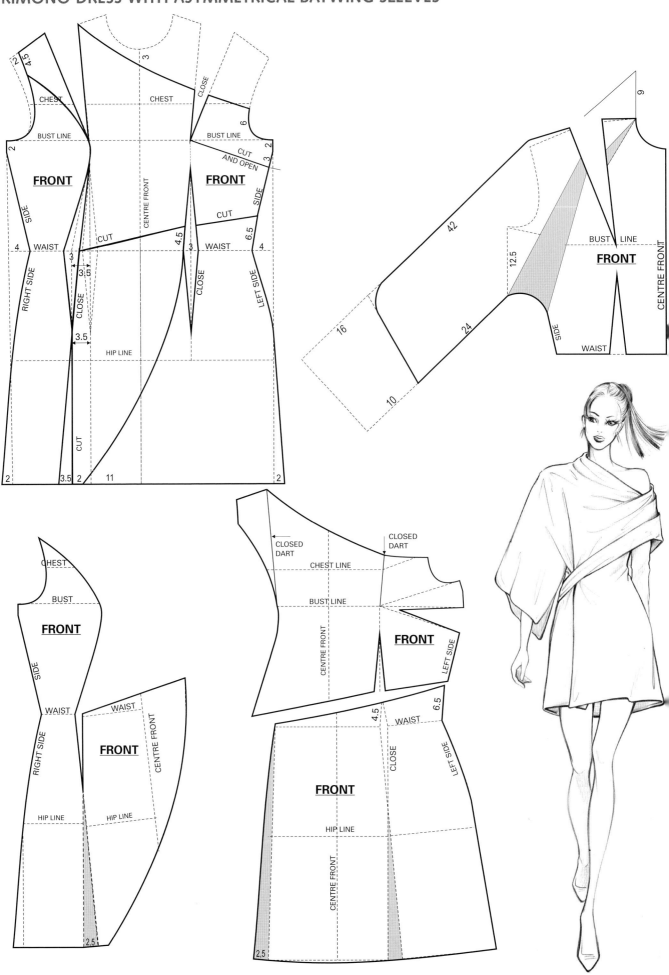

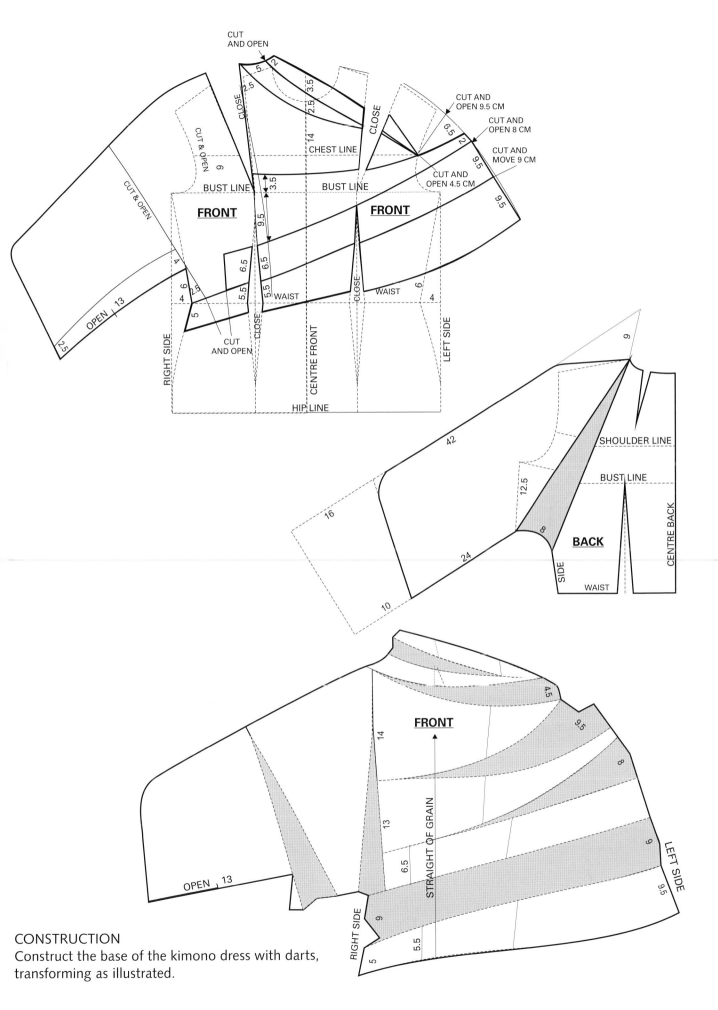

CONSTRUCTION
Construct the base of the kimono dress with darts,
transforming as illustrated.

KIMONO DRESS WITH ASYMMETRICAL BATWING SLEEVES

SCALE 1:10

BATWING BLOUSE AND TROUSERS SET

BATWING BLOUSE AND TROUSERS SET

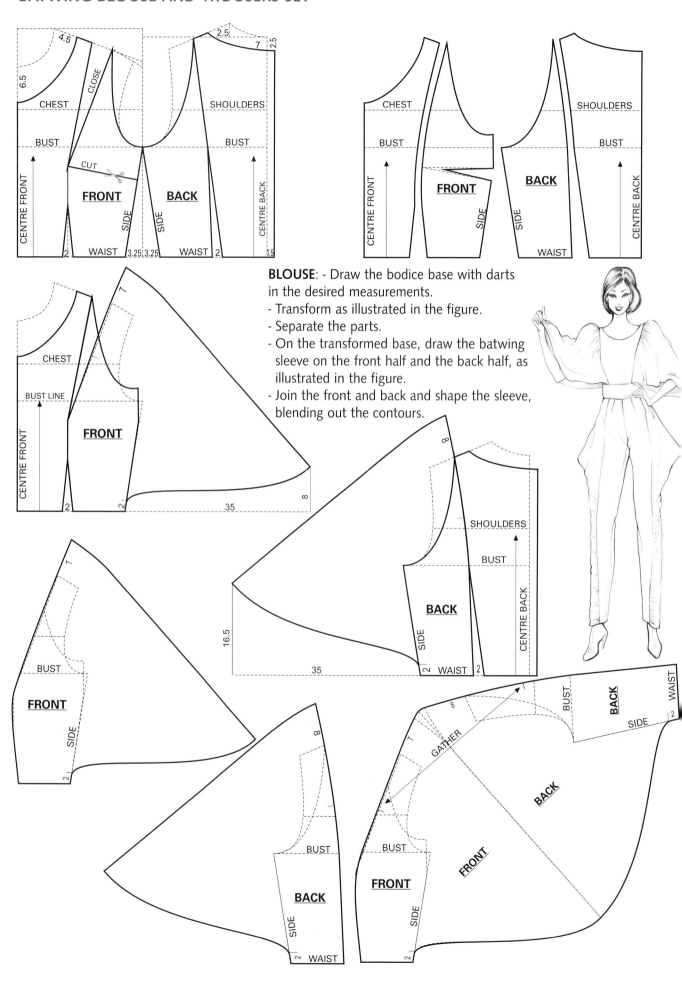

BLOUSE: - Draw the bodice base with darts in the desired measurements.
- Transform as illustrated in the figure.
- Separate the parts.
- On the transformed base, draw the batwing sleeve on the front half and the back half, as illustrated in the figure.
- Join the front and back and shape the sleeve, blending out the contours.

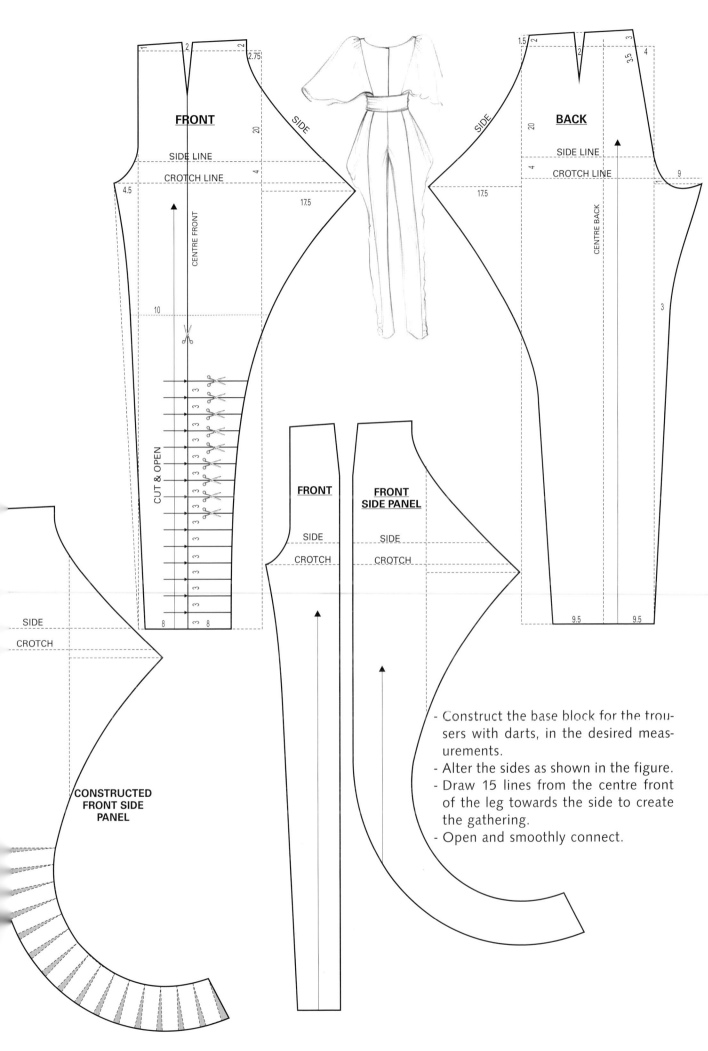

FRONT

SIDE LINE
CROTCH LINE
CENTRE FRONT
CUT & OPEN

20
4
4.5
10
2.75
17.5

3 3 3 3 3 3 3 3 3 3 3 3
8 3 8

BACK

SIDE LINE
CROTCH LINE
CENTRE BACK

1.5 2 2 3
3.5 4
20
4
9
17.5
3
9.5 9.5

FRONT

SIDE
CROTCH

FRONT SIDE PANEL

SIDE
CROTCH

CONSTRUCTED FRONT SIDE PANEL

SIDE
CROTCH

- Construct the base block for the trousers with darts, in the desired measurements.
- Alter the sides as shown in the figure.
- Draw 15 lines from the centre front of the leg towards the side to create the gathering.
- Open and smoothly connect.

TUNIC WITH GATHERED COLLAR

AND ENVELOPING "CAPE" SLEEVES

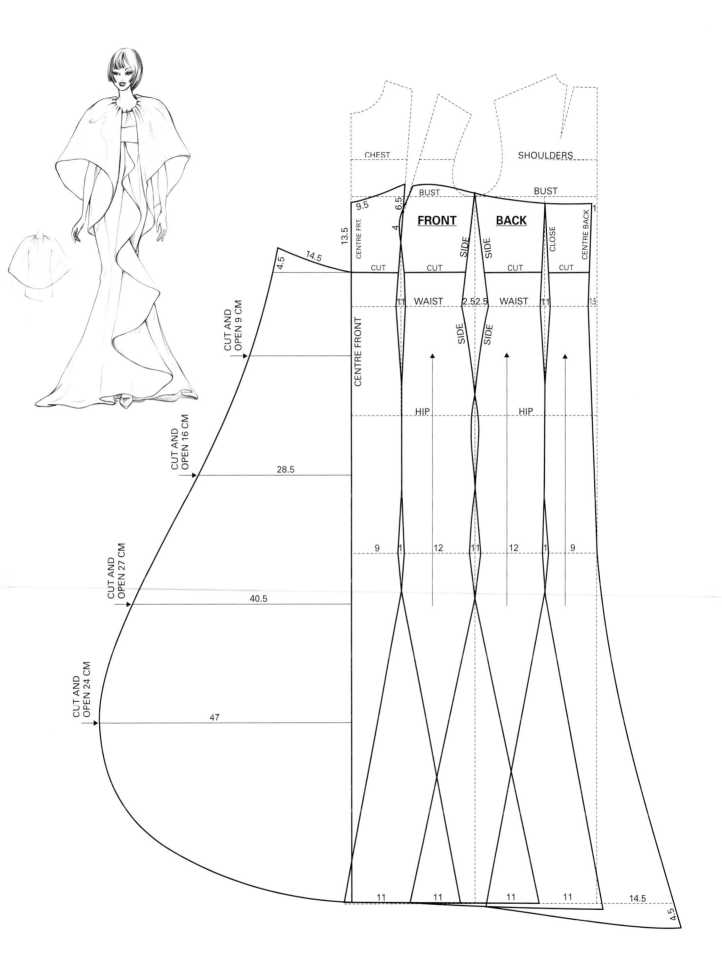

CHEST

SHOULDERS

BUST

BUST

9.5

6.5

FRONT

BACK

CENTRE FRT.

4

SIDE

SIDE

CLOSE

CENTRE BACK

1

13.5

14.5

CUT

CUT

CUT

CUT

4.5

11

WAIST

2.5 2.5

WAIST

11

1.5

CENTRE FRONT

SIDE

SIDE

CUT AND
OPEN 9 CM

HIP

HIP

CUT AND
OPEN 16 CM

28.5

CUT AND
OPEN 27 CM

9

1

12

11

12

1

9

40.5

CUT AND
OPEN 24 CM

47

11

11

11

11

14.5

4.5

CONSTRUCTION
Construct the base of the dress with darts, with the
appropriate ease, transforming as illustrated.

TUNIC WITH GATHERED COLLAR

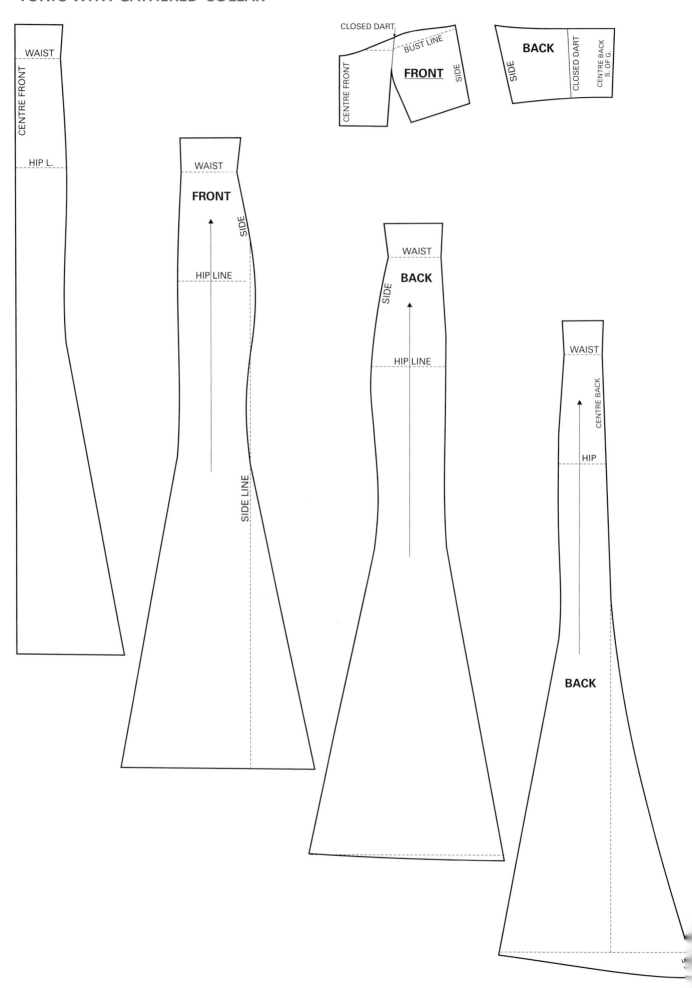

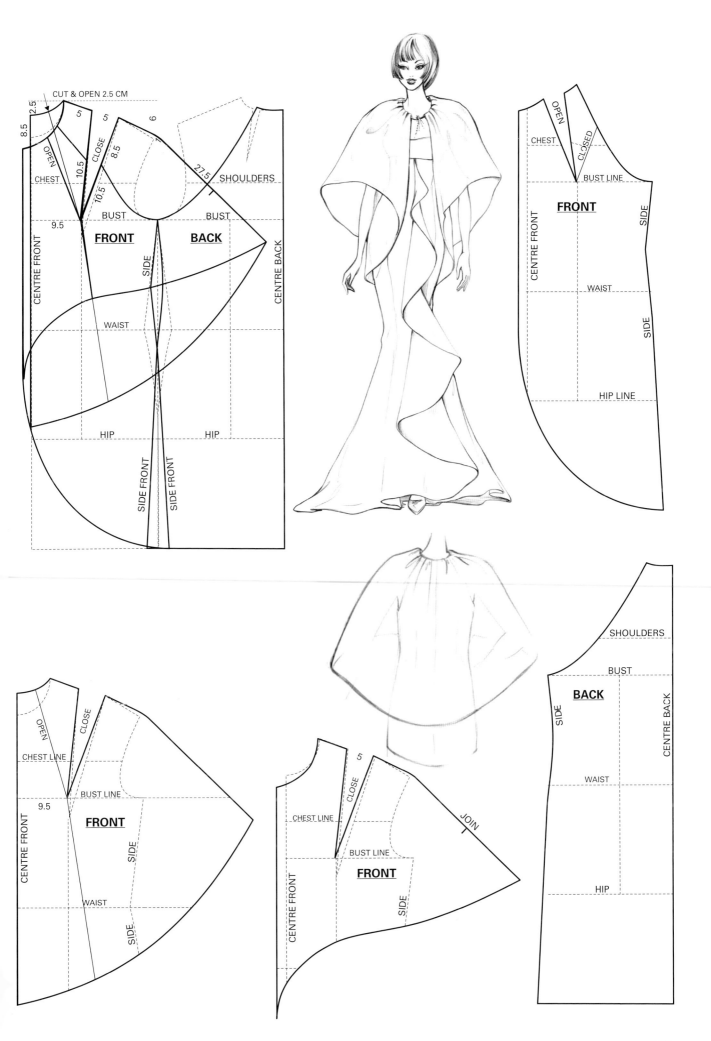

CUT & OPEN 2.5 CM

2.5

8.5

5

5

6

OPEN

CLOSE

10.5

8.5

7

27.5

SHOULDERS

CHEST

10.5

9.5

BUST

BUST

FRONT

BACK

CENTRE FRONT

SIDE

CENTRE BACK

WAIST

HIP

HIP

SIDE FRONT

SIDE FRONT

OPEN

CLOSED

CHEST

BUST LINE

FRONT

SIDE

CENTRE FRONT

WAIST

SIDE

HIP LINE

OPEN

CLOSE

CHEST LINE

BUST LINE

9.5

FRONT

CENTRE FRONT

SIDE

WAIST

SIDE

CLOSE

5

CHEST LINE

BUST LINE

JOIN

FRONT

CENTRE FRONT

SIDE

SHOULDERS

BUST

BACK

SIDE

CENTRE BACK

WAIST

HIP

TUNIC WITH GATHERED COLLAR

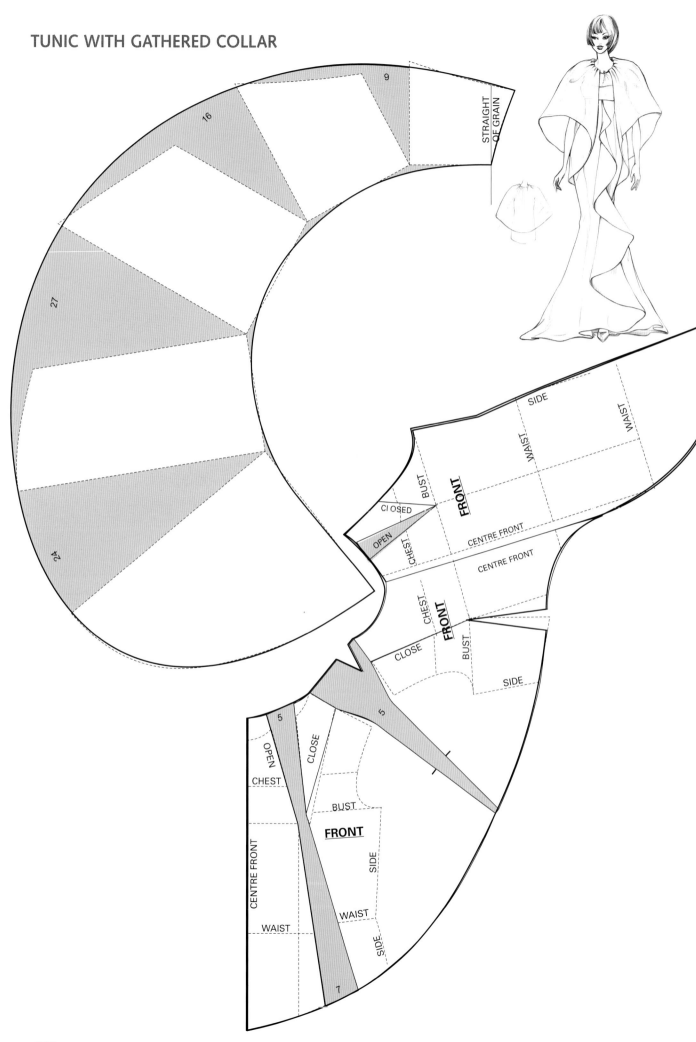

KIMONO-STYLE SUIT WITH FIT AND FLARE JACKET
WITH WIDE WING SLEEVES – SKIRT FLARED AT THE BOTTOM

KIMONO-STYLE SUIT WITH FIT AND FLARE JACKET

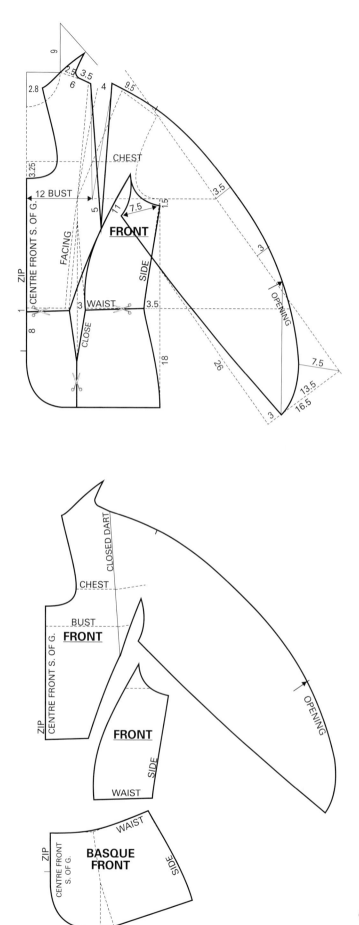

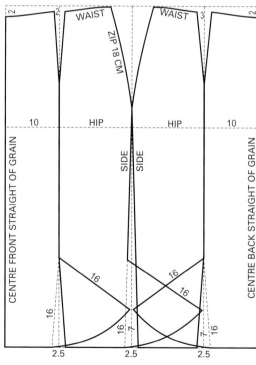

CONSTRUCTION
Construct the base kimono from the jacket with darts and the pencil skirt, transforming as illustrated.

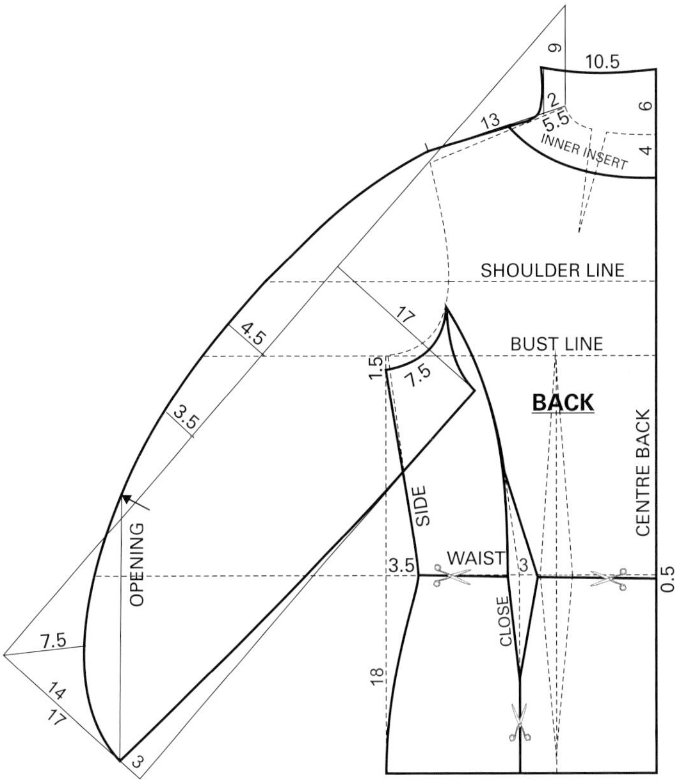
9
10.5
2
5.5
6
13
INNER INSERT
4
SHOULDER LINE
17
4.5
BUST LINE
1.5
7.5
BACK
3.5
SIDE
CENTRE BACK
OPENING
WAIST
3.5
3
0.5
7.5
CLOSE
14
17
18
3

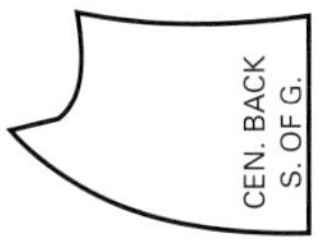
CEN. BACK
S. OF G.

INNER INSERT

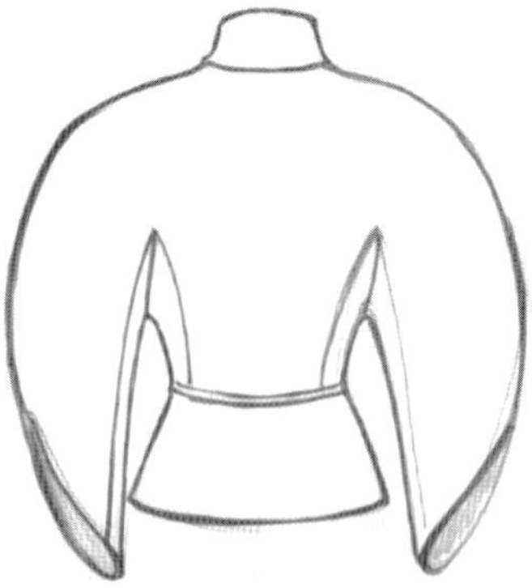

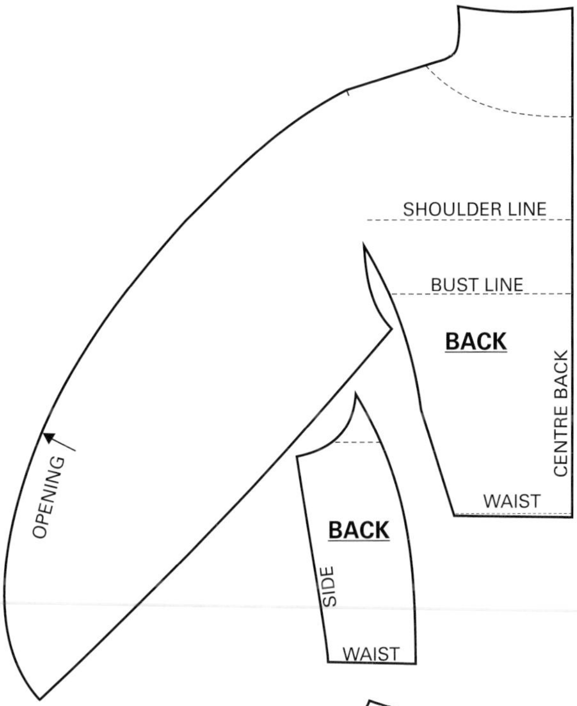
SHOULDER LINE
BUST LINE
BACK
CENTRE BACK
WAIST
OPENING
BACK
SIDE
WAIST

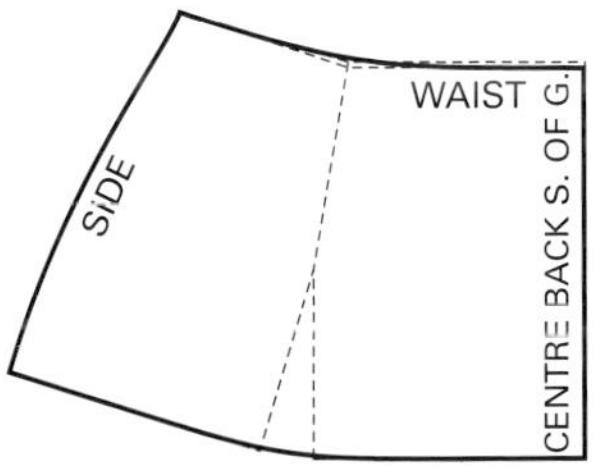
WAIST
SIDE
CENTRE BACK S. OF G.

BACK BASQUE

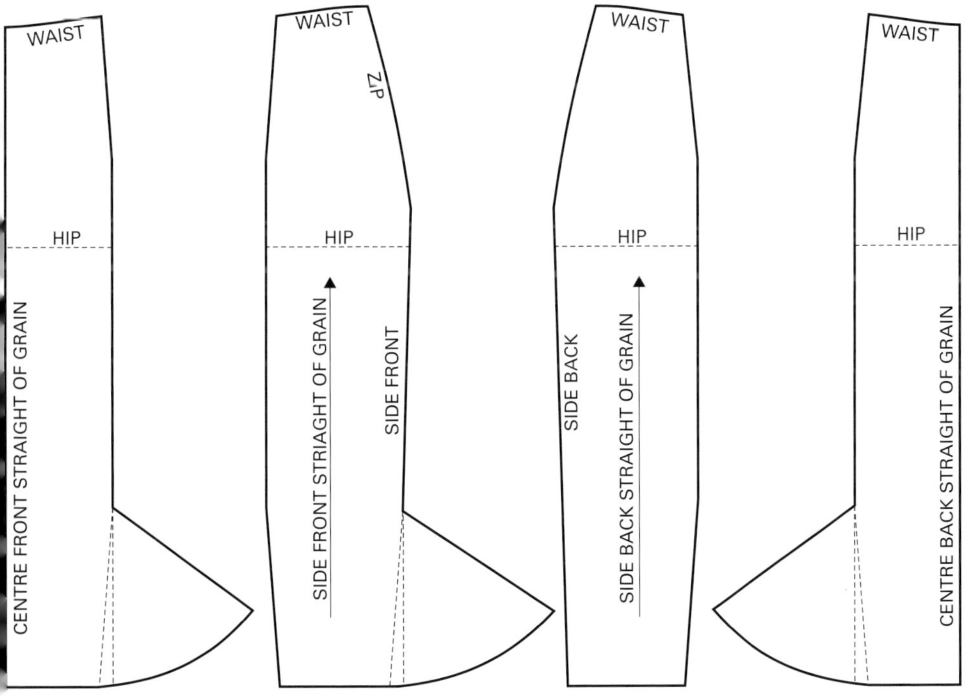
WAIST
HIP
CENTRE FRONT STRAIGHT OF GRAIN
WAIST
ZIP
HIP
SIDE FRONT STRAIGHT OF GRAIN
SIDE FRONT
WAIST
HIP
SIDE BACK
SIDE BACK STRAIGHT OF GRAIN
WAIST
HIP
CENTRE BACK STRAIGHT OF GRAIN

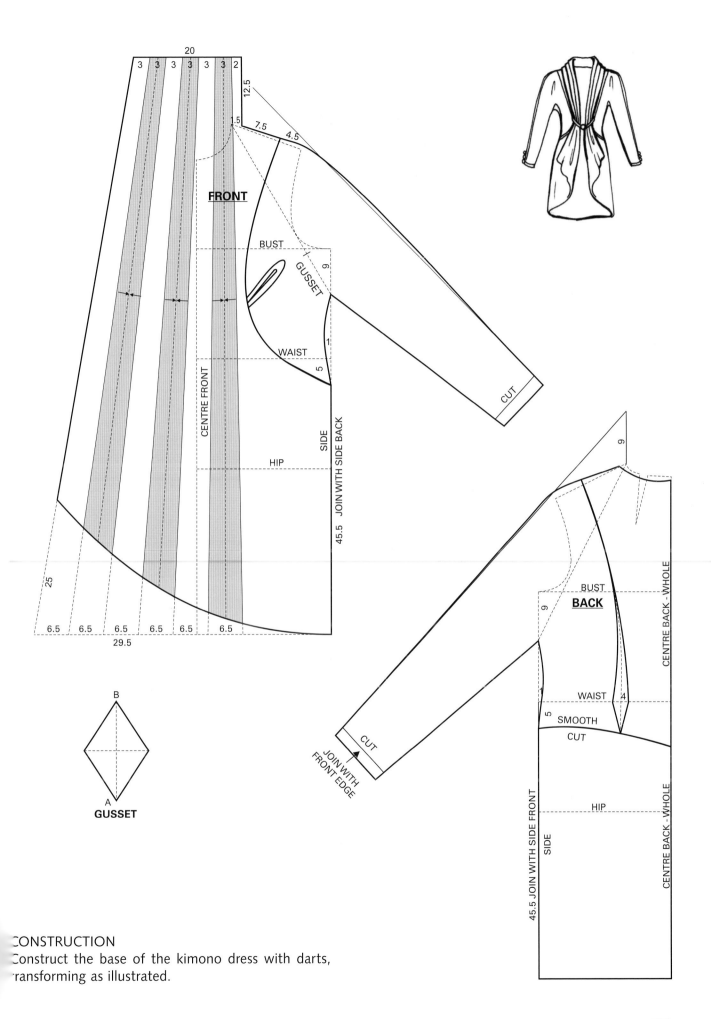

FRONT

20

3 3 3 3 3 3 2

12.5

1.5 7.5 4.5

BUST

GUSSET

9

CENTRE FRONT

WAIST

1

5

SIDE

HIP

45.5 JOIN WITH SIDE BACK

25

6.5 6.5 6.5 6.5 6.5 6.5

29.5

B

A

GUSSET

CUT

BACK

BUST

9

WAIST

4

5 SMOOTH

CUT

9

CUT

JOIN WITH FRONT EDGE

CENTRE BACK - WHOLE

CENTRE BACK - WHOLE

45.5 JOIN WITH SIDE FRONT

SIDE

HIP

CONSTRUCTION
Construct the base of the kimono dress with darts,
transforming as illustrated.

MID-THIGH JACKET WITH SHAWL COLLAR AND LOOSE FOLDS

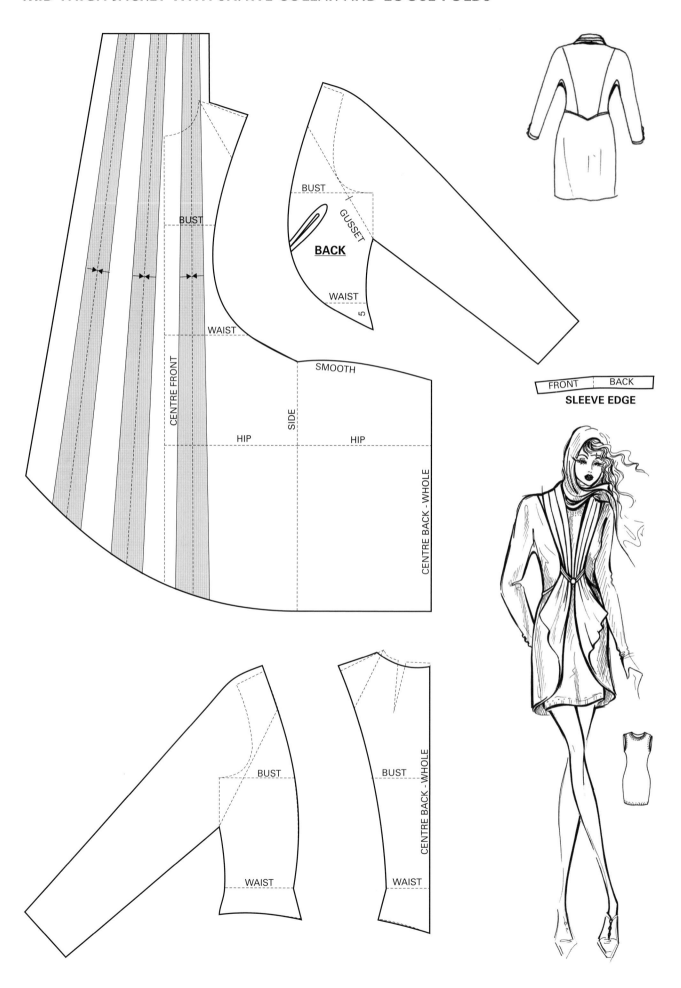

BUST

CENTRE FRONT

WAIST

BUST

GUSSET

BACK

WAIST

5

SMOOTH

SIDE

HIP

HIP

CENTRE BACK - WHOLE

FRONT | BACK

SLEEVE EDGE

BUST

BUST

WAIST

CENTRE BACK - WHOLE

WAIST

CAPELET DRESS
STAND-UP COLLAR, OPEN IN THE FRONT

CAPELET DRESS

FRONT

CLOSE CAPELET DART

CHEST

BUST

CLOSE

CENTRE FRONT

WAIST

BASQUE

SIDE

HIP

SLEEVE

FRONT   BACK

ELBOW LINE

JOIN WITH FRONT

SHOULDERS

BUST

BACK

CENTRE BACK

WAIST

BASQUE

SIDE

HIP

FOLD

EDGE OF BACK FASTENING

BASQUE, CLOSED FRONT

WAIST

SIDE

BASQUE, GATHERED FRONT

GATHER

WAIST

SIDE

BASQUE, CLOSED BACK

SIDE

BASQUE, OPEN BACK

SIDE

GATHER

WAIST

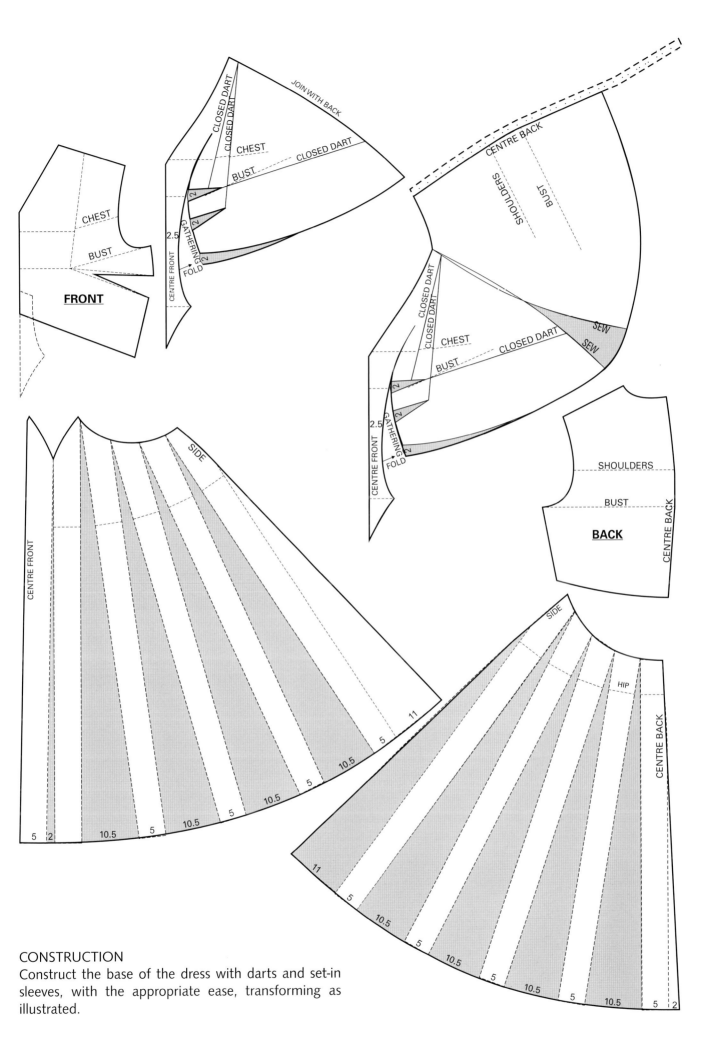

CONSTRUCTION

Construct the base of the dress with darts and set-in sleeves, with the appropriate ease, transforming as illustrated.

JACKET WITH GATHERED FOLDS ON THE FRONT
BUBBLE SKIRT WITH RUFFLES ON THE HEM

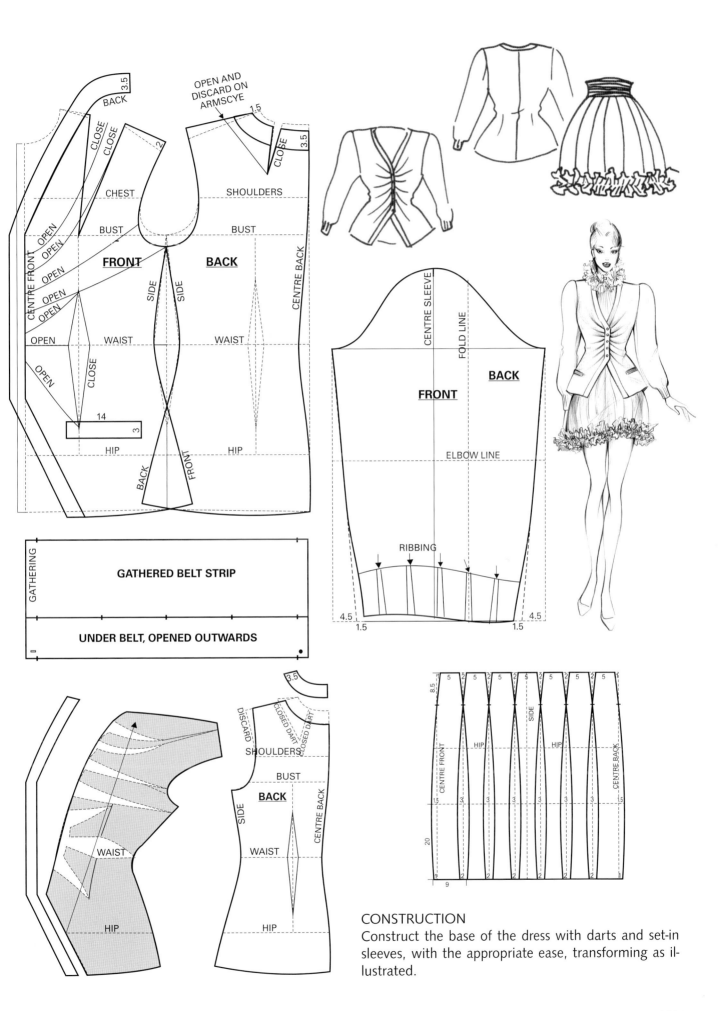

BACK 3.5

CLOSE CLOSE 2

OPEN AND DISCARD ON ARMSCYE 1.5

CLOSE 3.5

CHEST

SHOULDERS

CENTRE FRONT

OPEN OPEN

BUST

BUST

FRONT

BACK

SIDE SIDE

CENTRE BACK

OPEN OPEN

OPEN

WAIST

WAIST

CLOSE

OPEN

14

3

HIP

HIP

BACK

FRONT

GATHERING

GATHERED BELT STRIP

UNDER BELT, OPENED OUTWARDS

CENTRE SLEEVE

FOLD LINE

BACK

FRONT

ELBOW LINE

RIBBING

4.5

4.5

1.5

1.5

3.5

DISCARD

CLOSED DART

CLOSED DART

SHOULDERS

BUST

BACK

SIDE

CENTRE BACK

WAIST

WAIST

HIP

HIP

8.5

5 2 5 2 5 2 5 2 5 2 5

SIDE

CENTRE FRONT

HIP

HIP

CENTRE BACK

1.5

3

3

3

3

3

1.5

20

9

2 2 2 2 2 2

CONSTRUCTION

Construct the base of the dress with darts and set-in sleeves, with the appropriate ease, transforming as illustrated.

181

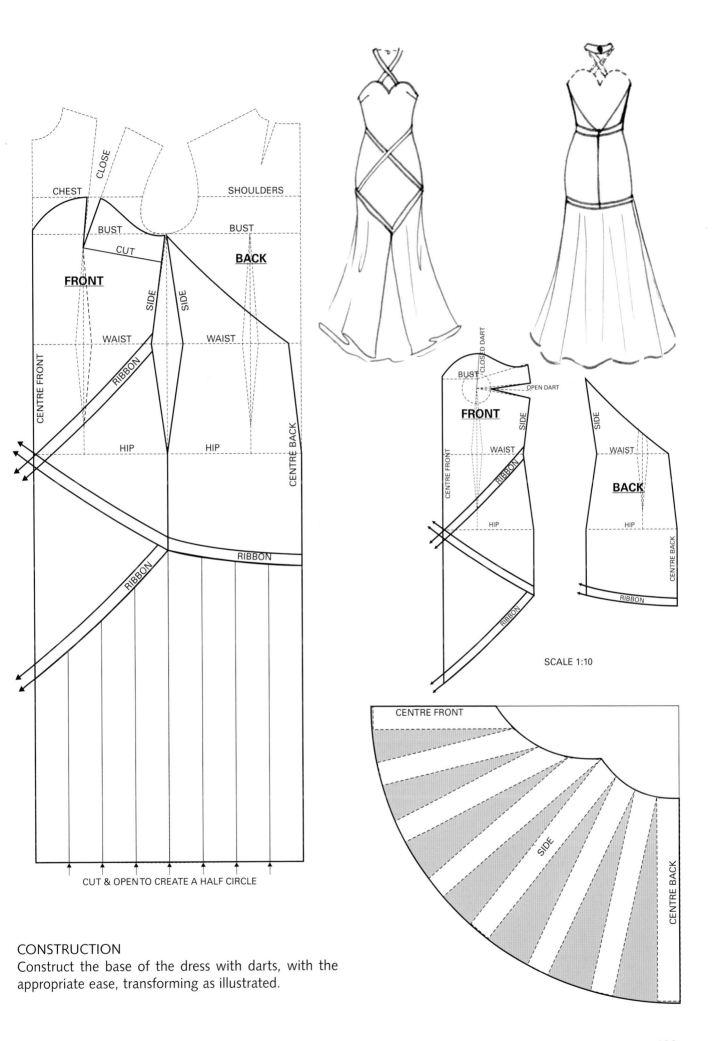

CHEST

CLOSE

SHOULDERS

BUST

BUST

CUT

BACK

FRONT

SIDE

SIDE

CENTRE FRONT

WAIST

WAIST

RIBBON

CENTRE BACK

HIP

HIP

RIBBON

RIBBON

RIBBON

CUT & OPEN TO CREATE A HALF CIRCLE

CLOSED DART

BUST

OPEN DART

FRONT

SIDE

SIDE

CENTRE FRONT

WAIST

WAIST

BACK

RIBBON

HIP

HIP

CENTRE BACK

RIBBON

RIBBON

SCALE 1:10

CENTRE FRONT

SIDE

CENTRE BACK

CONSTRUCTION
Construct the base of the dress with darts, with the
appropriate ease, transforming as illustrated.

183

DRESS WITH LEG OF MUTTON SLEEVES

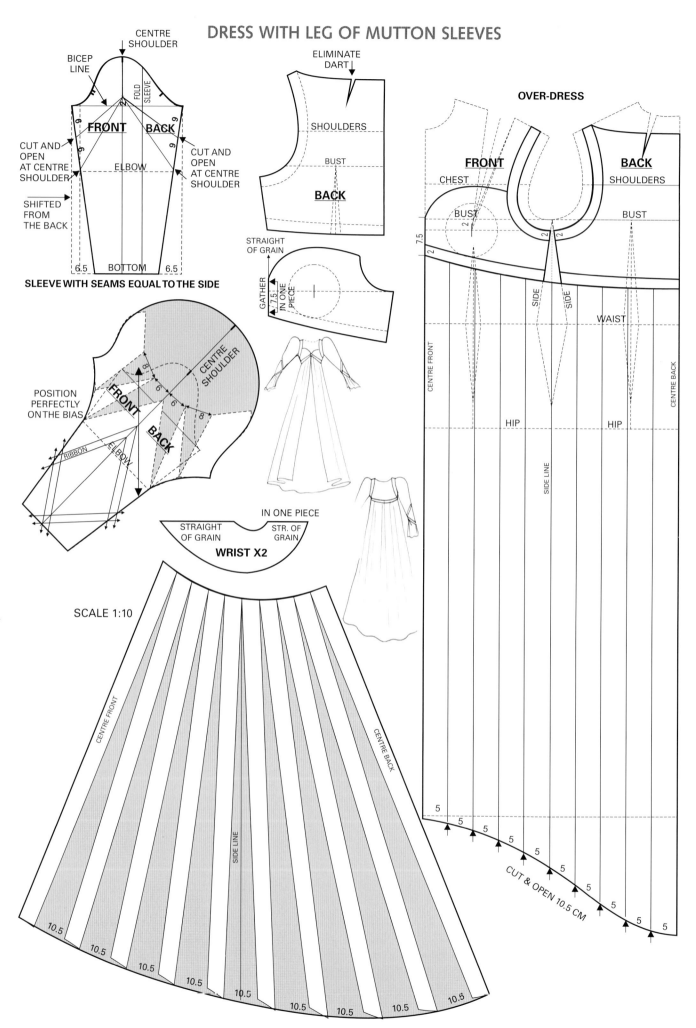

CENTRE SHOULDER

BICEP LINE

FOLD SLEEVE

FRONT   **BACK**

CUT AND OPEN AT CENTRE SHOULDER

ELBOW

CUT AND OPEN AT CENTRE SHOULDER

SHIFTED FROM THE BACK

6.5   BOTTOM   6.5

SLEEVE WITH SEAMS EQUAL TO THE SIDE

ELIMINATE DART

SHOULDERS

BUST

BACK

STRAIGHT OF GRAIN

GATHER   IN ONE PIECE   7.5

OVER-DRESS

FRONT   **BACK**

CHEST   SHOULDERS

BUST   BUST

CENTRE FRONT

7.5
2

SIDE   SIDE

WAIST

CENTRE BACK

HIP   HIP

SIDE LINE

POSITION PERFECTLY ON THE BIAS

CENTRE SHOULDER

FRONT   **BACK**

8   6   6   8

RIBBON   ELBOW

IN ONE PIECE

STRAIGHT OF GRAIN   STR. OF GRAIN

WRIST X2

SCALE 1:10

CENTRE FRONT

SIDE LINE

CENTRE BACK

10.5   10.5   10.5   10.5   10.5   10.5   10.5   10.5

5   5   5   5   5   5   5   5   5   5

CUT & OPEN 10.5 CM

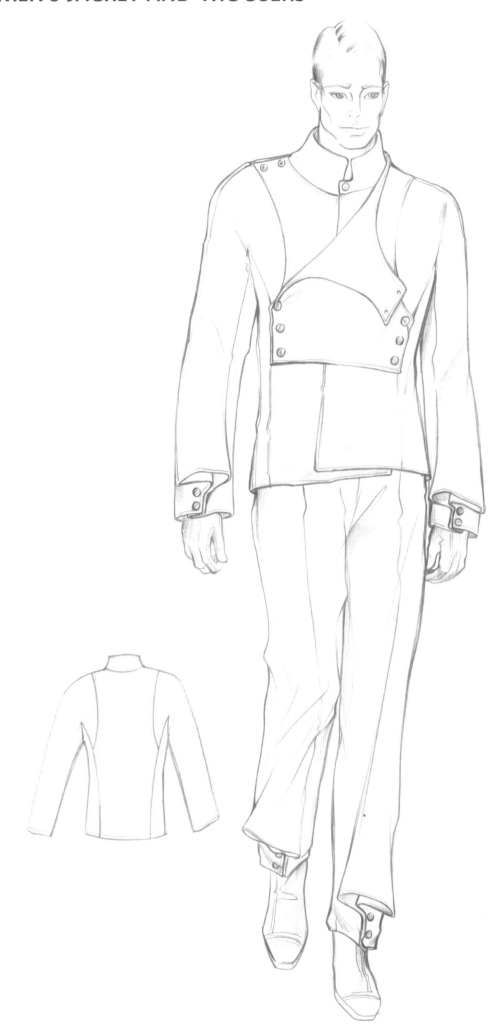

MEN'S JACKET AND TROUSERS

CONSTRUCTION
Construct the base of the men's jacket, set-in sleeves and trousers, with the appropriate ease, transforming as illustrated.

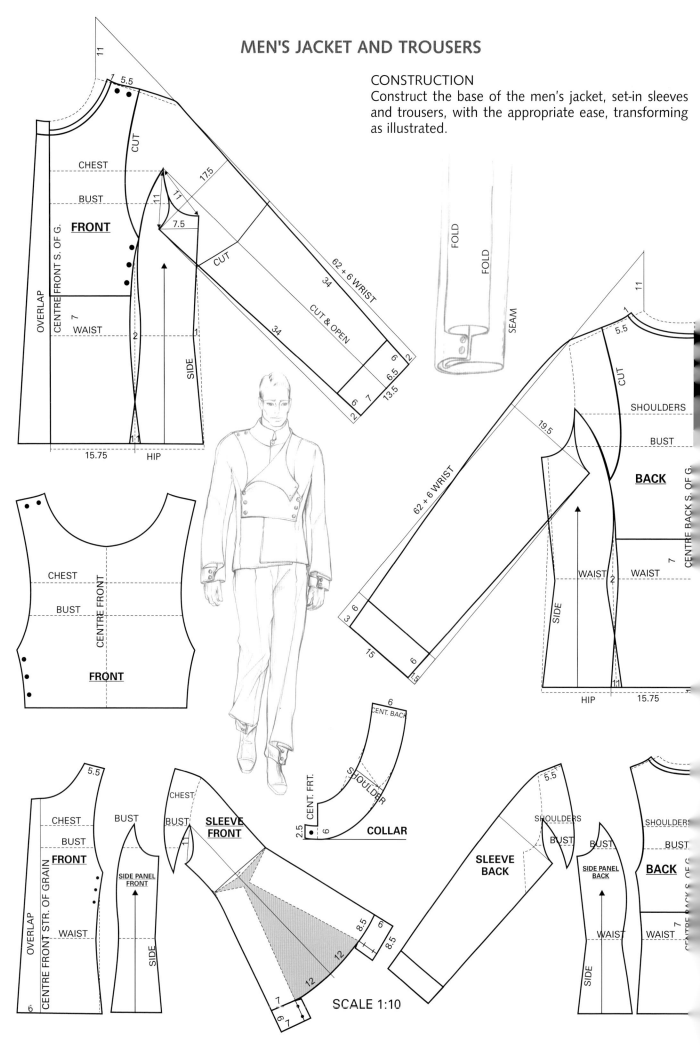

SCALE 1:10

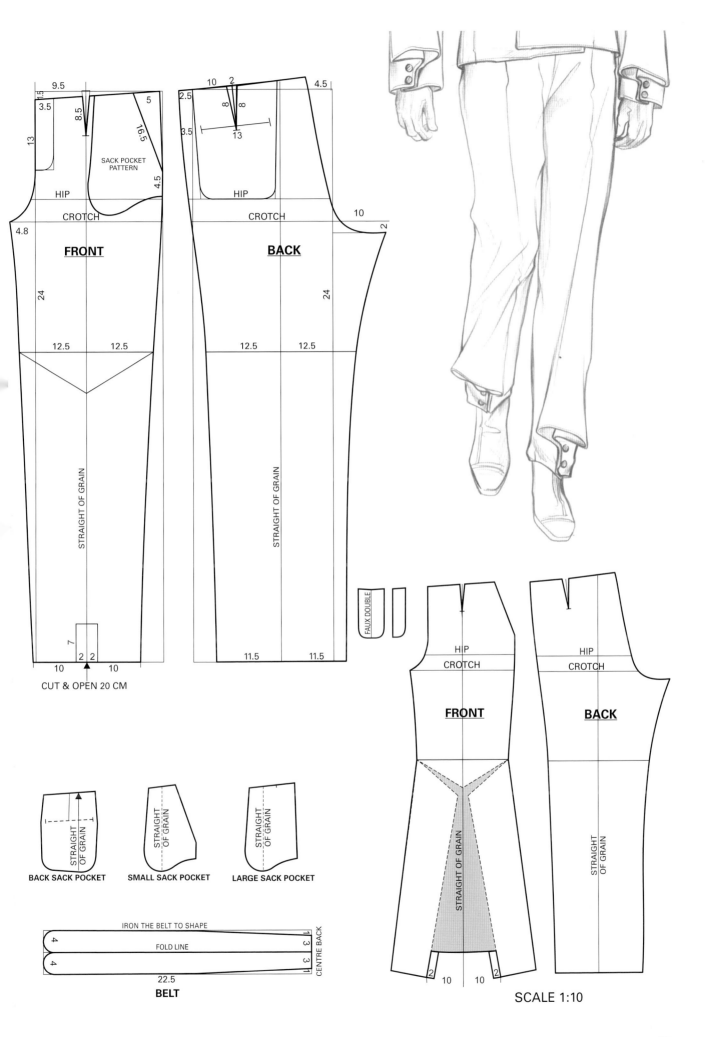

FRONT

BACK

SACK POCKET PATTERN

HIP

CROTCH

STRAIGHT OF GRAIN

CUT & OPEN 20 CM

BACK SACK POCKET

SMALL SACK POCKET

LARGE SACK POCKET

STRAIGHT OF GRAIN

IRON THE BELT TO SHAPE

FOLD LINE

CENTRE BACK

BELT

FAUX DOUBLE

HIP

CROTCH

FRONT

BACK

STRAIGHT OF GRAIN

SCALE 1:10

187

MEN'S JACKET WITH KIMONO SLEEVES

AND FRONT FASTENING

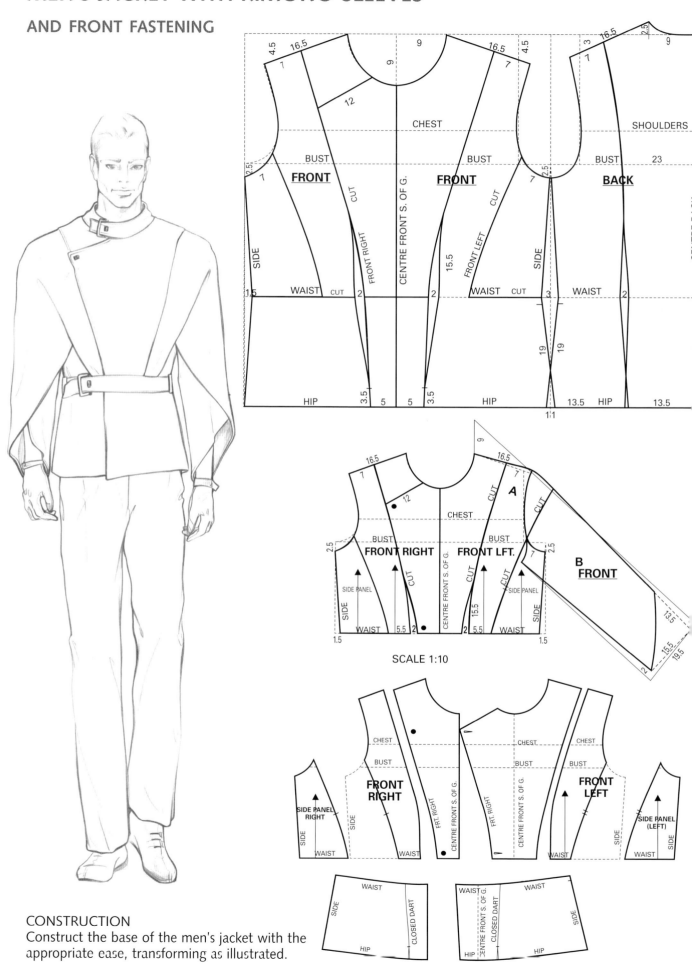

SCALE 1:10

CONSTRUCTION

Construct the base of the men's jacket with the appropriate ease, transforming as illustrated.

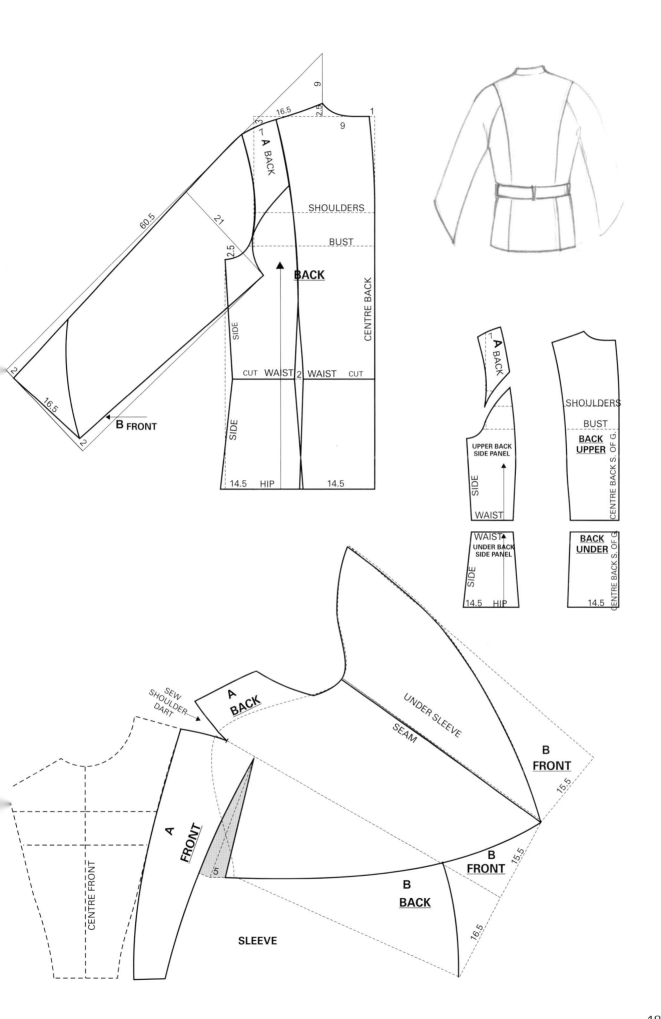

60.5

16.5

9

2.5

9

1

3

7

A BACK

21

2.5

SHOULDERS

BUST

2.5

BACK

CENTRE BACK

SIDE

SIDE

CUT WAIST 2 WAIST CUT

2

16.5

2

B FRONT

14.5 HIP

14.5

7

A BACK

SHOULDERS

BUST

UPPER BACK
SIDE PANEL

**BACK
UPPER**

SIDE

CENTRE BACK S. OF G.

WAIST

WAIST

UNDER BACK
SIDE PANEL

**BACK
UNDER**

SIDE

14.5 HIP

14.5

CENTRE BACK S. OF G

SEW
SHOULDER
DART

**A
BACK**

**A
BACK**

UNDER SLEEVE

SEAM

**B
FRONT**

15.5

A

**A
FRONT**

.5

**B
FRONT**

15.5

CENTRE FRONT

**B
BACK**

16.5

SLEEVE

MEN'S CLOACK WITH FOLD-BACK MOTIF ON THE COLLAR

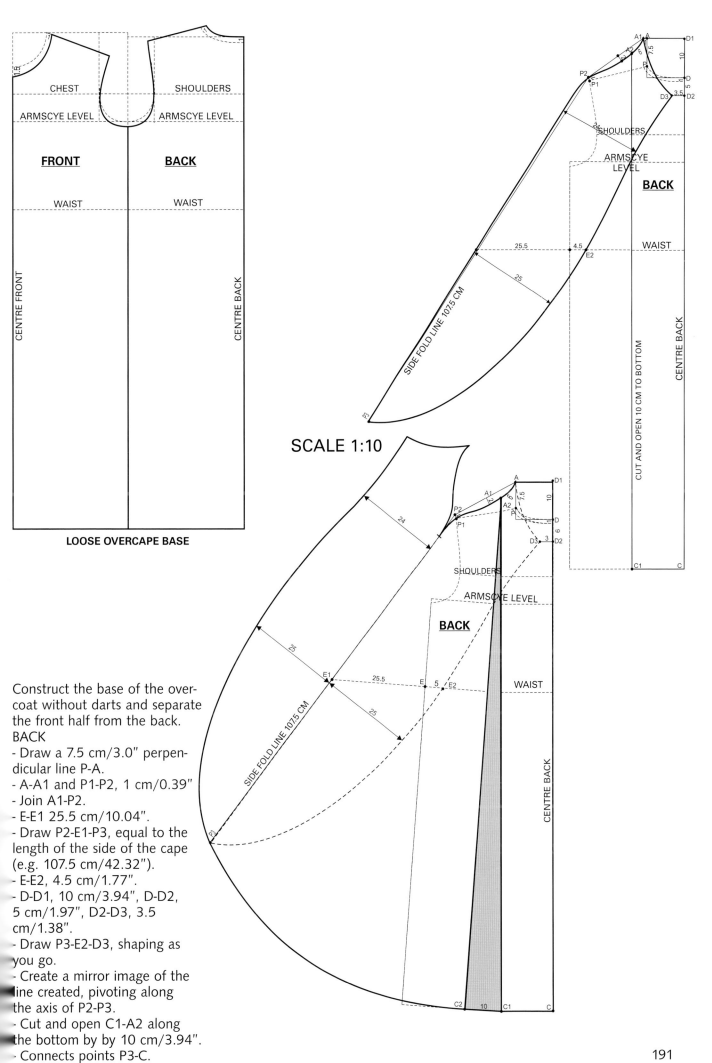

SCALE 1:10

CHEST   SHOULDERS

ARMSCYE LEVEL   ARMSCYE LEVEL

FRONT   **BACK**

WAIST   WAIST

CENTRE FRONT

CENTRE BACK

LOOSE OVERCAPE BASE

BACK

SIDE FOLD LINE 107.5 CM

CENTRE BACK

CUT AND OPEN 10 CM TO BOTTOM

Construct the base of the overcoat without darts and separate
the front half from the back.
BACK
- Draw a 7.5 cm/3.0" perpen-
dicular line P-A.
- A-A1 and P1-P2, 1 cm/0.39"
- Join A1-P2.
- E-E1 25.5 cm/10.04".
- Draw P2-E1-P3, equal to the
length of the side of the cape
(e.g. 107.5 cm/42.32").
- E-E2, 4.5 cm/1.77".
- D-D1, 10 cm/3.94", D-D2,
5 cm/1.97", D2-D3, 3.5
cm/1.38".
- Draw P3-E2-D3, shaping as
you go.
- Create a mirror image of the
line created, pivoting along
the axis of P2-P3.
- Cut and open C1-A2 along
the bottom by by 10 cm/3.94".
- Connects points P3-C.

191

MEN'S CLOACK WITH FOLD-BACK MOTIF ON THE COLLAR

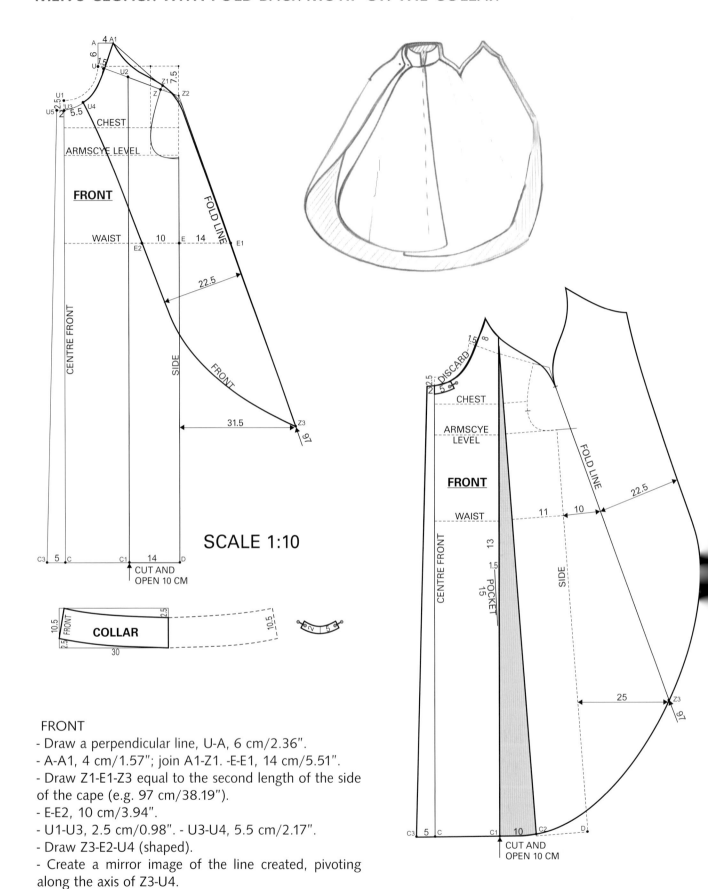

SCALE 1:10

FRONT
- Draw a perpendicular line, U-A, 6 cm/2.36".
- A-A1, 4 cm/1.57"; join A1-Z1. -E-E1, 14 cm/5.51".
- Draw Z1-E1-Z3 equal to the second length of the side of the cape (e.g. 97 cm/38.19").
- E-E2, 10 cm/3.94".
- U1-U3, 2.5 cm/0.98". - U3-U4, 5.5 cm/2.17".
- Draw Z3-E2-U4 (shaped).
- Create a mirror image of the line created, pivoting along the axis of Z3-U4.
- U3-U5, 2 cm/0.79". - C-C3, 5 cm/1.97".
- Join U5-C3.
- Cut and open C1-U2 along the bottom by 10 cm/3.94".
- Connect points Z3-C1-C3.

6. TAILORING CONCEPTS

LAYOUT AND CUTTING OF SILKEN AND TRANSPARENT FABRICS

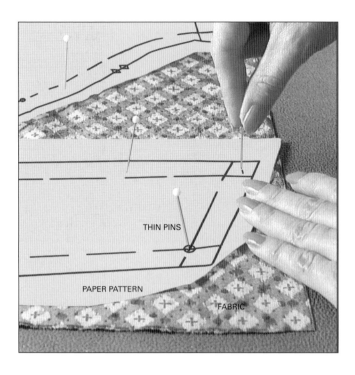

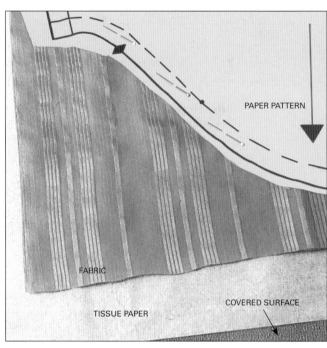

The fabrics used in high fashion are often more delicate than day-to-day wear and require special attention. Elegant colours, charming silks, beguiling transparencies, expert design and exclusive creativity, along with careful sewing, are the calling card of a well-made haute couture garment.

First wash and dry the transparent and silken fabrics to remove any starch. Then, to tighten them and avoid any problematic watermarks, press them with an iron at the appropriate temperature, and move on to laying out the pattern and cutting the pieces.

When cutting light or particularly thin textiles, it's helpful to cover the cutting plane with a piece of cotton fabric or, even better yet, to use a cutting table with a cork or upholstered work surface. By doing so, the fabric will not slide about and disturb the perfect execution of the cut.

The pattern should be fixed to the cloth with very thin pins (4-5 mm/0.16-0.20" in diameter) and the pattern paper should be cleaned of any traces of oil so as to not leave any marks. It is possible to find so-called silk pins, but they are still too thick for these fabrics.

To cut thin types of fabric such as these, you can use the "rotary cutter" with a blade that isn't too big, or a good pair of tailor's scissors with sharp blades. Cut the margins cleanly by using the rotary cutter, making sure not to move the fabric as you cut. It's best to put a plastic pad under the fabric when using the rotary cutter so that the cuts and margins are clean and direct. Tailor's scissors are also suitable for slippery, transparent fabrics, as the

curved shape of the handle allows the lower blade to be rested properly on the work surface as you cut.

The laying-out process
1. Fold the fabric with the right side facing out so that the less slippery surface is on the inside.
2. Lift the fabric by holding it along the fold and then let it fall to be sure of the accuracy of the crosswise grain.
3. Place a sheet of tissue paper over and under the fabric to better control it.
4. Pin the paper pattern by pushing the pins through the pattern's seam margins, the fabric and the cork work surface, so that the layers don't move. If you are using a cardboard table surface, don't use pins which are too thin as they will bend and be ruined.

Rotary cutter

Tailor's scissors

TABLE FOR SILKEN AND TRANSPARENT FABRICS		
Tools and techniques	Transparent, soft hand	Light silks
	Batiste, chiffon, Chinese silk, georgette	Charmeuse, crêpe de chine, jacquards, crepe-back satin, faile
	Transparent, dry hand	
	Organdie, organza, voile	
Sewing machine needles	8 (60 mm), 9 (65 mm) or 11 (75 mm)	8 (60 mm), 9 (65 mm) or 11 (75 mm)
Stitch length	12 to 16 to fit in each 2.5 cm	12 to 16 to fit in each 2.5 cm
Stitch length segment	From 2.5 to 2	From 2.5 to 2
Thread	Extra-fine in polyester, silk or di seta or mercerised cotton	
	These types of thread are used to sew undergarments, for machine embroidery or for quilting (use the finest thread possible)	
Hand-stitching needles	Measurements from 8 to 12	Measurements from 8 to 12
Interfacing	Lightweight non-woven, thermoadhesive fabric to sew, the same cloth, organza	Thermoadhesive knits, non woven transparent interfacing Maglia termoadhesiva, teletta, thermoadhesive or to sew, batiste, the same cloth, organza, organdie, lining
Special stitches	English, fine, whipstitch, double	English, whipstitch, double
Special hems	Whipstitch, rolled and whipstitched, rolled and sewn by hand, bordered with strips of knit fabric, with thin stitching, tight stitching	

Silken fabrics generally mean (even if incorrectly), all natural silk fabrics (or silk-like synthetics), such as acetate, polyester, nylon and rayon. High fashion garments usually are made of natural silk.

Silken textiles also includes: crepe de chine, cady, faille, charmeuse, and lightweight jacquard.

Shiny fabrics are particularly elegant, which makes them befitting to haute couture.

The shiny surface is either the result of the way the textile is woven, as is the case with satin, or of shiny fibres, as is the case with silk and acetate. There are also a few kinds of finishes which give a glossy look to certain fabrics, and it is possible to add metallic or sparkly threads to normal textiles to make them shiny and precious.

The main kinds of shiny fabrics are: satin, peau de soie, crepe-backed satin, taffeta, moiré taffeta, brocade, metallic fabrics, laminates (lamé), and sequined fabrics.

Transparent fabrics are very light and may have a dry or soft "hand". The main soft transparent fabrics are chiffon, Chinese silk, and georgette. Those with a dry hand, such as voile, organza, and organdie, are generally easier to cut. In general, transparent materials are delicate and require particular attention when they are being prepped and

sewn, ensuring that they are perfect and handled carefully, as anything done to the wrong side of the fabric is also seen on the right side. Therefore every detail from seams to hems, to facings must be done precisely and accurately.

Even the pattern must be appropriate to the delicate nature of the fabric. Patterns to be used for these textiles are those with soft, flowing lines, loose-fitting with details that enhance the garment such as draping, pleats, flounces and ruffles, while you also should avoid zips or inserted pockets as they are bulky and visible from the outside of the garment.

Pay close attention to parts cut on the bias as they tend to stretch out and are difficult to manage due to their slipperiness.

Fabrics with sequins or metallic fabrics require the use of simple patterns such as a simple, straight or slightly flared sack dress. You should thus avoid folds, gathering, darts, eyelets and fastenings. In addition, you'll need to remember that metallic fabrics or those with sequins might irritate the wearer's skin if they come in direct contact, so you'll need to line the garment, or at least the parts where there are seams.

HEMS AND TRIMS FOR DELICATE FABRICS

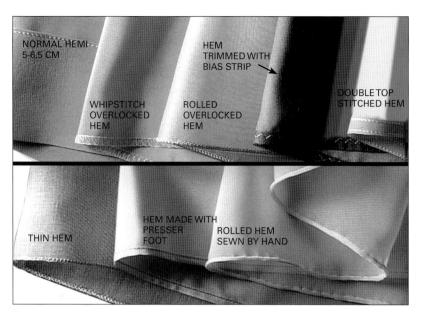

NORMAL HEM
5-6.5 CM

HEM
TRIMMED WITH
BIAS STRIP

DOUBLE TOP
STITCHED HEM

WHIPSTITCH
OVERLOCKED
HEM

ROLLED
OVERLOCKED
HEM

THIN HEM

HEM MADE WITH
PRESSER
FOOT

ROLLED HEM
SEWN BY HAND

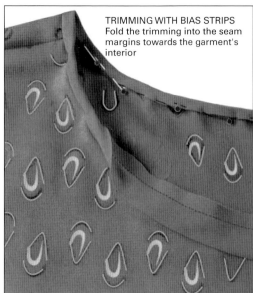

TRIMMING WITH BIAS STRIPS
Fold the trimming into the seam
margins towards the garment's
interior

HEMS

For silk and similar fabrics, you can apply normal hems, 5 to 6 cm (1.97-2.36") high, sewn with an invisible stitch or with a loosened catch stitch.

For flounces, bows and transparent textiles, it's best to use thin, small seams so as not to add any weight. This ensures that they fall better and that the seam isn't visible on the outside.

Small, thin hems can be created in three different ways:
1. A small rolled hem made with three-thread overlocker.
2. Whipstitch done on an overlocker on the cut edge.
3. Trimming on the cut edges with a lightweight, transparent bias cut knit, 1.5 cm/0.59" wide.

The last two hems are used for shirts and blouses which are tucked in to the waist of a skirt or trousers, while the first can be used for all garments.

Other types of hems which are slightly more difficult to execute are also often used for these fabrics.

- A stitched hem, with a 5 mm/0.20" margin on the wrong side with short, straight stitches, used for fabrics which tend to fray, even if the two seams are quite evident on the right side.
- A very fine hem, almost invisible, which is executed with a combination of straight and zig-zag seams, short 1.5 to 2 mm (0.06-0.08"). Keeping the fabric taut, as stitches made on thin fabrics tend to make them curl.
- A hem executed with the appropriate hemmer.
- A rolled, hand-stitched hem, which is labour intensive but is without a doubt the most refined and elegant.

TRIMMINGS

Garments made of transparent materials cannot have linings as they would be visible from the right side of the fabric and compromise their aesthetics. To finish and hide the borders and cut edges, ultra-light bias strip trimmings are applied. For quicker trimmings, cover the margins with a bias strip of light jersey and topstitch.

PROCEDURE

- After having cut the bias strip (seven times wider than the finished width of the trim, e.g. for a 6 mm/0.24" trim, cut a 4.2 cm/0.17" strip), fold the strip in half along the length, wrong side against wrong side, and iron.
- Draw the seam line on the part of the garment where the trim is to be applied and cut all of the edge.
- Pin the bias strip to the outside of the garment, matching up the edges and sew with a margin equal to the height desired for the trim.
- Fold the trim back towards the inside of the garment (see illustration) and lightly press.
- Affix the free margin of the trim in one of three ways:
a) with a seam in the groove where the bias strip was previously stitched;
b) with a topstitch along the right side, sewn along the edge of the trim;
c) with a slipstitch on the wrong side along the seam.

Sew the bias trimming

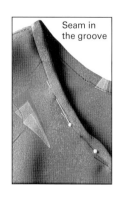

Seam in
the groove

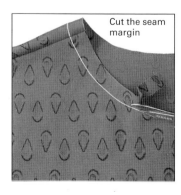

Cut the seam
margin

Topstitch

Slip stitch

TECHNIQUES FOR WORKING WITH LACE

Lace fabrics have an open, mesh or knit structure which has no straight of the grain and which does not unravel. For this reason, you can cut it freely, positioning the pattern in different ways. The seams do not need trims or edges and do not require special attention to the main motifs when trimmed with scissors.

Today, lace fabrics are generally machine made with cotton-polyester, nylon or acrylic threads. Many types of lace are given the name of the place in Europe where they were originally made by hand, including:
- Sangallo lace, which isn't a true lace, but a cotton or cotton-polyester fabric with openwork embroidery and satin stitch (broderie anglaise).

- Chantilly lace, with floral motifs surrounded by silk threads, on a thin mesh base.
- Venetian lace, made without a mesh background as found on the others, with heavy, interwoven threads in particular stitches and motifs joined with thread which gives them a three dimensional structure.
- Alençon lace, which is made on a transparent mesh base, with full motifs, contoured by a satin thread.

PATTERNS

Not all patterns are suitable for all types of lace, which should be chosen on the base of their weight and weave. For looser patterns and for flounces, lighter laces such as Chantilly are suitable; for simpler, more fitted patterns, it's best to use heavier laces such as Alençon.

In any case, it's always important to remember that:
- even if all laces should be dry cleaned and they rarely shrink, if the label says that it is washable, it's best to wash it before starting work, also because it will go along with the other fabrics;
- the parts of the pattern should fit within the width of the lace;

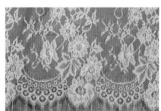
Chantilly lace

Alençon lace

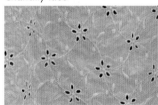
Sangallo lace

Venetian lace

- if you want to use a trimmed lace for sleeves, it will be necessary to choose a short sleeve pattern if the lace isn't long enough to make the long sleeves. As an alternative, you can apply the lace to a sleeve made in organza;
- there usually are no linings, pockets or even hems;
- it's possible to turn the pieces of the model as you wish to use a side as a finished margin, since lace has no straight of grain;
- if you want to add support or consistency to the lace, you can counter-line it with tulle, or by using a lining in a different colour. This further highlights the lace's design and hides construction details such as seams, darts, etc.;
- external margins can be finished with trimming, with an edge in lace, or an ultra-thin strip of bias-cut jersey;
- collars and cuffs should be cut in single layers, finishing the margins with trimmings or applied lace.

197

PATTERN LAYOUT

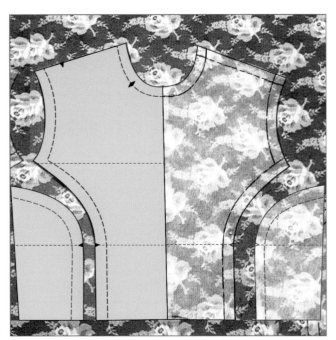

For whole parts, retrace the entire pattern on tissue paper or tracing paper, or even on a transparent piece of cloth.

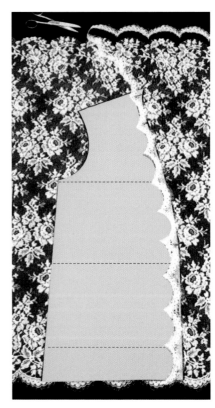

Along the curved edges, you can apply the scalloping previously cut off of the lace, resting the inner points of the scallops on the seam lines or hemlines.

Layout of the pattern on lace is an important step and should be done methodically and precisely. First of all, you must carefully inspect the details of the lace's motif, putting it over a piece of fabric in a contrasting colour to better see the design.

When laying out the pattern, remember that the main motifs should meet up along the seams and be positioned in the centre or be balanced along the larger parts of the pattern. If the motifs are all facing the same direction, you'll need to lay the pattern out in the same way as described for velvet fabrics.

CUTTING

After deciding how to use the motifs and the edges of the lace, but before the laying-out and cutting, think of the type of seam that will be used, which may be small if the lace has a design on the surface or overlapping if it has a large pattern. In this case, the pieces of the master pattern must be affixed with pins and cut in order. You can also use a combination of different seams on the same garment, in particular: a tight zig-zag or a double backstitch for the armscye; an overlapping stitch for the shoulders and the sides. It is absolutely essential that your pattern is lined up perfectly before cutting, because if lace is cut incorrectly it can't be corrected. For this reason, either make a test garment from inexpensive cloth before cutting the lace or reproduce the whole parts of the master pattern on to paper or transparent cloth.

This pattern (or the cloth), which will be used to cut the lace, should be laid out in a single layer, balancing the motifs in width and height on the larger parts of the garment, and centring the lace's most noticeable motifs on the centre front and on the bustline, taking the seams into consideration. Once you've found the ideal positioning, affix the master pattern with pins long enough to ensure it's stable.

EDGES AND SCALLOPING

To finish the edges, you must carefully analyse the lace's design and the edge of the master pattern. Understand if the edges or the main motifs can be shifted to the margins of the garment, such as in the hem of a skirt or in the sleeves, neckline, yoke, etc. On curved edges, you can apply the scalloping previously cut out from the lace, placing the internal points of the scalloping on the seamlines or hemlines.

Machine-sewn seams should be executed slowly, being extra sure that the points of the presser foot don't tear the lace. To avoid this, if you don't have the presser foot made for this purpose, you can cover the points of the presser foot with clear adhesive tape. During the sewing process, it's quite useful to put some tissue paper under the lace, thereby preventing the lace from getting dragged by the needle when the zig zag is being created.

PATTERNS FOR SEQUINED FABRICS

LAYING OUT
The placement of the pattern pieces on fabrics with sequins should be done by following the "direction" if the sequins, that is, the sequins should be done facing the bottom part of the garment (downward). To affix the model, in addition to pins, you will also need wide adhesive tape. This will help keep the sequins in place when you cut the fabric, making sure they don't fall down and break.

SEWING
Hand baste around the pattern with a loose stitch to transfer the pattern's outline to the back of the fabric. Then, just after cutting, make a supporting seam with the sewing machine along the face of the fabric with a 90/100 point needle, following along the seamlines of all the pieces in the direction of the sequins to ensure they aren't caught in the feed dog.
Recover any sequins that came off during the above steps and keep them to apply by hand where needed.

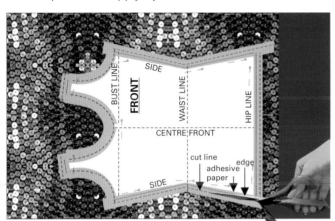

Position the master pattern with respect to the "direction" of the sequins and by affixing it to the fabric with adhesive tape as well as pins.

At this point you can sew the final seams with a sewing machine, adjusting the stitch length to 3/3.5 and changing the needle when necessary, which will be often seeing as the sequins will cause the needle to go blunt.

SUPPORT AND LININGS
Any plackets will have to be made with fabric for linings, and hems will also need to be done in lining fabric or with bias binding ribbon. Should the edges or neckline need added support, use pieces of cloth, not adhesive tape, as the sequins are heat sensitive. Just be sure to use interfacing that is appropriate to the type of garment being made.

PRESSING
Pressing or ironing fabric with sequins and metallic parts in general should be done with caution because they are made with heat sensitive elements. The best system is to press the seam with a thimble or with a bone folder or bit of rounded metal, and drag the tip of the iron along the seam, without using any water, and keeping the temperature relatively low. Avoid industrial presses as the steam would make the sequins less shiny.

Blugirl S/S 2011

MAINTENANCE
Garments with sequins should be dry cleaned, asking the dry cleaner not to use steam when pressing and to cold-dry the item. Avoid staining the spangles with alcoholic beverages, perfumes and other products which contain alcohol or trichloroethylene. Keep these garments in fabric and not plastic containers, as the polyethylene may dull the sequins.

SEQUINS
Patterns for fabrics with sequins or other beading, or metal elements, must be simple as they do not easily lend themselves to complicated cuts, folds, darts or gatherings, to zips or buttonholes. Fabric that is good for the application of sequins may be stretchy, in jersey, or light and transparent, such as chiffon. The garments made with these fabrics should be lined, at least on the parts which come in contact with the body, as they may be irritating to the skin or ruin undergarments.

R. Cavalli A/W 2012/13

B. Blass A/W 2009/10

7. BASIC DRAPING TECHNIQUES

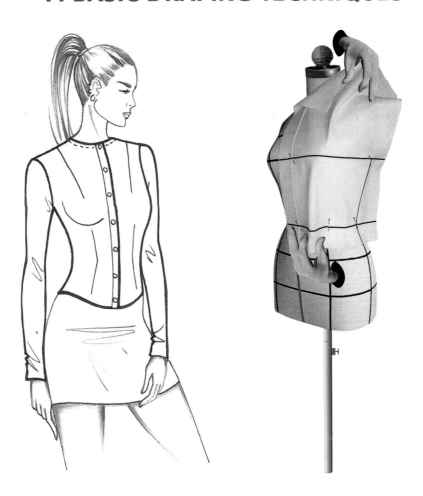

DRAPING

"Draping", or "moulage" or "modelage" in French, is a manual technique to create clothing patterns on three-dimensional forms. This technique is practiced by those who work in high fashion in Italy, though the practice is quite old in the tailoring traditions of established couturiers.

Unlike flat pattern making, which is more common and beings with a geometric design on a piece of pattern paper, the "moulage" technique involves adapting the fabric directly on the dress form to give it the sartorial shape desired through the use of pins and scissors. By doing so, a dress can be created from one piece of cloth, transforming the geometric shapes into flowing, perfect creations.

This system balances the fabric and the design, allowing the drawing to be seen in a tangible way, especially if it is complicated with lots of draped elements.

Moulage draping was used by the great French haute couture designers, such as Madeleine Vionnet (1876-1975), who was its pioneer from the 1920s to 1940s

In moulage draping, the garment gets its initial shape and volume directly on the dress form; it's a very instinctual, creative technique which allows the designer to have an preliminary idea of what the creation will be. It's like sculpting with cloth to bring it to life, and at the end of this "architectural" project, the whole will be immediately visible.

The pattern is made with rough cotton fabric which is shaped on the mannequin with pins that hold it in shape. While the draping is taking place, the eyes and hands interact, allowing for perfect understanding of the fabric, the body, and the interpretation and expression of fashion. There are numerous moulage methods which are used to make the pattern be as faithful as possible to the person's physical conformation.

The basic technique of draping which we'll use in this chapter is quite simple and, if the rules are followed, the result will be quite satisfying.

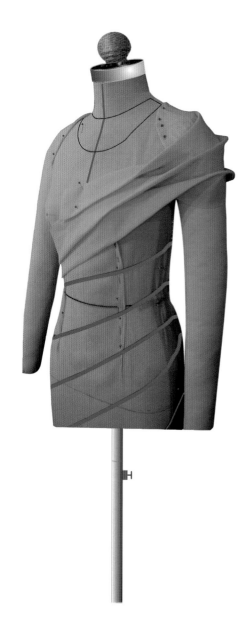

TOOLS AND EQUIPMENT

DRESS FORMS

In high fashion, the master pattern is created directly on a customised dress form. In this way, no subsequent changes will be necessary.

To create a pattern using the moulage technique, you'll need two types of dress forms: a standard dress form and an adjustable dress form.

Standard dress forms (fig. 1) can be customised by adding or removing padding to adapt them to the shape of a specific person's body, and in this case it will be exclusively used by that person. For garments made in regular sizes, standard, high-quality tailoring dress forms in the right measurements (depending on the clientele) are used. A good atelier will possess dress forms in all sizes.

Adjustable dress forms (fig. 2 and 3) are used to sidestep the problem of sizes. These dress forms are made of a shell divided in four parts with an internal mechanism that allows you to draw the parts closer or expand them through a dial which allows you to select the correct size. For female dress forms, a device also regulates the projection and size of the bust. To carry out the moulage draping, a strip of 1 cm adhesive tape must be applied to the dress form along the guidelines of the pattern, as will be explained in the following pages.

VARIOUS TOOLS

The scissors used for draping should have a 20-25 cm (7.87-9.84") blade and they should be kept sharpened. Their shape doesn't matter. Another pair of scissors, called pinking shears, (fig. 5) will also be necessary to create zig-zag edges. Pins are required for fixing and assembling the pieces of cloth or paper for the pattern. The most appropriate pin sizes are 3.5 cm (1.38") in length and 0.40 cm (0.16") in diameter, with or without a plastic heads (fig. 6). To keep your hands free, the best pincushion is the one that goes around your wrist and features a cushion or a flat magnetic surface (fig. 7).

The tracing wheel, also known as a pattern wheel, (fig. 8) is necessary to trace the lines of the cloth "blueprint" on the pattern paper.

The style tape (fig. 9) is a soft strip of satin or cotton 0.5-1 cm (0.20-0.39") in width which is applied to the dress form, indicating perpendicular lines and reference lines such as the bust line, the waistline, etc., as well as lines of patterns and garment sizes. The ribbon should be affixed to the dress form with pins.

Thumbtacks (fig. 10) allow you to fix the fabric model over the paper on a work surface.

You'll need two types of transparent rulers (fig. 11): a rigid one in Plexiglas 80-100 cm (31.50-39.37") to draw straight lines and a flexible one 40-50 cm (15.75-19.69") to mark measurements in curves.

Measuring tapes (fig. 12) should be of high quality and in the standard length of 150 cm (59.06").

Curved and square rulers (fig. 13) are used to draw and outline curved lines, create perfect corners and mark the straight of the grain.

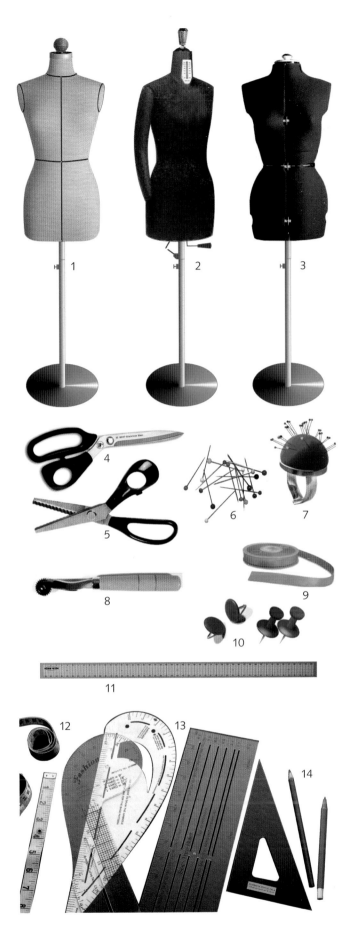

To draw lines on fabric, use special blue, red and black pencils (fig. 14), or even 2B soft pencils; to draw lines on paper, use an HB pencil. There are also black and red markers to accentuate the lines.

PREPARING THE DRESS FORM

The moulage technique is based on the use of the dress form as a tool to create all types of garments, even the most complex. For this reason, it's very important to pay close attention to its preparation with style tape. This will be the basis for how precise and perpendicular the lines, motifs and seams are, and they refer to the horizontal lines of the bust, the waist and the hip. The style tape may be in cotton or a synthetic material. It should be 5-10 mm (0.20-0.39") wide and can be fixed with pins, with thumbtacks or using adhesive tape. Generally the tape on the centre front and the centre back is in a single colour (light blue or red), while all the rest are another colour (black).

PROCEDURE

The first strip of tape should be put square on the centre back.
- At the shoulders, define the centre of the back.
- With a pin or thumbtack, affix at the central point at the height of the shoulders.
- Use a triangle ruler to make sure it's at a right angle, and affix at the bottom with another pin or thumbtack.
- Proceed in the same way for the tape on the centre front.
- Check that the line in the centre front is equidistant on the right and left side from the tape in the centre back.

Horizontal tape
After attaching the two vertical central strips of tape (front and back), move on to positioning the horizontal lines.
Waist tape: This tape should be placed very carefully and with a lot of attention, as it is the reference line for all the other horizontal pieces.
- Affix the tape with a thumbtack or pin at the centre of the vertical line at the proper height.
- Square the tape and affix it with a thumbtack or a pin on the side.
- For perfectly horizontal tape, use a ruler resting on the ground and, after having positioned and affixed a pencil at the height of the waist, rotate the dress form on its base.

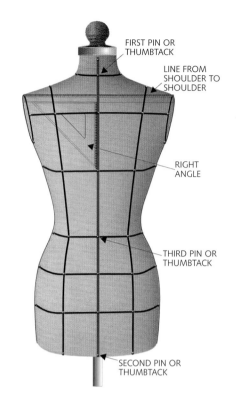

FIRST PIN OR THUMBTACK

LINE FROM SHOULDER TO SHOULDER

RIGHT ANGLE

THIRD PIN OR THUMBTACK

SECOND PIN OR THUMBTACK

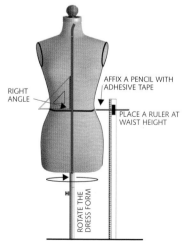

RIGHT ANGLE

AFFIX A PENCIL WITH ADHESIVE TAPE

PLACE A RULER AT WAIST HEIGHT

ROTATE THE DRESS FORM

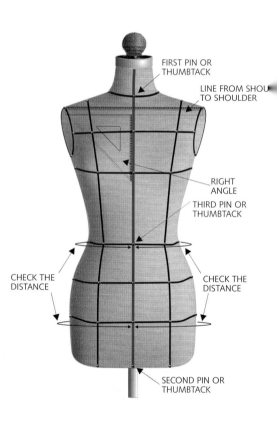

FIRST PIN OR THUMBTACK

LINE FROM SHOU TO SHOULDER

RIGHT ANGLE

THIRD PIN OR THUMBTACK

CHECK THE DISTANCE

CHECK THE DISTANCE

SECOND PIN OR THUMBTACK

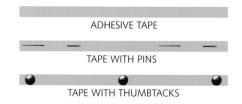

ADHESIVE TAPE

TAPE WITH PINS

TAPE WITH THUMBTACKS

HORIZONTAL TAPE

- Bust line: this tape, like all the other horizontal strips, is applied like that at the waist. It should be placed at the most-protruding point of the bust.
- Hip line: this should be positioned 20 cm/7.87" (see the table in volume 1) from the waist line, at the most protruding part of the buttocks.
- Abdomen line: should be positioned halfway between the waist line and hip line.
- Chest and shoulder line: should be placed 7 cm/2.76" from the bust line.

OTHER TAPE

- Side shoulder line: affix the tape at the base of the neckline at the very edge of the shoulder. Pass the tape through the centre of the armscye and affix it to the waist line and at the bottom, ensuring that it's perfectly equidistant from the centre front and centre back.
- Front and back dart lines: these dart lines should be set at a distance from the centre back and the centre front which is equal to ½ of the bust divergence (eg. 19:2 = 9.5 cm/3.74").
- Start by affixing the tape on the bust line at the distance established (9.5 cm/3.74").
- Affix the tape on the shoulder halfway between the neckline and the very edge near the armscye.
- Affix the tape on the hip line and at the bottom at the same distance as the thumbtack placed on the bust line (9.5 cm/3.74");
- Affix the tape on the waist line at the same distance;
- Place other thumbtacks or pins along the entire length of the tape to make sure its secure.
- Armscye: to establish the form of the armscye, follow the form of the dress form, staying 1-2.5 cm/0.39-0.98" above the line of bust tape. Keep a base width of the sector of approximately 11 cm/4.33", unless otherwise your pattern says otherwise.
- Neckline: for the neck, follow the seam of the dress form's lining and affix the tape with thumbtacks or pins so that it doesn't move.
- Dart lines in different positions: the front bust darts and those on the waist can be placed in various positions and directions, according to the needs of the pattern. The main positions are: on the neckline, on the armscye, on the side and at the waist. In addition, darts can be split, made to flow into seams or into gathering.
- Particular lines for the shape of the collar or motifs: to make it easier to create certain shapes on the neckline or motifs, you can place the tape corresponding to the outlines.

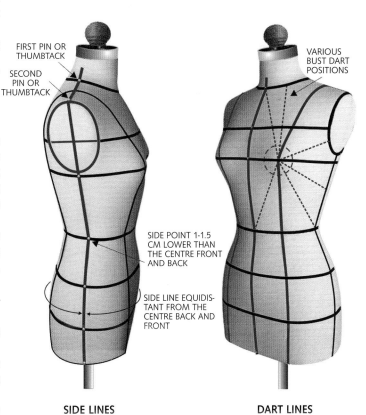

FIRST PIN OR THUMBTACK

SECOND PIN OR THUMBTACK

VARIOUS BUST DART POSITIONS

SIDE POINT 1-1.5 CM LOWER THAN THE CENTRE FRONT AND BACK

SIDE LINE EQUIDISTANT FROM THE CENTRE BACK AND FRONT

SIDE LINES　　　**DART LINES**

SPECIAL LINES

FABRIC AND PINNING

MOULAGE CLOTH

To get a good final result for the desired pattern, the cloth used for moulage draping must have a few specific structural characteristics. In particular:

1. It must be firm and not too thick, nor elasticised, or else it may skew the pattern's outline.

2. It must be white, or another neutral yet light colour.

3. It must be flexible and not too tight of a weave, so that the pins can be inserted easily.

4. The canvas cloth must not wrinkle easily; it must be decatised and ironed well.

5. The fabric's size must correspond in warp and weft to the width of the garment which you wish to make, plus an ease in both directions to carry out the draping.

You can easily find cloth which meets the above characteristics for sale in a good fabric shop.

DRAPING PINS

Even the pins are quite important to properly carry out moulage draping.

The pins suitable for this process should have:

1. a diameter of approx. 0.40/0.45 mm (0.015/0.017") as they will be easier to use;

2. a length of approx. 35/40 mm (1.38/1.57") to ensure the surface of the fabric is flat and uniform.

PINNING

Pinning the fabric on the dress form should be done with utmost attention and skill, and should be considered as a substitution for the seam.

There are three main pinning methods:

1. Horizontal
2. Vertical
3. On the bias

Each of these methods should be used for various positions. The distance between one pin and the next should be approximately 3-3.5 cm (0.12-0.14"), remembering that the pattern's assembly lines should be precise and clean, as this will determine the proper outcome for the final garment. Be extra careful not to skew the fabric when pinning.

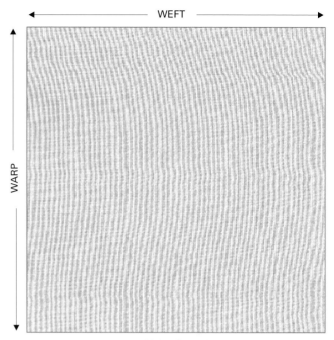

MOULAGE CLOTH

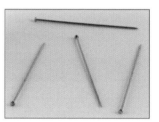

TAILOR'S PINS   PINS WITH PLASTIC HEADS

PINNING FABRIC FOR MOULAGE

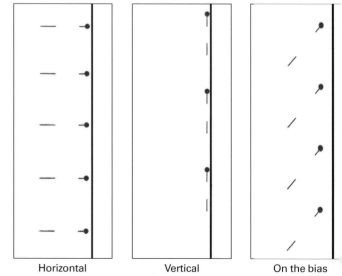

Horizontal   Vertical   On the bias

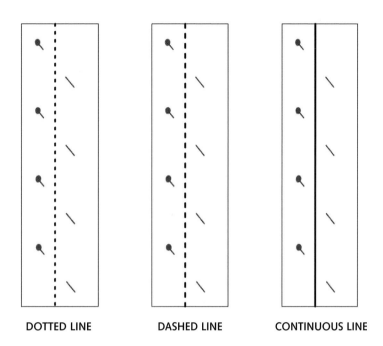

DOTTED LINE   **DASHED LINE**   **CONTINUOUS LINE**

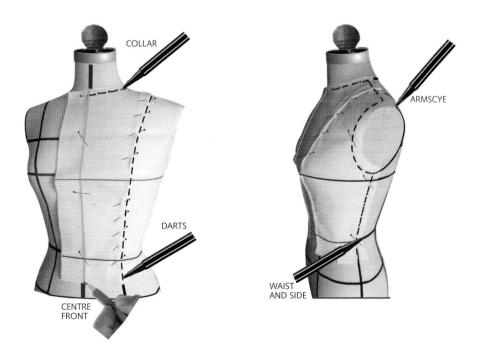

COLLAR

DARTS

CENTRE FRONT

ARMSCYE

WAIST AND SIDE

MARKING

Marking is the act of signalling, on the fabric, the edges, the centre front and centre back, the darts and the seams of the garment with small points, dotted lines or continuous lines. Marking the fabric should be done according to the position of the pins used to affix the fabric to the dress form and for the various operations required by the draping.

This marking operation is useful, first and foremost, to prepare all the lines and marks necessary to create the master pattern with the fabric mounted on the dress form. For this reason, it's very important to be precise and make very clear marks.

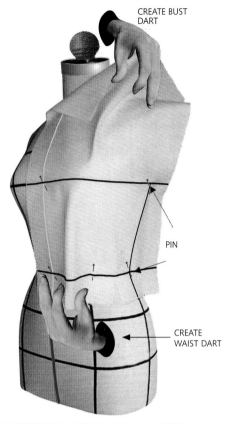

CREATE BUST DART

PIN

CREATE WAIST DART

POSITIONING FABRIC ON THE FRONT

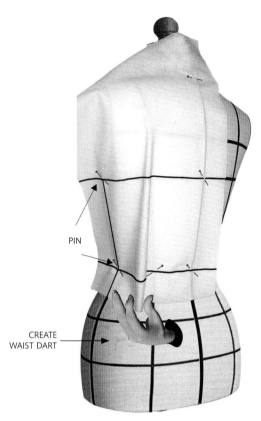

PIN

CREATE WAIST DART

POSITIONING FABRIC ON THE BACK

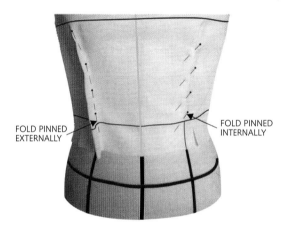

FOLD PINNED EXTERNALLY

FOLD PINNED INTERNALLY

POSITIONING OF THE FABRIC ON THE DRESS FORM AND THE CREATION OF FRONT AND BACK DARTS

The positioning of the fabric on the dress form is very important, as this will determine the proper outcome of the garment.

The steps involved in positioning the fabric are:

FRONT

1. Position the fabric on the dress form, making the fabric's centre front line meet the vertical centre front tape line on the dress form, and matching up the horizontal lines of the waist and bust.

2. Affix the fabric first in three points on the centre front at the neckline, the bust and the waist, then on the side line at the height of the waist line and at the base of the armscye, lastly, on the shoulder, making the lines of the fabric meet those of the tape on the dress form.

3. Take the excess fabric on the waist point, corresponding to the ribbon on the dress form in the position of the dart with your fingers and fold it towards the side.

The edges of the dart should align with the tape.

Then affix it with pins along the entire length of the dart. The fabric should be perfectly flush with the dress form.

4. Carry out the same operation for the bust dart, making the line of the dart align with the line of the tape on the dress form in the darts' position.

Note: There are two ways to sew or pin the two parts of the dart when draping: one by positioning the seam on the inside of the bodice, the other on the outside.

The first is used more often and thus we will use this method for our patterns.

The second is used for more complex patterns and requires double pinning which we'll explore later on.

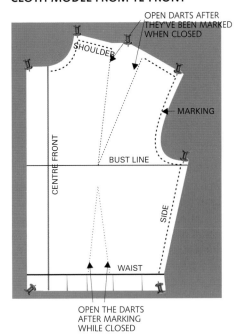

CLOTH MODEL FROM TE FRONT

OPEN DARTS AFTER THEY'VE BEEN MARKED WHEN CLOSED

SHOULDER

CENTRE FRONT

BUST LINE

MARKING

SIDE

WAIST

OPEN THE DARTS AFTER MARKING WHILE CLOSED

PIN AND MARK THE FRONT

NECKLINE MARKING

CLOSED DART MARKING

CENTRE FRONT

CLOSED DART MARKING

CLOSED DART MARKING

SHOULDER MARKING

SIDE LINE MAKRING

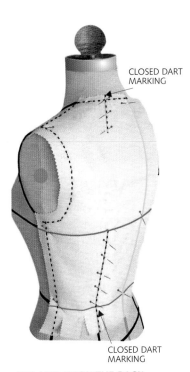

CLOSED DART MARKING

CLOSED DART MARKING

PIN AND MARK THE BACK

JOIN BACK TO FRONT

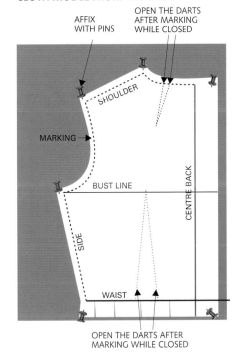

CLOTH MODEL FROM THE BACK

AFFIX WITH PINS

OPEN THE DARTS AFTER MARKING WHILE CLOSED

SHOULDER

MARKING

BUST LINE

CENTRE BACK

SIDE

WAIST

OPEN THE DARTS AFTER MARKING WHILE CLOSED

MARKING THE FABRIC

After having completed the pinning, carefully and precisely hand mark the fabric, with a marker, along the tape lines placed on the dress form: that is, along the lines of the centre back, the centre front, the side, along the bust and waist dart lines, making dashed lines or a series of relatively large points.
These demarcation lines will then be used to draw the definitive lines for the pattern, using the ruler and the curvilinear ruler.

FRONT AND BACK FABRIC PATTERN

Remove the marked-up fabric from the dress form, carefully lifting all the pins, and affix it on a flat board (which should be prepared in advance), and prudently pass over the lines once again, checking that all the seam margins are the right measurements along the entire perimeter of the model. It's a good idea to then copy over the model to pattern paper so you can save it to use in the future.

LAPELS

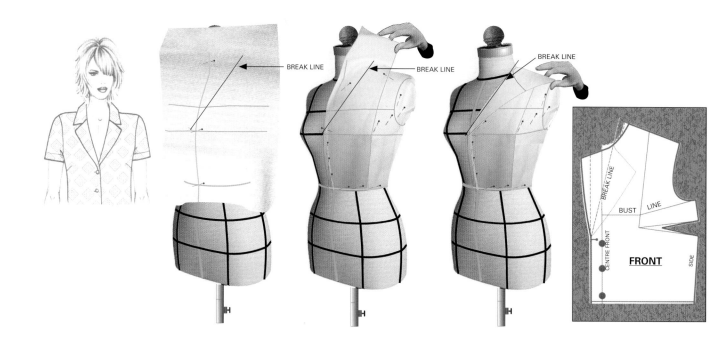

LAPELS, WITH OR WITHOUT FACING

To create the lapels according to the moulage method:

1. Prepare a sufficiently large rectangular piece of fabric (lapel plus facing, if any).
2. Position it on the dress form after marking the guidelines.
3. Fold the fabric for any facing which won't be detached.
4. Mark the break point, create any necessary darts and mark the outline of the lapel.
5. Disassemble the fabric and create the pattern on a flat surface.

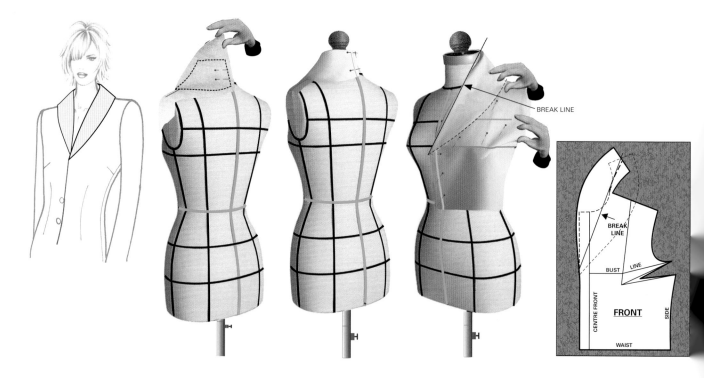

SHAWL COLLARS

Similarly, to make a shawl collar with the moulage method:

1. Prepare a sufficiently large rectangular piece of fabric according to the shape and height of the collar.
2. Position it on the dress form after having marked the guidelines.
3. Pin the collar on the CENTRE BACK.
4. Mark the break line, create any necessary darts and mark the outline of the collar.
5. Disassemble the fabric and create the pattern on a flat surface.

BUST DART MERGED INTO A GATHERED NECKLINE

The bust dart can be distributed over the bodice's entire neckline, creating a gathered effect.

The moulage draping method here is similar to that of the base with darts, but instead the space is distributed along the neckline, affixing it bit by bit with pins. Mark along the dress form's tape, disassemble the fabric and position it on a flat board, affixing it adequately with pins. Then create the pattern on paper.

FABRIC PATTERN (FRONT)

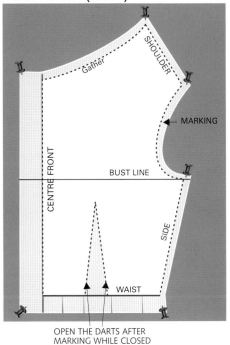

SHOULDER DART MERGED INTO THE BUST AND WAIST LINES

The bust dart placed on the shoulder can be shifted to all the positions previously shown for flat patterns. Using the moulage draping method, carry out the steps on a dress form or on the client, distributing the darts to the desired positions.

After positioning as desired, mark along the tape on the dress form, disassemble the fabric and position it on a flat board, affixing it adequately with pins or thumbtacks. Then create the pattern on paper.

FABRIC PATTERN (FRONT)

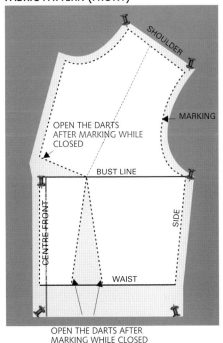

SET-IN SLEEVE

To construct an set-in sleeve using moulage draping, you will need to attach the arm to the dress form. However, before attaching the arm, you'll need to understand how to position the set-in sleeve and define the sleeve lines with respect to those of the bodice. It is important to note that using the draping method, the sleeve is made of just one piece of fabric, paying special attention because the front and back curve of the sleeve crown are not the same.

Thus, you cannot use moulage on half a sleeve.

MOULAGE STEPS

- First establish the height and the base line for the armscye with a piece of tape, based on the depth desired for the garment.
- Place a strip of tape on the dress form along the centre sleeve line and the shoulder width line.
- Prepare a piece of fabric in the desired sleeve length, width equal to the circumference of the arm+ease+2

cm/0.79" margin along the entire perimeter.
- Draw the Centre Sleeve line with the back approx. 2 cm/0.79" wider; the height of the Armscye line equal to that of the dress form; the shoulder width line.
- Position and pin the assembled sleeve on the armscye and mark by following the tape on the dress form.
- Pin the centre sleeve on the centre shoulder, aligning them perfectly with respect to the dress form, and mark the sleeve crown.
- Disassemble the sleeve and perfect the line of the sleeve crown.
- Trim the sleeve crown leaving a seam margin along the armscye and along the length.
- Assemble the sleeve with the bodice, paying careful attention that the lines of the armscye and the width of the shoulders line up.
- Dismantle the sleeve and transfer the outlines to a paper pattern.

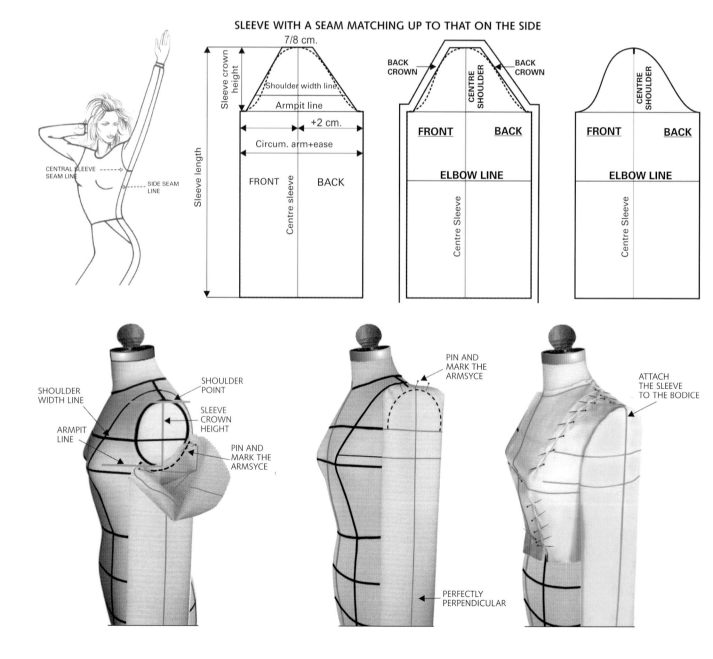

SLEEVE WITH A SEAM MATCHING UP TO THAT ON THE SIDE

SHIT WITH A GATHERED NECKLINE

To create this pattern using the moulage method:
1. prepare a piece of fabric in the desired length plus the cm necessary for the desired gathering along the top and the width equal to ½ bust circumference + the gathering cm + 2-3 cm / 0.79-1.18" for the construction margins.
2. mark the lines for the bust, waist and CENTRE FRONT (or CENTRE BACK).
3. position the fabric on the dress form, following the tape lines on the form, and pin it in place.

4. evenly distribute the excess fabric along the neckline and affix it with pins.
5. cut the armscye and the neckline, leaving the seam margins.
6. remove the fabric from the dress form, position it on a piece of pattern paper, pass over the marks on the fabric once again and transfer them to the pattern paper.
Repeat the above steps for the back.

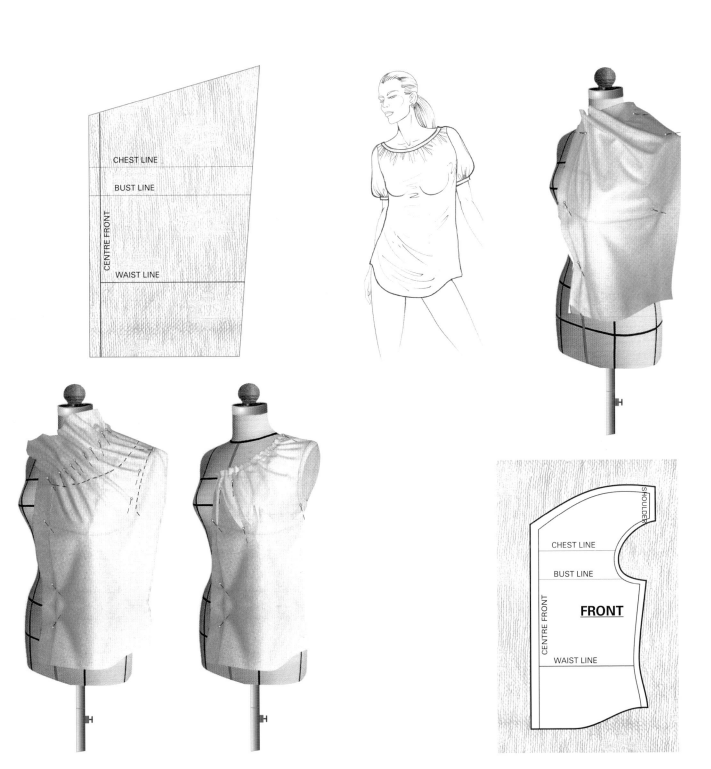

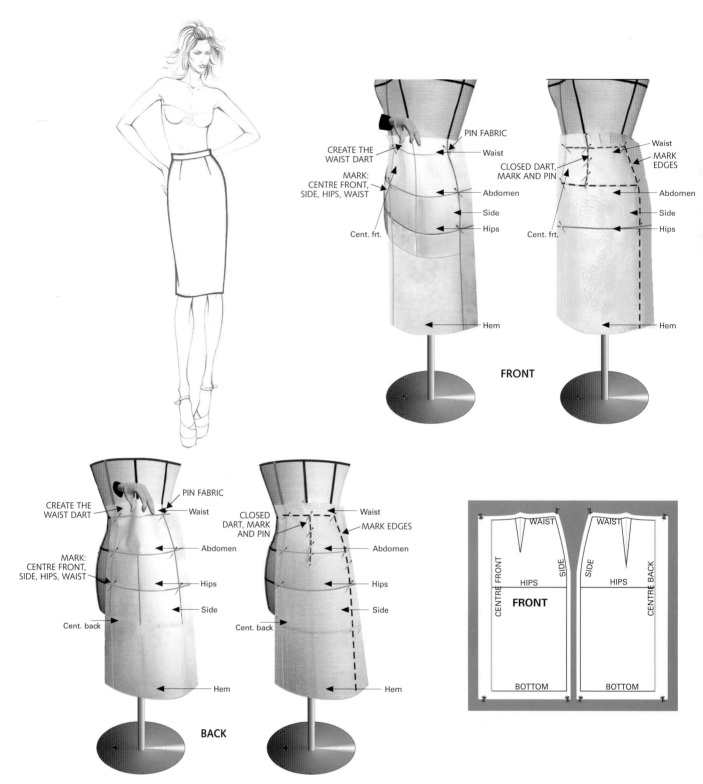

FRONT

PIN FABRIC
CREATE THE WAIST DART
Waist
MARK: CENTRE FRONT, SIDE, HIPS, WAIST
Abdomen
Side
Cent. frt.
Hips
Hem

CLOSED DART, MARK AND PIN
Waist
MARK EDGES
Abdomen
Side
Cent. frt.
Hips
Hem

BACK

CREATE THE WAIST DART
PIN FABRIC
Waist
MARK: CENTRE FRONT, SIDE, HIPS, WAIST
Abdomen
Hips
Side
Cent. back
Hem

CLOSED DART, MARK AND PIN
Waist
MARK EDGES
Abdomen
Hips
Side
Cent. back
Hem

CENTRE FRONT | WAIST | SIDE | WAIST | CENTRE BACK
HIPS — **FRONT** — HIPS
BOTTOM | BOTTOM

THE PENCIL SKIRT

To make the pencil skirt using the moulage draping method, you'll need to prepare two pieces of fabric, one for the front half and one for the back half, in the desired length + 4-5 cm /1.57-1.97" and with the width equal to ½ hip circumference + 3-4 cm / 1.18-1.57".

PROCEDURE

- Prepare the fabric by marking a vertical line along the centre front, a horizontal line 3 cm / 1.18" from the edge to indicate the waist and another horizontal line at the height of the hip.
- Position the fabric on the dress form, making the lines on the centre front, the waist and the hip meet up and pin along the centre front line.
- Make sure the fabric is closely adherent to the dress form and pin along the side line at the height of the waist and hip.
- Define the waist dart naturally and pin it.
- Mark a curved dotted line along the side, the waist and the dart.
- Do the same for the back.
- Remove the fabric from the dress form and re-trace the dotted lines using the curvilinear ruler if necessary.
- Remove the pins and create the paper pattern from the fabric model, faithfully and precisely tracing all the lines.

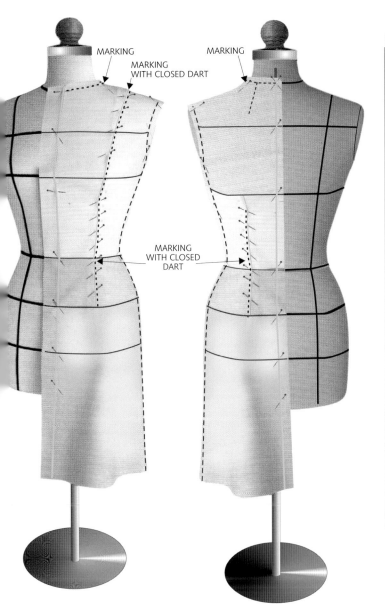

MARKING

MARKING
WITH CLOSED DART

MARKING

MARKING
WITH CLOSED
DART

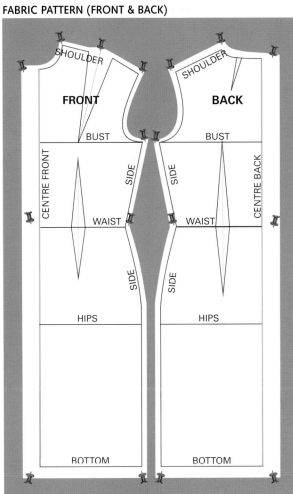

SHOULDER

FRONT

BACK

BUST

BUST

CENTRE FRONT

SIDE

SIDE

CENTRE BACK

WAIST

WAIST

SIDE

SIDE

HIPS

HIPS

BOTTOM

BOTTOM

- Mark a dotted profile line along the side, the waist and the darts.
- Remove the fabric from the dress form and re-trace the dotted lines using the curvilinear ruler if necessary.
- Remove the pins and create the paper pattern from the fabric model, faithfully and precisely tracing all the lines. To complete the dress using the moulage method, you'll need to prepare two pieces of fabric, one for the front half and one for the back half, in the desired length + 4-5 cm / 1.57-1.97" and with a length equal to 1/2 hip circumference +3-4 cm / 1.18-1.57".

RAGLAN SLEEVES

To make a raglan sleeve using the moulage draping method, after having made the base of the bodice with or without darts and with set-in sleeves, with the client's specific measurements or on a dress form in the desired size, complete the following steps:

1. Draw the outline of the front of the raglan sleeve in the desired shape, starting from the armscye until the front neckline.

2. Repeat for the back of the bodice.

3. Draw the centre shoulder, bringing it forward by approx. 1 cm / 0.39".

4. Draw a line down the centre of the sleeve starting from the centre shoulder until the bottom.

5. Disassemble the bodice and cut the parts of the sleeve along the lines drawn to shape the raglan sleeve on the front and back, after having made a few notches to facilitate the construction.

6. Pass over the lines once again, using the curvilinear ruler as an aid.

7. Mark notches along the centre sleeve line.

8. Cut the sleeve along the centre line, dividing the front from the back and write the indications for reference.

9. Create a dart on the sleeve crown and smoothly round out the pattern's rough edges.

10. Transfer the fabric sleeve to a paper pattern, tracing all the notches and adding the seam margins.

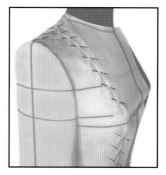

BODICE WITH SET-IN SLEEVE

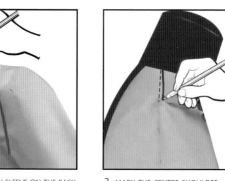

1. MARK THE RAGLAN SLEEVE ON THE FRONT

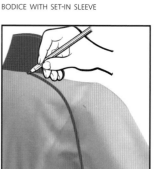

2. MARK THE RAGLAN SLEEVE ON THE BACK

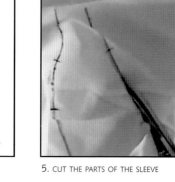

3. MARK THE CENTRE SHOULDER

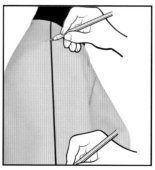

4. MARK THE CENTRE SLEEVE

5. CUT THE PARTS OF THE SLEEVE

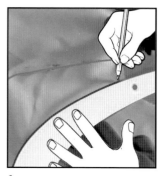

6. RE-TRACE THE LINES

7. MARK THE NOTCHES

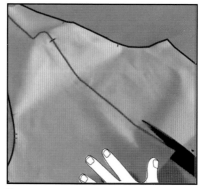

8. CUT THE CENTRE SLEEVE

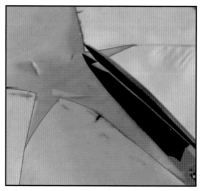

9. CREATE THE DARTS AND ROUND THE CORNERS

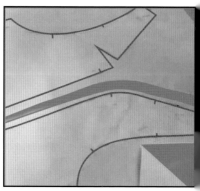

10. COPY TO PATTERN PAPER

DRESS MADE WITH THE MOULAGE TECHNIQUE

FRONT

On the front, draw the lines to position the shoulders, bust, waist, hips, centre front, and calculate the proportions of the seams and motifs.

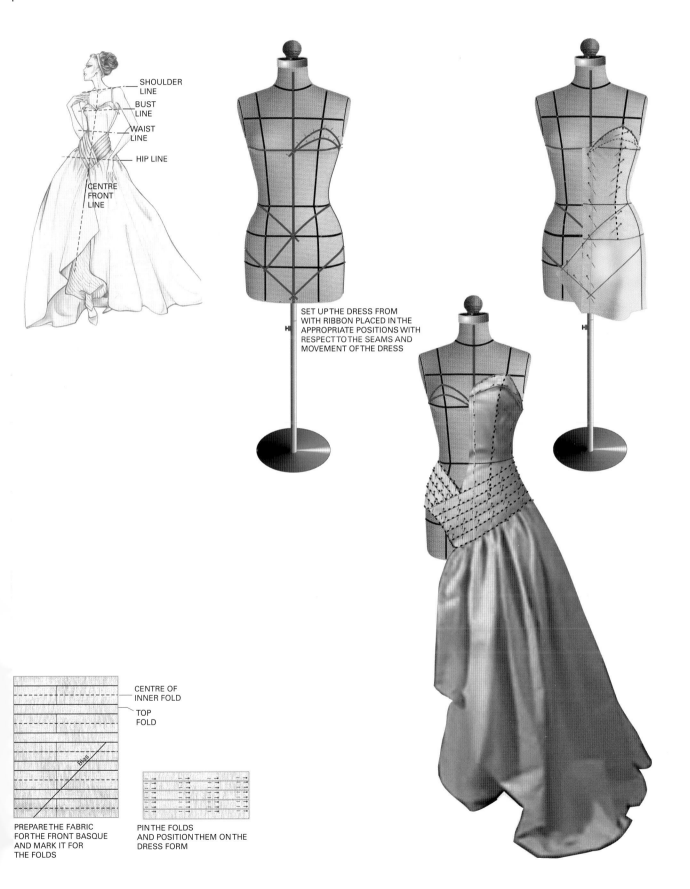

SHOULDER LINE

BUST LINE

WAIST LINE

HIP LINE

CENTRE FRONT LINE

SET UP THE DRESS FROM WITH RIBBON PLACED IN THE APPROPRIATE POSITIONS WITH RESPECT TO THE SEAMS AND MOVEMENT OF THE DRESS

CENTRE OF INNER FOLD

TOP FOLD

PREPARE THE FABRIC FOR THE FRONT BASQUE AND MARK IT FOR THE FOLDS

PIN THE FOLDS AND POSITION THEM ON THE DRESS FORM

BACK

On the back, draw the lines to position the shoulders, bust, waist, hips, centre back, and calculate the proportions of the seams and motifs.
- Cut the pieces of soft fabric a bit larger than the part of the pattern to follow.
- Position and affix the fabric with pins on the dress form, respecting the layout of the tape.
- Construct the darts following the tape lines and affix with pins.
- Mark the lines for the wing for the bust, trim it, leaving a margin, and pin along the edges.
- Mark the basque, following the appropriate tape on the dress form.
- Position the fabric for the skirt, gathered and prepared in advance, and pin it bit by bit along the front and back of the basque.
- Mark the cuts, the darts, and the motifs with a dashed line.
- Remove the various pieces of the pattern from the dress form and create the paper pattern as explained previously.

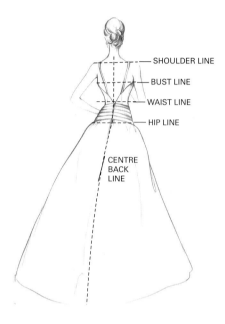

SHOULDER LINE
BUST LINE
WAIST LINE
HIP LINE
CENTRE BACK LINE

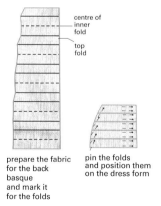

centre of inner fold
top fold

prepare the fabric for the back basque and mark it for the folds

pin the folds and position them on the dress form

BACK

8. PAINTING ON FABRIC

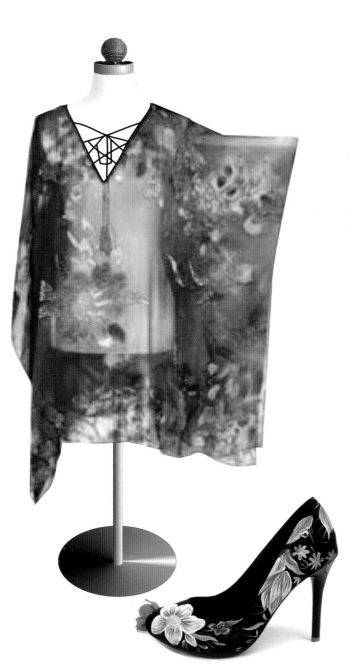

INTRODUCTION

With this chapter, I wanted to give students who have attended at least three years of fashion design, patternmaking or tailoring/seamstress courses, who are looking for an attractive variation and way to bring more value to their creations through painting on fabric, the foundation for another skill set and specialisation in the wonderful world of fashion and clothing which surely will be advantageous.

What I call without hesitation "applied art" will bring much satisfaction to students and those who practice it. Naturally, the results depend on one's mastery of the technique (through countless freehand exercises) and imagination. These two elements are closely linked, be it in creating drawings and subjects, or in intuiting how these, through various elaborations with the right materials, may translate into graphic embellishments to enhance the garment and create an original, exclusive look. Painting on fabric allows you to transform a sim-

ple garment into a unique, inimitable object, expressly dedicated to one person.

What pushed me to write this chapter for the fourth book of *Fashion Patternmaking Techniques* was, more than anything else, the number of requests coming to me from trainees, designers and patternmakers, still in school and with degree in hand, as well as many others. Here I offer the most of what my experience has taught me and lessons from a few of my teachers who have worked in this field for some time. Anyone who follows these short lessons, even if the material here is far from complete, will learn the basic techniques of painting on fabric, illustrated simply and therefore executable by all students to good results in a short amount of time.

I hope that this chapter is useful to my readers, from whom I gladly accept constructive suggestions and critiques to help me better meet their needs.

TOOLS MATERIALS AND HOW TO USE THEM

For excellent, "professional" results, the choice of tools and materials should be made with the necessary foresight and without trying to save money on the quality and reliability of the products bought. You should thus buy appropriate materials and products from a reputable brand, suitable for your purposes, and adopt the correct procedures.

Black pencils should be soft and pass easily over the surface of the fabric.

Light-colour pencils, usually white, sky blue, yellow or orange, should also be soft and of high quality.

The rubber and pencil sharpener you can find easily in any stationary shop.

Tracing paper is necessary to copy, with a soft pencil, the outline of the subject to be painted, then pass over it again, flipping it over to the other side of the sheet, with light pressure on the pencil. You can skip this step if the fabric you're using is very light in colour or transparent, copying the design directly onto its surface. The best result is obtained by using a light box, placing the design and the fabric on its surface and carefully tracing the image.

The most frequently used paintbrushes are "cat's tongue" (round) no. 6 and sable no. 5/6 brushes for blending and adding finishing touches.

Paint brushes should always be washed well and dried carefully every time you stop working. Remember that the paint used on cloth dries easily, so leaving your brush dirty for just ten minutes will ruin it.

Paint brushes should be kept in a jar of water to make sure the bristles don't bend and get ruined. And once they're dried properly, they should be kept upside down in a jar or flat in a box.

Always use the same brush to mix colours.

Every time you change colour, wash the brush and dry it with a clean rag.

Never use a wet brush. It will form halos on the fabric which are difficult to get rid of.

For stencils, it's helpful to have a few extra brushes, because these are always to be used dry. In fact, they don't dry quickly when changing colours.

Cups or palettes: these accessories are used to hold the paint in just the right amount so as not to waste any. Remember to wash them and dry them carefully each time you stop working.

The water which is kept in a glass or in a jar should always be clean and it's a good idea to replace it often with clean water.

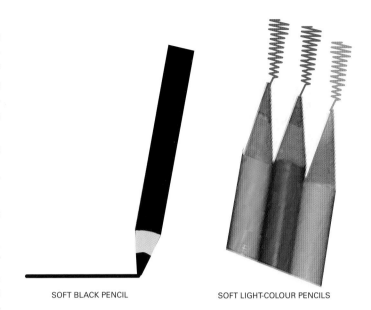

SOFT BLACK PENCIL   SOFT LIGHT-COLOUR PENCILS

TRACING PAPER

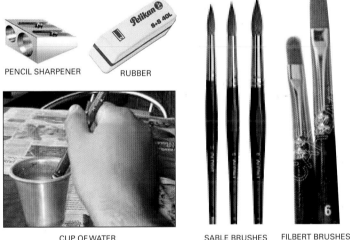

PENCIL SHARPENER   RUBBER

CUP OF WATER   SABLE BRUSHES   FILBERT BRUSHES

RAG TO CLEAN BRUSHES   CUPS OR PALETTES FOR PAINT

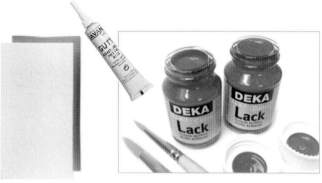

PAINT

You'll find numerous brands of paint for sale in special ised stores; be sure to ask specifically for that to use on fabric. The most commonly found brand to use or fabric is "Deka", and more specifically: white, red no. 407, blue no. 408, yellow no. 402, black and gold There are three categories of paint: opaque – transpar ent – pearlised.

Paint containers should always be kept closed so thei contents don't dry out.

- The container should be shaken well before use;
- Only pour as much paint as you will need in the cur or palette so you don't waste any.
- Always use the colour blend made throughout the day, making sure to mix it every so often and to add a few drops of water when needed.

If you happen to have some of the mixed colour lef over, and you would like to use it the next day, cover the cup or palette with a piece of polyethylene film or aluminium so that the paint doesn't come in contact with the air.

For dark fabrics, before creating your figures, add a white base coat to make them a bit brighter.

Absorbent paperboard: should be placed under the fabric you'll paint on. You can find sheets of card board, usually measuring 50x7 cm (19.69x2.76") ir most stationary shops.

They should always be used dry to avoid dirtying the fabric.

Frames and support: the fabric to be painted shoulc be placed and stretched properly over a frame which can be made of wood or stiff cardboard. Always put a piece of paper or blotting paper underneath, so as tc absorb the extra paint.

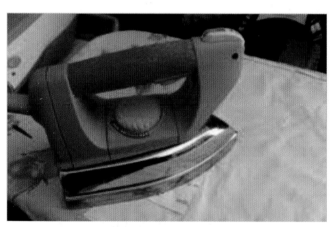

Iron: once you've finished painting, it's a good idea to leave the garment to dry for about 48 hours. The painted fabric should then be dry pressed with an iror to set the paint. Be sure to iron on the back of the fabric at a temperature appropriate for the fabric used, even putting an extra piece of fabric between the iror and the garment. Once you've done this, the garment can be washed with warm water or even in the wash ing machine. Do not dry clean the garment.

Fabric that is most suitable for decoration is that in a solid colour or with stripes that are very far apart, or with large squares. Every type of fabric can be paintec on, but those made of natural fibres – cotton, linen, silk, and hemp with a dense weave – work best. Silk re quires denser paint and lighter pressure with the brush. Leather and buckskin can also be decorated.

Before painting the fabric, make sure it isn't starched, and it's always best to wash it in hot water or ever boil it in a lye bath and rinse very well. Paint applied tc starched fabric will disappear after the first wash. Press the fabric well, removing every crease.

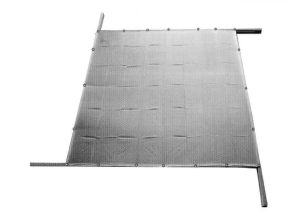

SKETCHING THE SUBJECT

When choosing a subject to decorate your garment, it's best not to seek out complex elements, mistakenly thinking that the more complex the image is, the prettier it will be. Rather, look towards simplicity, coherence and balance in the composition, trying to express it harmoniously on the fabric, will the purest understanding of "art".

In any case, before choosing the colours and paints, it's a good idea to ensure you are properly acquainted and familiar with creating the design free hand - painting is a bit like drawing with a brush, so it's quite important to dedicate some time to freehand drawing exercises, repeating the image you've chosen numerous times. For those who aren't quite at the necessary skill level to create the design directly on the fabric, it's possible to use a copy and transfer system with tracing paper:

After having copied the outline of the design with a marker on tracing paper and flipping it over onto the fabric, pass over the back of the design, lightly applying pressure to a grease pencil. In this way, a faint print of the figure to be painted will remain on the fabric. If the fabric to be decorated is light in colour or transparent, you can skip this step by placing the fabric directly on top of the image and lightly copying it on the fabric surface.

You can get an even better result by copying the image using a light box: a box containing fluorescent lightbulbs, with one side made of glass. Place the design and the fabric on the glass and closely trace the outlines, which will be easier to see, even with darker fabrics. On dark fabrics, you will want to use a soft pencil in a light colour.

Remember that this is a hand-crafted process and thus more precious and valued, but in terms of products made and time investment, it isn't competitive with industrial processes. It should be approached with a different spirit, that is, not worrying about counting the time it takes to complete the "output" at the end of the day. In short, don't rush, it's the only way you'll get the satisfying results you are hoping for.

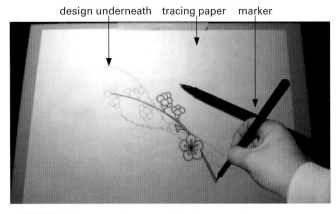

design underneath   tracing paper   marker

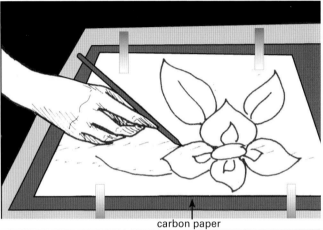

carbon paper

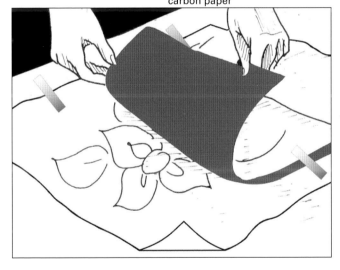

Copying with carbon paper

You should be able to find tracing or graphite paper for tracing by hand, which has a lighter layer of ink and thus more easily cleaned.

Place the design on a properly ironed piece of fabric, aligning the lines in the centre, and set it with a few pins or, better yet, with paper which is adhesive on only one side. Insert the tracing paper between the design and the fabric and properly affix all the sides so that it's all properly secured. By tracing the design with a biro pen with a fine point, the line will be more precise (if you don't want to make a mess of the design to use it later, use a pen which has run out of ink).

Reproduction by dusting

Another method, used in particular for delicate fabrics, involves first copying the design on a piece of paper and then poking holes in its outlines with a needle. Position the paper, sprinkle the design with a special dust (light or dark according to the colour of the fabric), using a pad similar to a powder puff. When the sheet of paper is removed, a thin line of dots will remain, less visible than the marks made with carbon paper.

Before removing the design from the fabric, carefully lift up the carbon paper and check to make sure all the details have been transferred to the fabric without shifting the placement of the carbon paper itself.

DECORATION AND THE FIGURE

Each type of fabric has its own set of qualities and characteristics in terms of its "drape" and "movement". In other words, each textile takes on a certain set of folds and falls in a specific way. It's necessary therefore to accurately study the way the fabric adheres to the figure when it wraps around the body and the way in which the drape forms when the fabric is not touching the body. It's very important to remember that it is always the figure which brings a certain tone to inspiration and creation, so various fabrics and various decorative images must adapt and harmonise with it. Each person's artistic sensibility, paired with a good understanding of human anatomy, should be starting points as to what are the subjects which will lend the best outcome to your creation.

Among the various subjects, a special homage should be made to fruits and grains, especially for the fierceness and impetuosity of certain colours: the reds and yellows of geraniums and poppies, of corn or sunflowers, used to bring full colour to these motifs. Even the water of the Mediterranean or the ocean, in their tranquil transparencies or their acute intensities, can be interesting and suitable themes for prized fabrics.

The common denominator, especially as far as Italian designers (who excel in this field) are concerned, is a graceful romantic atmosphere, never maudlin or cloying. Flowers and leaves, sometimes neat and sometimes exquisitely stylised and barely hinted at, until they become liquid stains of colour which dilute and soften: roses, daisies, narcissus, delicate, balanced corollas, ferns and trellises, soft floral ideas which dissolve in nimble brushstrokes.

These may be the themes placed on regal, prized fabrics which you'll decorate, fragrant, sophisticated homages to feminine grace which, by the beauty of nature, tap into the depths of the spirit.

If a garment is painted by hand and the drawing's or painting's motif is repeated, it will never be exactly like the garment painted before it, even with the same motif. The blending of the colour in a particular part or the line impressed upon the fabric by the painter's hand will, no matter what, be unique. I hope that more people choose this type of art, appreciating it for all of the value it holds.

EXECUTING THE "FLAT" TECHNIQUE
ON TAFFETÀ

The "flat" technique of painting involves coating paint on the fabric in a uniform, homogenous manner, filling small or large spaces delimited by an outline with a single colour, trying to be "quick".

Pure colour, taken directly from the paint containers or just diluted depending on the decoration, is applied first, yet not allowed to dry completely so as to allow other colours to amalgamate with them. Once dried, you can then proceed to blur between them, create shadows, highlights, outlines, etc.

Description:
The flat technique was used on this silk taffeta dress. Warm tones of yellow/orange and gold were applied to the fabric with a pearlised silk effect. The colours used to make the stylised flowers on a branch are lemon yellow shaded with Chinese red, while the branches themselves are a mixture of brown and white for the central branch and pure brown for the two side branches. The sides of the flowers were then outlined with gold.

Brushes used: no. 02-04 soft round with a fine point. Fabric paint.

1. Copy the image of your choice to the tracing paper with a fine-point permanent marker.
2. Stretch the fabric properly and affix it to a rigid frame with drafting tape, placing a white sheet of paper under it, preferably absorbent.
3. For the central flower, I've applied the orange colour using lemon yellow with Chinese red and brush no. 04. For the buds, I spread the lemon yellow colour with a touch of Chinese red. Before the paint dried, I applied a small brushstroke on the external part of the buds with the red paint, blending it with an almost-dried brush. The central branch was made by mixing brown and white, while the side branches are pure brown.
4. Be careful when using the gold paint, as it is very pasty and should be diluted as necessary to make it fluid on the fabric – the same amount of attention which is paid when diluting the other colours so as not to irreversibly stain the fabric. Let the entire painting dry completely.
5. Iron the back side of the fabric with a dry, hot iron for two or three minutes, placing a piece of white paper beneath. Do not use any steam!

Wash with warm water or follow the instructions from the fabric paint's manufacturer.

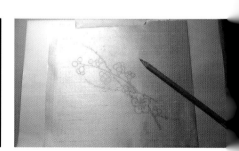

THE FLAT TECHNIQUE
ON SHANTUNG SILK

For this dark fabric, you'll want to use white paint as a base and then, afterward, use a neutral pearlised coat to bring out the effect.

The pearlised paint should be diluted very little, otherwise it will lose its lustre, and it may be necessary to apply two coats, letting the first dry before applying the second.

Details have been brought out with pure black paint. Brushes used: no. 02-06 soft round with a fine point.

227

DECORATION TECHNIQUES USING BLENDING

STEPS

FOR LIGHT COLOUR FABRIC
1. Place an absorbent sheet of paperboard under the fabric.
2. Draw the outlines of the motif on the fabric.
3. Prepare the paint necessary in the appropriate trays and adjust their density as needed by adding a few drops of water.
4. Apply the paint for the decoration with the appropriate brush according to the design's size, holding the fabric in place with your left thumb and index finger (or right hand if it's more comfortable) so as to avoid affixing the fabric with thumbtacks or pins which might ruin it.

FOR DARK FABRIC
1. Follow steps 1 and 2 above for light colour fabric.
2. Prepare the white paint in the appropriate tray, in the required density.
3. Apply the white paint uniformly on the inside of the design and let it dry completely.
4. Decorate as with light colour fabric:

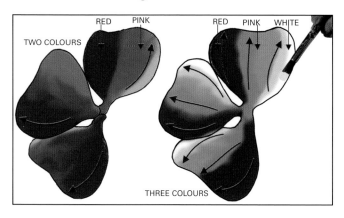

PROCEDURE

To create decorations with shade gradients, the colours should be applied "flat", that is, filling an outlined space with a single colour, trying to be "quick".
To then add the blending, take the following steps:
1. Apply the first, lightest colour. Immediately after, apply the paint with a darker tone to the part where you'd like the blending, proceeding with the brush from the darker part towards the lighter part without dipping into the paint and always moving in the same direction.
2. If the blending is too dark, clean the brush well, dip it in the light colour and proceed in the reverse order (from light to dark).

THREE-COLOUR BLENDING
You can also use three colours for blending: 1. the lighter colour, 2. the darker colour, and 3. white paint. The white added to the other two colours will make the decoration brighter.
It should be applied opposite the dark colour.
With a dry brush, after having carried out the steps described above, blend the colours first starting from the dark part towards the light part and, on the other half, the light part towards the dark.
Keep in mind that if the design is large, it's a good idea to decorate it one piece at a time. If it's a flower, work petal by petal.
For dark fabric the procedure is the same, but you'll need to apply a white base coat and let it dry completely first.

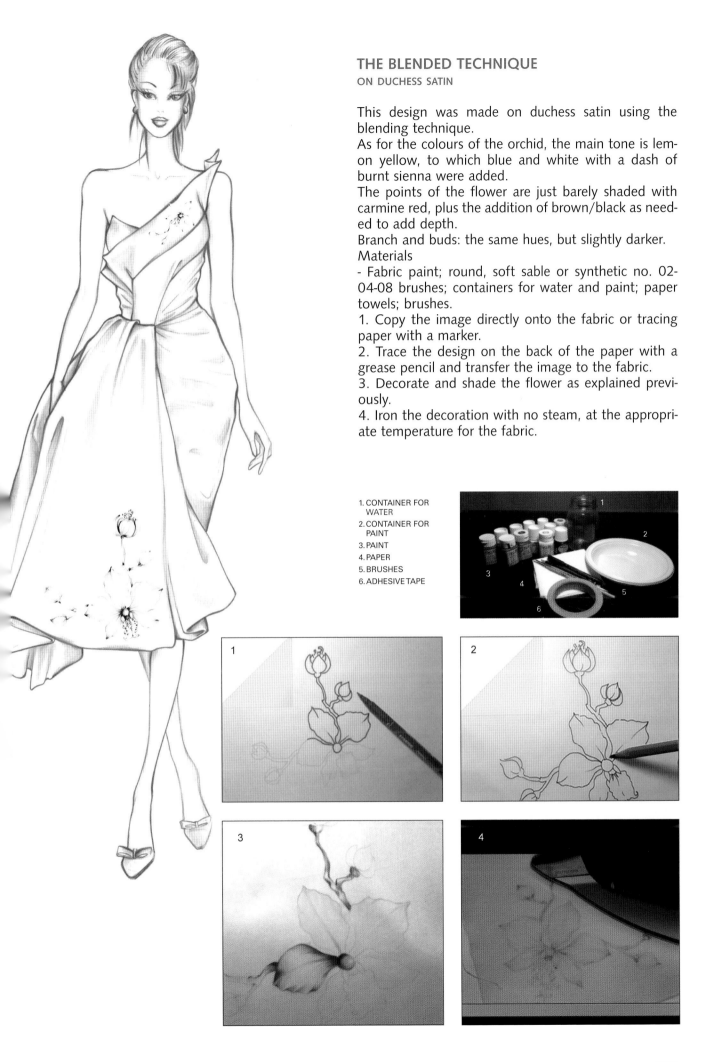

THE BLENDED TECHNIQUE
ON DUCHESS SATIN

This design was made on duchess satin using the blending technique.

As for the colours of the orchid, the main tone is lemon yellow, to which blue and white with a dash of burnt sienna were added.

The points of the flower are just barely shaded with carmine red, plus the addition of brown/black as needed to add depth.

Branch and buds: the same hues, but slightly darker.

Materials

- Fabric paint; round, soft sable or synthetic no. 02-04-08 brushes; containers for water and paint; paper towels; brushes.

1. Copy the image directly onto the fabric or tracing paper with a marker.
2. Trace the design on the back of the paper with a grease pencil and transfer the image to the fabric.
3. Decorate and shade the flower as explained previously.
4. Iron the decoration with no steam, at the appropriate temperature for the fabric.

1. CONTAINER FOR WATER
2. CONTAINER FOR PAINT
3. PAINT
4. PAPER
5. BRUSHES
6. ADHESIVE TAPE

THE BLENDED TECHNIQUE
ON TRIPLE ORGANZA

This design has been applied to triple organza, using the blending technique as it lends itself quite well to this type of fabric. Both the paint and the brush flow easily along the surface and blend well.

For this peach branch, I've used the vermilion red paint with bright red on the points and some white. The paint is shaded and blended until the darkest colours to give the flowers depth, while the light reflections make use of the light colour of the fabric.

The centre of the flower was brightened with a bit of orangish-yellow to give it a bit of light, while ochre and brown were used for the pistils. The branch and the leaves were shaded by blending blue, yellow and ochre.

Brushes used: soft no. 02/06, round with a fine point. Fabric paint.

THE BLENDED TECHNIQUE
ON PURE SILK ORGANZA

The blending technique was used here on pure silk organza.

Pay careful attention to this type of fabric because, as it is very light and transparent, you only need a little bit of paint and you can eventually take it up again by adding some more to the fabric after the previous layer is dry.

The colour used for the small flowers is bright blue with a bit of added violet; the centre part is lightened with yellow/orange blended with hazel/brown.

For the vine tendrils and for the leaves, leaf green blended with yellow was used.

Brushes used: soft no. 02/04, round with a fine point. Fabric paint.

THE BLENDED TECHNIQUE
ON SILK SATIN

This image was painted on silk satin, which is easily suited for the blending technique as the paintbrush flows over the surface easily and blends easily.

The paint used for the flowers are pepper red/vermilion red, lightened with white where necessary, while in the shadows the red paint was mixed with brown to create a chiaroscuro effect.

The branch and the leaves, on the other hand, are yellow with added blue and ochre on the tips, blending green/brown in the darker parts to add depth.

Brushes used: soft no. 02-06-08, round with a fine point. Fabric paint.

THE BLENDED TECHNIQUE
ON PURE SILK ORGANZA

The blending technique was used here on pure silk organza.

Pay careful attention to this type of fabric because, as it is very light and transparent, you only need a little bit of paint and you can eventually take it up again by adding some more to the fabric after the previous layer is dry.

The colour used for the small flowers is carmine red with a bit of added yellow; the centre part is lightened with yellow/orange blended with hazel/brown.

For the vine tendrils and for the leaves, leaf green blended with yellow was used.

Brushes used: soft no. 02/04, round with a fine point. Fabric paint.

THE BLENDED TECHNIQUE
ON SILK CHIFFON

Pay close attention to this type of fabric, attaching it well to the frame as it moves about easily.
The colours used for these bellflower sprigs are pepper red mixed with white, as is also found on the ribbon, while the vine features yellow/blue with a bit of sienna, blended delicately. The paints used here were not diluted.
Brushes used: no. 02-04.
Fabric paint.

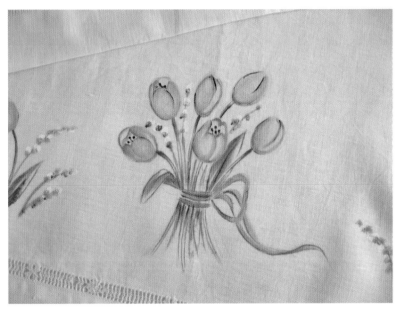

THE FLAT AND BLENDED TECHNIQUE
FOR LIGHT SATIN

Painting on this light satin, I opted for the "flat and blended" technique. In this case, because I was painting butterflies, I applied a neutral pearlised coat of paint over the entire subject, which I let dry. I then applied other paints over the pearlised paint, such as green, light blue and ochre. You can see that this gave all the other colours a pearlised look, for a greatly satisfying effect.

The finishing touches were the butterfly body with some grey/black, with white/black on the wings.

Brushes used: soft no 02-04-08 round, with a fine point.

FABRIC PAINT

Required: light satin fabric, fabric paint: pearlised neutral, leaf green, brown, black, white, yellow, ochre & grey

Brushes: sable or synthetic, round with a fine point, no. 02-04-08

Containers for water and for paint; paper towels; permanent black marker, tracing paper; a rigid frame of cardboard or a wood board; masking tape; HB-8B pencil to trace the design to the fabric.

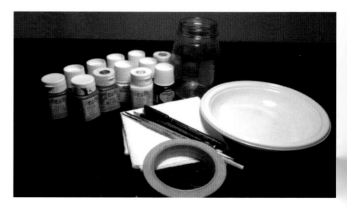

1. Copy the design on the tracing paper with the permanent marker, tracing along the back of the sheet with an 8B pencil.
2. Securely affix the fabric on a rigid frame with some masking tape, putting a sheet of paper underneath. Transfer the design to the fabric with the pencil.

PAINT AND PRESS

Pass over the entire design, in this case the butterfly, with a clear pearlised paint using a no. 08 brush and let it dry completely. At this point, we'll blend some other paint on top. Create shading on the butterfly's wings with the green paint, starting from the exterior and following the design, leaving a clear area. Continue on in this way, darkening the colour with brown/black/green. With the no. 02 brush, make the lines on the butterfly's wings and body with grey/black, adding touches of light with the white paint. Finish lightly around the edges. Let dry completely.

Iron the fabric inside out with a hot iron (dry, with no steam) for two or three minutes, with a sheet of white paper underneath. Never use the steam!
This method helps to set the colours in the fabric.
Wash with warm water or follow the paint manufacturer's instructions.
Paint the butterflies with a no. 08 brush, passing from the neutral, pearlised paint to continue on with the brown/black/green paint using a no. 02 brush.
Press the fabric with a dry iron at the appropriate temperature for the fabric used to set the paint.

THE STENCIL TECHNIQUE

Stencilling is one of the most simple techniques, in that by using cut-out acetate or heavy cardboard we can create truly wonderful decorations.
The stencil is placed over the fabric and secured well with the masking tape.

REQUIRED MATERIALS: fabric (preferably natural fibres such as cotton, linen, silk, etc.), here we've used Hollywood Jacquard.
Fabric paints: brown, burnt Sienna, black.
Brushes: round, fine point no. 02, two brushes per stencil.
Containers for water and for colours, paper towels, permanent black marker, tracing paper, a rigid support (thick cardboard or a wood board), masking tape, HB/8B pencil, clear adhesive tape (to create the stencils), scalpel type blades, a straw.

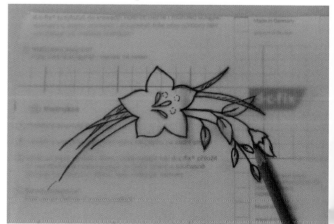

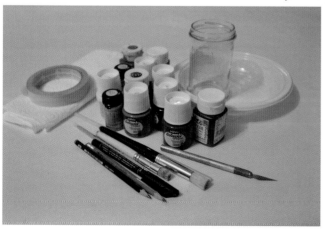

Copy the subject directly to the fabric or tracing paper with a marker.

On the back of the sheet of paper, trace with a grease pencil to transfer the design to the fabric.

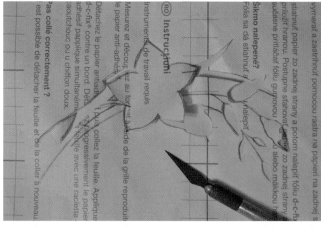

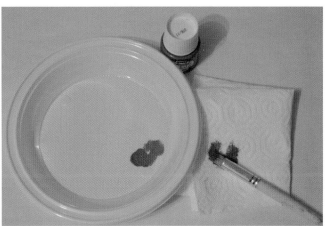

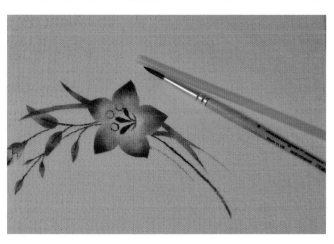

239

THE STENCIL TECHNIQUE
ON CRÊPE DE CHINE

On this fuchsia crêpe de chine fabric, I used the stencil technique. The colours used for the stylised flowers are orange, red/orange, burnt sienna/orange, and ochre/white.

For the branch, I used a leaf-green paint with lemon yellow.

After having drawn, cut and affixed the stencil to the fabric, proceed to colouring it in.

The brush for the stencil should be dipped into the mixed colour, dabbed on a rag, and patted onto the stencil until you get the desired shading.

The sides of the flowers have been outlined with an ochre/white colour, while the pistils are in black.

Gold was then used for the finishing touches along the edges.

Brushes used: no. 02-06 and brushes for stencils.

Fabric paint.

Clear adhesive tape.

Scalpel type cutter.

240

THE SERTI TECHNIQUE ON SILK

The serti technique is one based, more than anything else, on interplays of colours. In fact, with this technique it is rather difficult to obtain results with precise details or with homogenous colour tonalities. For this reason, the serti technique is particularly suited for creating simple subjects, geometric forms and floral motifs.

To carry out the serti technique, you will need: "gutta" (a transparent, liquid resist to create the edges of the design); an applicator bottle with a fine tip; thinner with a dropper; a glass container; a small stick; a piece of cloth as large as you'd like; silk paint or other types of dyes for this purpose. Serti is a technique with closed forms and subtle features: the liquid colours, applied with a brush, fill the surface of the fabric contained by the outlines created by the resin, known as "gutta".

Gutta is a viscous, waterproof mass which blocks the colour from passing from one part of the design to the other. It is the element which defines the serti technique. It can be found sold in small plastic applicator bottles (or in larger refill bottles), which have a changeable tip in various sizes. It comes in various colours, but the most common ones are: clear, gold, pearlised, black, and in various colours. The fabric to be decorated should be thin, silk is ideal.

Before application, the liquid should be prepared in a glass container, including the thinner with the dropper, mixing with the small stick until you get the right consistency.

Stretch the silk over a frame and affix with small clamps, but there are other alternatives. Once the drawing has been transferred to the silk, draw all the outlines with the gutta, using the inserted tip or by poking a small hole with a pin (according to the brand of gutta). Always hold the gutta at a slight angle, as you would a pencil. By lightly squeezing the applicator bottle, the liquid flows onto the silk through the hole in the tip. When applying, you should be able to feel the point of the tip scraping over the surface of the silk, proceeding carefully and slowly.

Let it dry completely before applying the paint. A thin line of paint dries in 10 to 20 minutes. To speed up the drying times, you can use a hair dryer, but be sure to keep it at a safe distance from the fabric/gutta. After you've finished using the dispenser, clean the tip and seal the opening so that the liquid paint inside doesn't dry out. To help make the edges of the design more recognisable, given that the gutta is clear, you can also use gutta with a bit of colour (which can generally only be found in certain pearlescent colours). Keep in mind that the pearlescent or coloured gutta will remain on the fabric, while the clear gutta disappears after the first wash.

Silk paint is usually very watery and easy to mix amongst them.

They are applied with the brush directly to the fabric or prepared in various mixtures on a small tray or plate. When they are applied to the fabric they harmoniously mix together. Various techniques can be carried out using these paints.

They are set with an iron, without any steam, and should be washed in warm water or according to the directions provided by the manufacturer.

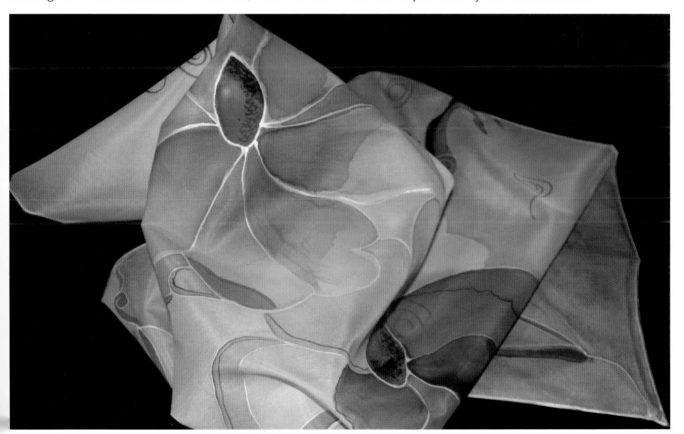

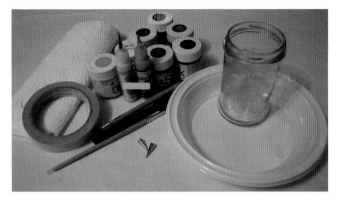

Prepare everything as needed to carry out the process: a glass container, a small stick, a piece of cloth as large as you'd like, silk paint or dye, gutta, an applicator bottle with a fine tip, the thinner with a dropper, brushes, the fabric to be painted, tracing paper, pencils, paper towels, and the frame.

The gutta should be applied slowly and carefully along the edges of the design, keeping the tip at a 45° angle. If necessary, you can use pre-coloured gutta. The thin line of the gutta will dry in 10/20 minutes, according to the size of the project. After having used the applicator bottle, be sure to clean the tip well so that the contents don't dry out.

Choose the subject to paint and carry the design over to the fabric with a soft pencil, directly, using a light box or overhead projector if possible, or a makeshift one of a piece of glass or Plexiglas resting on two boxes with a light bulb below. The light box will be quite useful, especially for dark fabric.

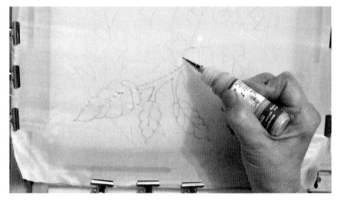

The silk paint should be applied after making sure the gutta is completely dry, using a soft, round sable brush directly on the fabric, or by preparing the various mixtures on a tray or palette, adding a few drops of thinner. If applied directly to the fabric, they'll mix gracefully.

As an alternative to drawing directly on the fabric, you can proceed by copying the image onto tracing paper. If you do so, after flipping it over onto the fabric, pass over the edges again with a soft pencil. Before proceeding with the above steps, first affix the silk tightly on a frame, attached with a few clamps so as not to ruin the fabric.

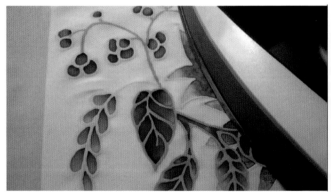

To set the colours, use a dry iron, never using the steam feature. Iron on the back of the fabric, waiting 48 hours from the time the paint has dried, using a temperature appropriate to the fabric. After ironing, you can wash the garment in warm water or in the washing machine, but never dry clean so as not to ruin the colours.

EXAMPLES OF PAINTED SILK

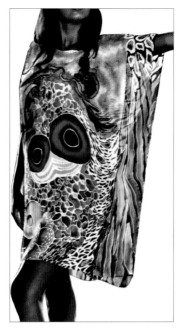

A blue silk scarf with a hand-painted paisley design Hand painted dress by La Rocca

Painting on silk. Works by Olga Sobolevska.

BATIK DECORATION

Batik, also known as artistic expression through wax, is a way to dye fabric using a resist technique. That is, the areas which are not to be dyed are coated with wax or through other water-resistant materials such as clay, resin, vegetable pastes, or starch, while the non-coated parts are dyed. The results of this effect can be truly impressive. It's a method that has its roots in the mists of time, and now we'll see how to do it.

There are two variations of the technique: the first involves working on a piece of fabric stretched over a frame, the second involves gathering the fabric in various parts, and once secured in that position, dipped completely in the dye.

The tools and materials needed for batik are: brush - wax - paraffin - fabric dye - container - an iron - pots – cotton cloth - and, for traditional batik, you'll need a specific pen-like tool called a *canting* or *tjanting*, which is a type of metal spout attached to a wooden handle. The melted wax is placed inside the vial, from which it is poured out through a spout, the tjanting, or two or three spouts (the tool used to create parallel lines). The brush is needed to cover broad swaths with wax. Then, there are also stamps to recreate the same motif. You'll also need a wax heater and an embroidery frame to keep the fabric stretched tight when applying the wax.

Traditionally, a light fabric is used for batik, generally textiles with a thin, regular yarn, which allows for the design to be executed precisely. Today, however, batik can also be done on paper. The fibres that make up the fabric should accept the dyes well; natural textiles work best, generally silk, cotton, and linen. Only a few synthetic materials can be used, such as viscose and rayon.

Remove the starch from the fabric by washing it and, after it's dry, affix it to a frame.

Wax-resist

After prepping the design, apply the melted wax to the parts which you do not want to be dyed. The wax, penetrating the fabric's fibres, will make them impermeable, blocking the dye from leaving any colour. You can use the canting, or even brushes, metal stamps (cap or tjap), wood sticks, blocks of wood with a row of needles (complongan), or the canting with a single spout or multiple spouts according to the effect you are aiming for.

Once the wax is dry, submerge the fabric in a tub that contains the dye bath according to the instructions on the dye packet, for approximately 20 minutes at a temperature of 40 to 50 °C (104 to 122 °F). Remove the cloth from the water, rinse it with cold water and, after it's dried again, put it back on the frame and repeat the process. For each colour of dye, you'll have to add a new layer of wax and use a new dye bath. The wax is then removed with the heat, putting the fabric between a few layers of paper (newspapers) and ironing it to melt the wax, which is absorbed by the paper.

Tjanting.

Double and triple tjanting.   *Wax heater with thermostat.*

Frame and brush to spread the wax.

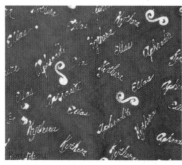
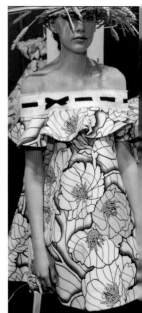

Fabric painted using the batik technique.

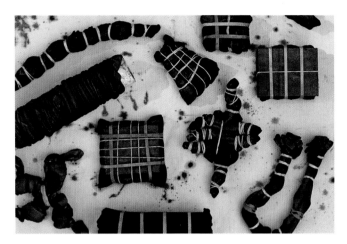

The second technique is the ancient Japanese technique of *shibori* or tie-dye or *plangi* (an ancient term used mostly in Indonesia), while in Italy it is called *mal tinto* (poorly dyed) or *tecnica a nodi* (the knot method). The latter method varies slightly from the one above, which places more emphasis on the wax rather than the knots. Usually this method is used for very large designs, but it is also possible to create lots of smaller motifs and thus to create a wide variety of effects, a visually tangible synonym of an art form with satisfying, elegantly elaborate impact. With shibori, the design is created through folds or the introduction of elements to the fabric before it's dyed. Thus it is considered a resist-dyeing technique, like batik, and it has been exported and adopted around the world, with similar or quite different results, which are often simpler and less refined. It's certainly simpler to do, easy enough for those who aren't particularly skilled or trained at drawing. The fabric is gathered in various points and in various ways, and once the knots are affixed, it's dipped entirely in the dye. The dye isn't able to enter the tightly gathered parts of the fabric, creating entirely unique designs and effects. If you decide to use new, just-bought fabric, wash it and let it air dry in the sun to get the best results. By doing so, you'll eliminate any residual dyes left over from its production. When the fabric is dry, quickly press it with a hot iron so as to get rid of as many wrinkles as possible. At this point, you can choose the types of dyes and colours you want to use. We recommend first folding the fabric in half width-wise, then in half again length-wise. Knot the corners of the fabric, then, if you want to create even more of an effect, add more knots scattered throughout the fabric in a more or less disorderly manner.

You can swap out the knots with rubber bands and twine. The more the cloth is knotted, the greater the impact will be. In this way, the knots will block the colour from being absorbed by the tied cloth.

Once you've finished this step, prepare the dyebath. Take the appropriate dye and completely dissolve it in a tub of warm water, mixing with a wooden spoon. Submerge the fabric, pressing it downwards with the spoon. As for the time to let it soak, closely follow the instructions on the dye packet. Once the necessary amount of time has passed, take the fabric and rinse it thoroughly, until the water running off it is completely clear. Then remove all the ties, knots and strings and lay the fabric out in the sun to air dry. Let it dry before using it.

You will even be able to make very colourful, original designs by subsequently dipping the fabric in other colours. Thus, it's a good idea to choose a light-colour fabric so that you will have full control and more choices as to the final result.

The tub with Dupont's "rouge sang" dye, where the tied and knotted silk is dipped. At right is the final result, showing the resulting designs on the fabric.

To create this painting on a soft, silky cotton t-shirt, first draw as you please on the shirt, then hand sew along the design. The shibori technique was used along the neckline, with stitching around the edges, tight on the inside. The swirls are made by the ori-nui technique, gathering the drawn line by sewing along the spiral. The fabric is then dipped in the dyebath. Lastly, the seams are removed to reveal the final product.

9. TECHNICAL CONCEPTS

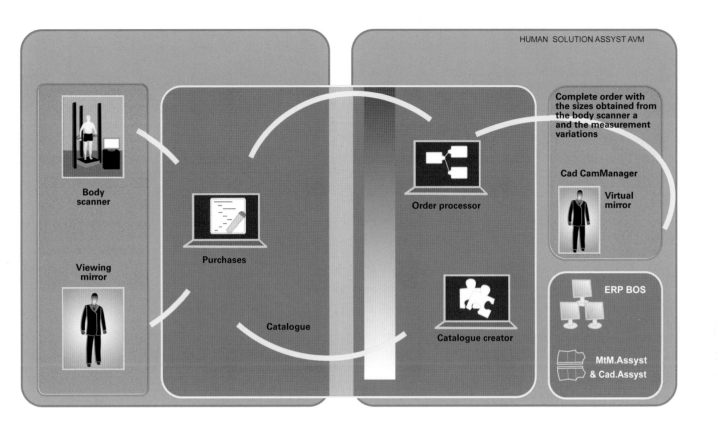

HUMAN SOLUTION ASSYST AVM

Body scanner

Viewing mirror

Purchases

Catalogue

Order processor

Catalogue creator

Complete order with the sizes obtained from the body scanner a and the measurement variations

Cad CamManager

Virtual mirror

ERP BOS

MtM.Assyst & Cad.Assyst

3D CAD FOR CLOTHING

Among the relatively recent computing technology related to fashion, there are 3D CAD programs for clothing which offer advanced three-dimensional design techniques. The fashion industry, as we know, is a complex environment. Collections are developed in ever-shorter time spans and the garments have to fit the greatest number of customers possible. Many partners in various countries often work together and the quality and costs must be just right. In this context, the right technology makes all the difference. There is software which provides benefits in relation to "fit". Everyone has a different shape, different measurements and body types, yet an item of clothing sold in today's market must adapt to as many people as possible. For this reason, fashion designers need to have the most possible data on the sizes and the shapes of the human body. This data is supplied by a few companies, such as Lectra System, AVM, FK System and others. Such information can be analysed online and is available in the CAD program as well as physically in the shape of fashion dress forms. This means that producers can make decisions on solid foundations according to the target group and the relative fit of the garments being developed in their collections. This allows companies to be even more innovative than ever.

3D product development has become a crucial element in competitive challenges. With 3D software, the garment's virtual design is available even before the first sample is sewn. Often the image quality seen with certain software is surprising and, in an exceptional feature, the garment is simulated exactly as it would on a real person. The design is identical to that shown on the CAD screen. The material's properties and even the way it drapes are both perfect, as well as the sizes

and individual forms correspond exactly to that in the 3D CAD program. With these types of 3D CAD applications, companies can create their design 20-30% faster. The fashion industry can look ahead to other innovations which facilitate daily tasks.

The creation of a pattern requires years of experience. This is the point in which the designer's idea is combined with the company's fit philosophy to give rise to an industrial product to be made in large quantities. There are many variations which can be produced: colour, shape, patterns, trimmings, just as is true for the sizes. All of these requests make the pattern maker's work very complex, and errors are quite costly. On one hand, they shouldn't happen, but on the other, the pressure to shorten production times can be intense. This is where CAD for clothing comes in. This isn't just any CAD program, as is made clear from how a patternmaker can work efficiently, which tasks can be automated, and how the product and the pattern's information can be combined seamlessly.

A few new software programs are able to provide a high level of efficiency in the pattern's creation, so much so that even experts and professionals can increase their working speed by approximately 20-30%, thanks to its various inherent functions.

Order configurator – All of the client's info and the order itself are centrally managed through the 3D system. The options to be selected (the pattern, the material, the colour, etc.), can be added with the configurator. It's also possible to view a preview of the design selected and the always up-to-date product catalogue, including the available materials and designs.

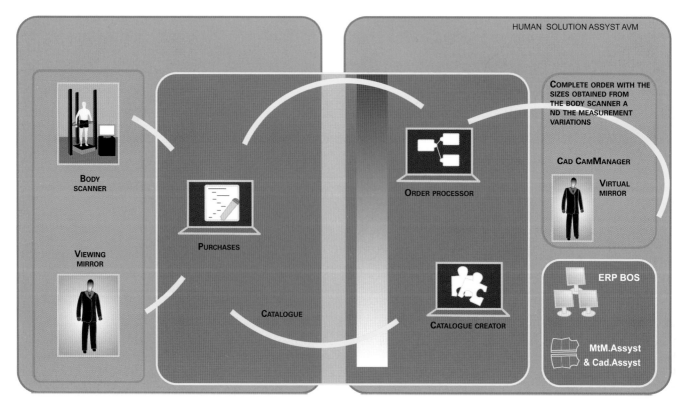

3D SCANNER - MEASUREMENTS

The 3D scanner, in addition to being much quicker than taking manual measurements, is also very precise and consistent. The scan is done in the store in just a few seconds, with a procedure that doesn't involve any physical contact. During the scan, the customer should stand completely still, allowing the equipment to quickly reveal the measurements. By doing so, the information taken will be accurate and without any errors, be it in a table or in the person's 3D scanatar.

Today, even in the world of fashion, nothing in the pattern-making process is done without using CAD. In recent releases, 3D CAD programs for the clothing-manufacture industry have been united in a single program, not just for planning and viewing 3D samples in real time, but also quickly and efficiently communicate with the partners of the project. In particular, with this software you can:

1) Create a pattern from scratch, immediately shown in 3D.
2) Quickly modify and convert a 2D pattern into 3D.
3) Implement changes to 3D patterns in even less time.
4) Position the garment on the three-dimensional mannequin in one single click.
5) Assemble the pieces, quickly and simply, with fast and precise sewing.
6) Create multi-layer clothing.
7) Choose different fabric and patterns for each model.
8) Get the perfect results from the fabric on the virtual mannequin.
9) Create the rendering in real time.
10) Create videos and virtual 3D books online.

11) Have something which is compatible with all CAD programs.
12) Share your projects with multiple partners.

DIGITAL MEASUREMENTS

Mass customisation, that is, the process in which you provide a made-to-measure product for a customer, is the new market trend in which products are quickly changed one at a time to meet clients' various needs. It is a valid competitive strategy to maximize the client's satisfaction and minimize warehousing costs. Even if a bit of time is necessary to get the customer's consent and, in particular, establish a serene collaboration between all parties involved. The potential offered by a full body scanner is enormous; it is precisely for this reason that industrial and commercial sectors have begun moving in this direction. The main goal of such research, carried out in recent years, is that of making this technology usable by a greater number of people and reducing costs. The result is a purchasing system with very low costs, to be installed at the company (boutique, tailor or industrial) and manageable by the same company and/or 3D software supplier remotely. A garment can be considered customised only if it is made to fit the precise measurements of the client.

The client is measured in the store with the 3D scanner, entirely without physical contact. In addition, the client's individual preferences can be included in the order. The measurement procedure creates a digital "twin" (in the 3D scanner), which is an exact image of the customer. This scan allows another program to be used at the store: a virtual trying-on simulator, called Virtual Mirror, in which the client sees his own 3D scan which then wears which s/he has chosen in the precisely correct measurements. In this way, the client can verify, in real time and in terms of looks, the cut and the fit, before it is prepared and packaged. This new form of sales cannot but help to be met with the approval of buyers and ensure success for the 3D system.

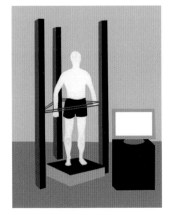

The 3D scanner now comes in smaller sizes for used in stores. The procedure lasts just a few seconds, and acquires 40 measurements from the body, complete automated and according to current standards. In addition, it now also includes technical characteristics to evaluate posture and to determine the customer's size.

PLUS SIZES

People who, due to their body type, wear plus sizes (also called "curvy") are not always able to find suitable garments in stores. They know how difficult it can be to navigate the world of roomier sizes, where the information and data printed on garment tags are completely different from standard sizes. Unfortunately, there aren't any shared standards and the measurements of plus sizes can change from one brand to the next.

Plus sizes are essentially divided in two categories: calibrated and conforming. They are established by referring to the body's measurements, including:
1. bust circumference;
2. hip circumference;
3. waist circumference;
4. shoulder width;
5. height.

Calibrated sizes are essentially those of standard sizes, but larger, especially adapted for those with narrow shoulders and large hips.

CALIBRATED SIZING

Marina Rinaldi and Persona have calibrated collections which start at size 15 and go up to 27.
Size 15 = IT 44-46 (UK 12-14); size 17 = IT 46-48 (UK 14-16); size 19 = IT 48-50 (UK 16-18); size 21 = IT 50-52 (UK 18-20); size 23 = IT 52-54 (UK 20-22); size 25 = IT 54-56 (UK 22-24); size 27 = IT 56-58 (UK 24-26); size 29 = IT 58-60 (UK 26-28).
Elena Mirò, Fiorella Rubino and Luisa Viola produce conforming patterns starting at size 39 (a very roomy Italian size 46/UK size 14) and go up to 51 (39-41-43-45-47-49-51).
This book includes a chapter to illustrate the ideal lines and appropriate volumes for subjects who use the "conforming" sizing to emphasize their feminine qualities and minimising their defects while seeing overall balance.
The method used to create the base patterns remains unchanged, while the structure of the conformed subject should be analysed, with ideal measurements obtained from sizes or made to measure.
The conforming dress block with darts on the bust should be carried out with an appropriately increased ease.

PLUS SIZE CHART

IT standard	44	46	48	50	52	54	56	58	60
conforming	15	17	19	21	23	25	27	29	31
calibrated	37	39	41	43	45	47	49	51	53

INTERNATIONAL SIZE CHART CONVERSIONS: EUROPEAN, AMERICAN, JAPANESE AND INTERNATIONAL SIZES.

IT	UK	USA	EU	INTERNATIONAL
48	16	14	44	L-XL
50	18	16	46	XL-1X
52	20	18	48	1X-2X
54	22	20	50	2X
56	24	22	52	3X
58	26	24	54	4X
60	28	26	56	5X
62	30	28	58	6X
64	32	30	60	7X

StylModa D

Pattern info sheet

Season	Brand	Line	Plus size category
A/W 2015-16	StylModa D	Sub-line	Casual

Date and pattern dept.	Pattern Det. Cod	Washed base Snap fastenings	Definitive Pattern Cod.	DNN
A/W 2015-16				

Finishing	No. of pieces	Comm. size
Washed - 40° cond. - do not iron	7	42

Item/Variation

D3A/8 1Cot00

Presentation fabric

Label/tag

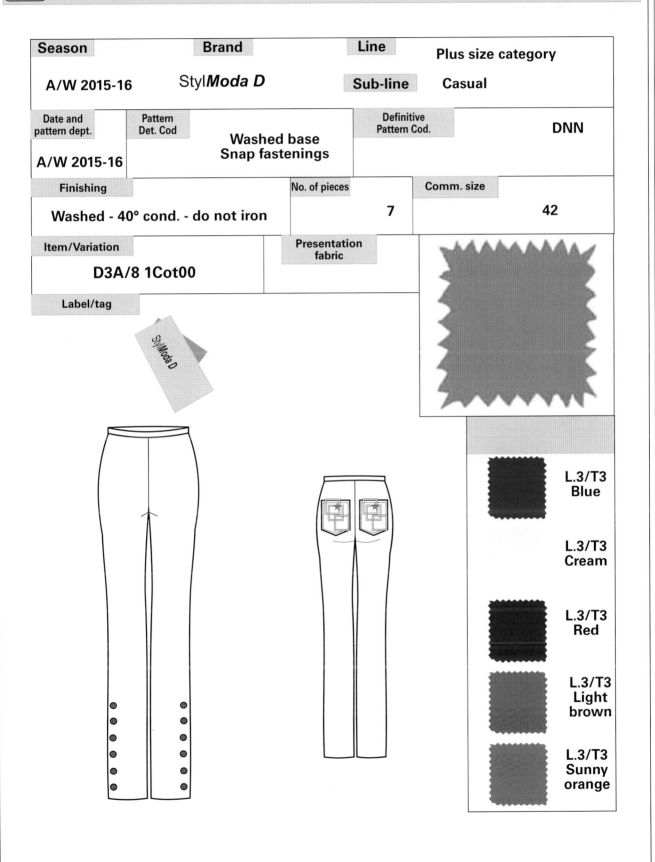

L.3/T3 Blue

L.3/T3 Cream

L.3/T3 Red

L.3/T3 Light brown

L.3/T3 Sunny orange

StylModa D

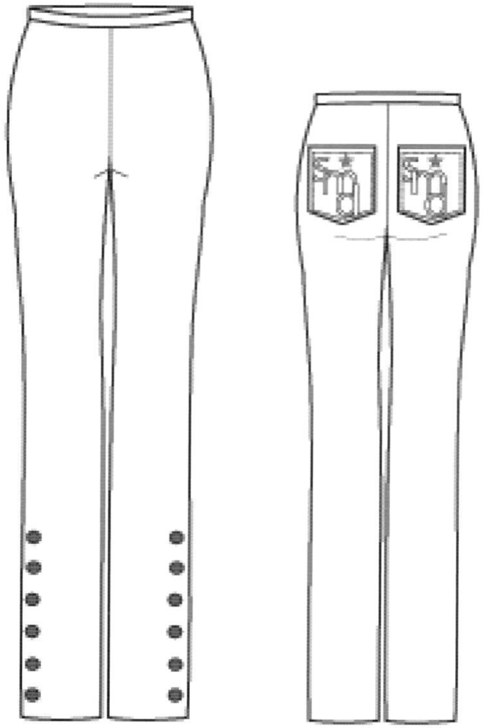

	Season	Line	Category women's tailored	Brand
		Sub-line		

Garment colour	COL. 2	COL. 4	COL. 5		M	L	XL	XXL
Blue	Cream	Yellow	40% darker than the garment colour		10	5	3	3
Light green	White	Dark Green	Light grey		15	8	3	2
Black	Cream	Yellow	Dark grey		10	6	3	1
Olive green	Light grey	Bordeaux	40% darker than the garment colour		10	5	3	1
Quantity	2,010							
BOX	88	Assorted pieces per box						

Colours

1. Blue
2. Cream
3. Yellow
4. 40% Darker Blue
5. Light Green
6. White
7. Dark Green
8. Light Grey
9. Black
10. Dark Grey
11. Olive Green
12. Bordeaux
13. 40% Darker O. Green

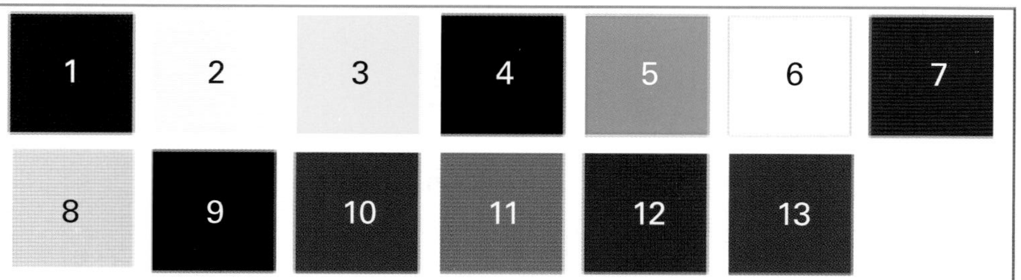

1	2	3	4	5	6	7

8	9	10	11	12	13

Description

Colour 1 -
Colour 2 -
Colour 3 -
Colour 4 -

Styl*Moda D*

Labelling sheet

Season	A/W 2007-08	Brand	Styl*Moda D*	Line	Plus size category

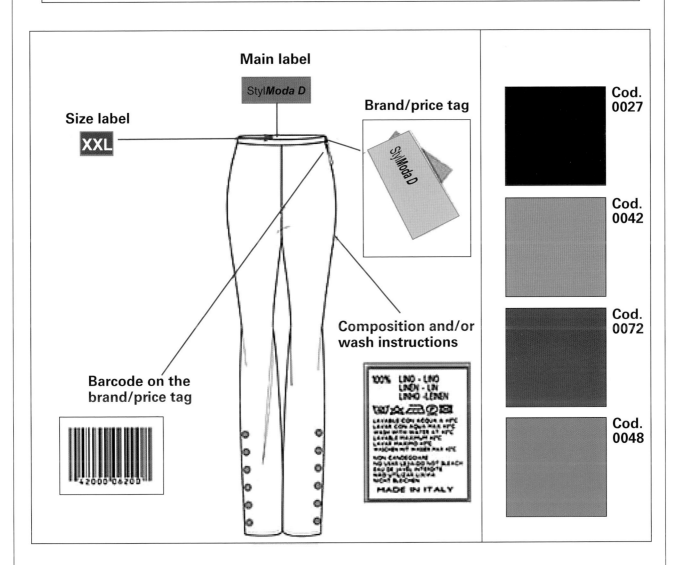

Main label

StylModa D

Size label

XXL

Brand/price tag

Composition and/or wash instructions

Barcode on the brand/price tag

Cod. 0027

Cod. 0042

Cod. 0072

Cod. 0048

Button photo

Button description

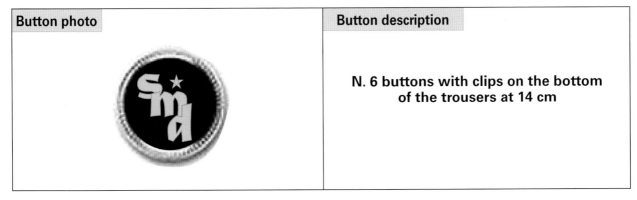

N. 6 buttons with clips on the bottom of the trousers at 14 cm

Styl*Moda D*

Order sheet

Collection: **A/W 2007/09** Pattern/Item: **D8A/3 100 cot.** Line: **Category: plus size**

Price: **€ 15**

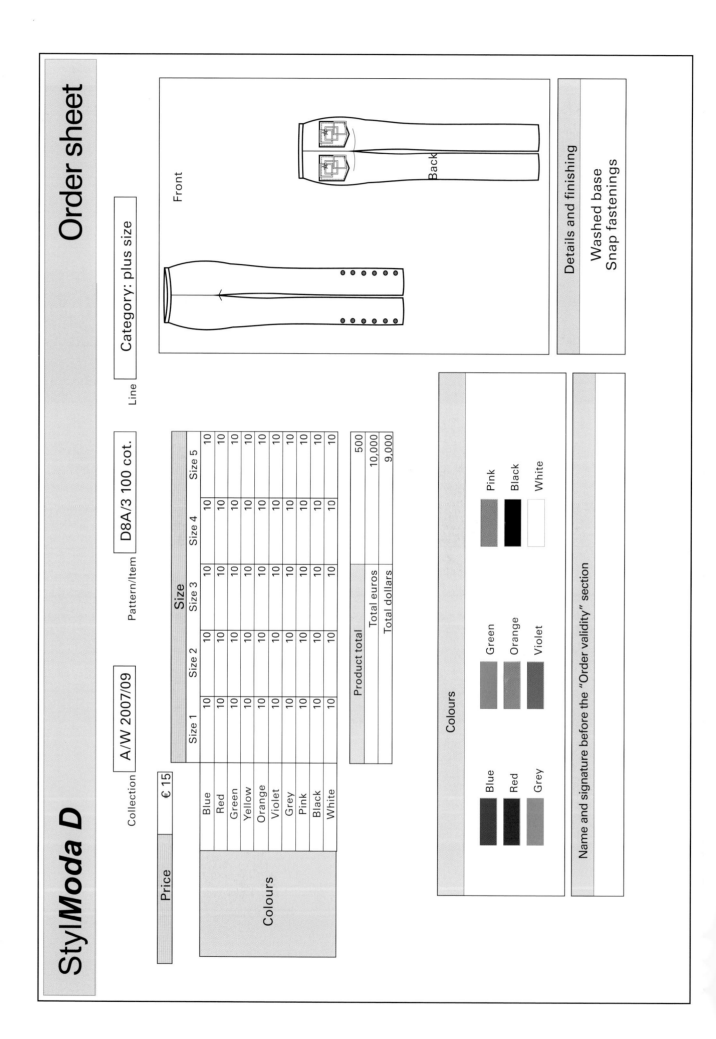

Front

Back

Colours

Colours	Size				
	Size 1	Size 2	Size 3	Size 4	Size 5
Blue	10	10	10	10	10
Red	10	10	10	10	10
Green	10	10	10	10	10
Yellow	10	10	10	10	10
Orange	10	10	10	10	10
Violet	10	10	10	10	10
Grey	10	10	10	10	10
Pink	10	10	10	10	10
Black	10	10	10	10	10
White	10	10	10	10	10

Product total	500
Total euros	10,000
Total dollars	9,000

Colours

Blue   Red   Grey   Green   Orange   Violet   Pink   Black   White

Name and signature before the "Order validity" section

Details and finishing

Washed base
Snap fastenings

OTHER PROMOPRESS TITLES

FASHION PATTERNMAKING TECHNIQUES [Vol. 3]
How to make jackets, coats and cloaks for Women and Men

Antonio Donnanno
Illustrations by Elisabetta Kuky Drudi

ISBN: 978-84-16504-18-3

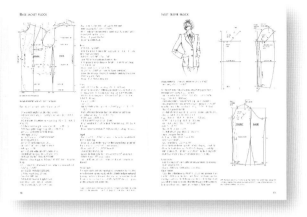

We guide readers through and examine the various procedures for transforming bodices through dart manipulation and study techniques for creating volumes, draping, and fitted patterns. Moreover, we introduce: techniques for creating patterns for knit fabrics; basic dress blocks; sleeve styles for shirts and dresses; basic blocks for men's vests and jackets; size grading for tops and dresses and the fundamentals of pattern layout.

FASHION PATTERNMAKING TECHNIQUES [Vol. 2]
How to make shirts, undergarments, dresses and suits, waistcoats and jackets for Women and Men

Antonio Donnanno
Illustrations by Elisabetta Kuky Drudi

ISBN: 978-84-15967-68-2

This title guides readers through the various procedures to transform bodices, create volumes or draping, and fitted patterns using different fabric types, styles and size grading. It offers a comprehensive technical analysis of the structures of tops, pants and dresses.

PATTERNMAKING IN PRACTICE
A step by step guide

Lucia Mors de Castro

ISBN: 978-84-92810-07-9

Using four basic garments (skirts, dresses, jackets and coats), this volume explores contemporary patternmaking in detail and explains how to draw, cut and mount patterns. This book teaches how to customize and adapt basic models and recreate patterns from pictures. It describes the traditional methods used and today's advanced body-shaping techniques.

FASHION PATTERNMAKING TECHNIQUES [Vol. 1]
How to make skirts, trousers and shirts Women / Men

Antonio Donnanno
Illustrations by Elisabetta Kuky Drudi

ISBN: 978-84-15967-09-5

This volume offers a wealth of in-depth knowledge relating to pattern design, beginning with a detailed study of people's measurements and builds, textile technology and tailoring terminology. It also explores making patterns for men and examines making alterations for different sizes.

FASHION DRAWING COURSE
From Human Figure to Fashion Illustration

Juan Baeza

ISBN: 978-84-15967-06-4

This book analyses the most useful techniques for drawing the human figure in the context of fashion design. It offers in-depth explanatory texts and illustrations.

OTHER PROMOPRESS TITLES

FASHION SKETCHING
Templates, poses
and ideas for fashion
design

Claudia Ausonia Palazio

ISBN: 978-84-16504-10-7

This book offers every type
of silhouette and pose of
women, men and children
so that designers can
produce sketches that are
faithful to the human figure.

FASHION DETAILS
4,000 Drawings

Elisabetta Kuky Drudi

ISBN: 978-84-92810-95-6

This title by best-selling
author Elisabetta Drudi
contains everything you
need to discover how to
make accurate drawings
of a wide range of fashion
elements.

COUTURE UNFOLDED
Innovative pleats, folds
and draping in fashion
design

Brunella Giannangeli

ISBN: 978-84-92810-55-0

This book is a complete
sourcebook that explores
the multiple possibilities of
fabric manipulation. The
pictures of the folds that
appear in this book show
different types of fabric
suitable for each technique.

**FABRICS IN FASHION
DESIGN**
The way successful
fashion designers
use fabrics

Stefanella Sposito

ISBN: 978-84-15967-05-7

This is the definitive
reference guide to all the
major types of fabric in circulation today, featuring more
than 1600 stunning photographs that show how the most
successful fashion designers work with fabrics.

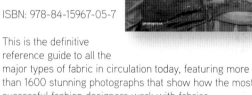

**DETAILS IN FASHION
DESIGN**
Collars & Necklines

Gianni Pucci

ISBN: 978-84-16504-17-6

This book presents 1,200
images focusing on collars
& necklines. This title
contains an extensive
selection of the styles,
trends and cutting-edge
designs.

HATS & CAPS
Designing Fashion
Accessories

Gianni Pucci

ISBN: 978-84-92810-90-1

Hats & Caps comprises of
more than 1,200 fashion
and styles photos. It
provides a complete and
current account of the
designs displayed on
runways.

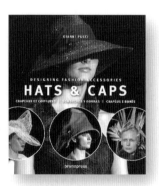